FROM TORPEDOES TO AVIATION

# FROM TORPEDOES TO AVIATION

## Washington Irving Chambers and Technological Innovation in the New Navy, 1876–1913

STEPHEN K. STEIN

THE UNIVERSITY OF ALABAMA PRESS
*Tuscaloosa*

Typeface: AGaramond

∞

The paper on which this book is printed meets the minimum requirements of American National Standard for Information Sciences-Permanence of Paper for Printed Library Materials, ANSI Z39.48-1984.

Library of Congress Cataloging-in-Publication Data

Stein, Stephen K.
From torpedoes to aviation : Washington Irving Chambers and technological innovation in the new Navy, 1876–1913 / Stephen K. Stein.
p. cm.
Includes bibliographical references and index.
ISBN-13: 978-0-8173-1564-1 (cloth : alk. paper)
ISBN-10: 0-8173-1564-0
1. Chambers, Washington Irving, 1856–1934. 2. United States. Navy—Officers—Biography. 3. Naval art and science—Technological innovations—United States—History—19th century. 4. Naval art and science—Technological innovations—United States—History—20th century. I. Title.
V63.C39.S74 2007
359.0092—dc22
[B]

2006033985

*To Carolyn*

# Contents

# Illustrations

# Acknowledgments

I wish to express my sincere appreciation to Dr. Allan R. Millett for his encouragement, insight, and guidance. Thanks also go to Dr. John F. Guilmartin and Dr. William R. Childs, for their comments, suggestions, and guidance. I also benefited from the astute observations of several anonymous reviewers who saved me from some minor errors and pointed me in important directions. Kathleen McDonough at the Manuscript Division of the Library of Congress, Rebecca Livingston at the National Archives, Gregory Plunges at the Northeast Regional Branch of the National Archives, Evelyn Cherpak at the Naval War College Library, Beverly Lyall at the Nimitz Library at the U.S. Naval Academy, and Robert Henshaw at the Naval Historical Center are all gratefully acknowledged. Without the unstinting support of my wife, Carolyn, completion of this book would have been impossible.

# FROM TORPEDOES TO AVIATION

# Introduction

The career of Washington Irving Chambers, from 1872 to 1919, spans a unique and formative period in the development of the U.S. Navy. He entered the Naval Academy during the doldrums, the years of obsolete, often rotting ships; he left the service after it had developed a large, world-class fleet of modern battleships, supplemented by increasing numbers of aircraft. Chambers was one of the navy's "young Turks"—a group of late nineteenth-century officers united by a common affinity for technology and progress who fought for administrative reforms and new technologies despite the many technical, bureaucratic, and personal obstacles placed in their paths. They recognized that changing technology required a complete transformation of the fleet and a simultaneous reform of the navy's administration and educational institutions. They fought for higher education for officers, the adoption of modern managerial and administrative practices, strategic planning, improvements in armor, ordnance, and ship design, and the adoption of new weapons and weapons systems that ranged from torpedoes to submarines and aircraft.

While Chambers began his career participating in the classic operations of the old navy, "showing the flag," policing the seas, and protecting trade, even in the early years of his career he worked to reform and modernize the navy. He participated actively in the process of technological innovation that transformed the navy's warships and the simultaneous process of professionalization that transformed its officer corps. He worked on torpedoes and their guidance systems, produced designs or conceptual designs for several new warships including a prototype all-big-gun battleship, supervised the trials of new submarines, and tinkered with a host of inventions. He worked in several of the institutions of the new, professional navy during their formative years including the Office of Naval Intelligence, the Naval War College, and the General Board. Throughout his career, he kept abreast of the latest scientific developments and worked to educate his fellow officers. As an instructor at the Naval War College and in his writings, Chambers helped redefine the role of the navy in society and change its strategy and guiding principles. He pushed for legislation to fund and build modern battleships, acquire overseas coaling stations, build a canal across Central America, and subsidize the merchant marine. He pressed the navy to hold frequent tactical exercises that stressed concentrated firepower, to replace coal with fuel oil, to build transports and supply ships to support long-range operations, acquire new weapons and technologies, and aggressively fund research and development.

Chambers's most important contribution came at the end of his career when the navy appointed him to guide its embryonic aviation program in 1910. Along with pioneer aviator and inventor Glenn Curtiss, Chambers guided a coalition of enthusiasts and pioneers that popularized aviation and convinced a growing number of naval officers and politicians of its importance to the navy. In 1910, they arranged the first take-off from and landing of an airplane on to a ship. Over the next two years, Chambers laid the foundation for a growing naval aviation program and carefully cultivated a select group of officers to carry on his work. He also sought to perfect an autopilot system, radio communication, and other important technical details of flight and built a catapult to launch planes from ships. Chambers served in this position until 1913, when the navy placed him on the retired list for lack of service at sea. As one of his friends later wrote, he was "a victim of his devotion to naval aviation."[1]

Yet, the navy needed his expertise and kept him on active duty. For the next six years, he assisted the succession of junior officers who replaced him. During these years, he worked tirelessly to create the National Advisory Committee for Aeronautics, which would guide aeronautical research for the next several decades. Increasingly shunted aside by the service's bureaucracy, Chambers slowly drifted into obscurity, while still struggling to advance aviation research and enlarge and modernize the navy's growing air arm.

Officers in those years struggled to adapt new technologies, management techniques, and administrative structures to the navy's needs, to develop new missions for the fleet, and to create a new vision for the future. These transformations mirrored those of the American people in the Progressive Era as they adapted to a new industrialized, urbanized, and bureaucratized society—a society increasingly dominated by professionals who ranged from social workers to engineers. Like their counterparts in civilian life, many naval officers sought to rationalize and harmonize life within the service, to make it more efficient, and prepare it for "the coming century, when America would assume far-reaching world responsibilities."[2]

Technological innovation proved a painstaking process with many false starts and wrong turns, often hindered by low budgets and bureaucratic inertia. The navy ignored many innovators, filing and often forgetting their reports and letters. Conservative officers often channeled innovation into less threatening areas, or managed to isolate new ideas, technologies, and weapons and prevent their spread. Occasionally reformers disagreed on the pace and direction of reform and quarreled with one another, further confusing the already complex and convoluted task of modernization.

Determined innovators responded to opposition by stepping up their arguments and popularizing their ideas widely, often through the press. They forced their opponents to confront their arguments, and debate them, though the consequences to the innovators' careers could be severe. They worked to win other officers to their causes and to recruit junior officers to continue the struggle. Innovators proved most successful in convincing the navy to adopt technologies that fit within its existing doctrine and strategic paradigms. Officers who advocated heavier ordnance or improved fire control met with relatively little resistance. Those who advocated radically new technologies such as the submarine and airplane, though, encountered substantial opposition, but Chambers and others persevered in the struggle. Successful innovation or reform did not result from sudden, radical change, but rather from slow progress, as their adherents steadily gained support among senior officers or were themselves promoted into positions of authority from which they could implement change.

Chambers's career provides a window into the process of technological innovation within the navy. Chambers helped bring about the two most momentous transformations the U.S. Navy has undergone in its history. In the first, he helped like-minded officers convince Congress and the public to abandon the nation's traditional naval strategy of coast defense and commerce raiding and replace it with a new strategy built around battleships and fleet engagements. In the second, he laid the groundwork for naval aviation and the eventual replacement of the battleship by the aircraft carrier as the backbone of the fleet. Chambers helped design and build several of the ships of the new navy, worked to perfect the new technologies it needed, and helped create the new strategy and tactics that would guide their conduct in war.

Chambers occupied a central place in the process of reform and technological innovation of these years, and his struggles typify the problems reformers faced. His career during this period of constant flux shows an officer struggling to master new technologies while simultaneously using his mastery of technology to further his career and improve the navy. The changes and internal struggles that accompanied the development of the new navy both helped and hurt his career. He pushed for innovation and reform throughout his career, yet fellow reformers who disagreed with him on the direction of technological innovation united with conservative officers to limit his influence and push him out of the navy. Forcibly retired ("plucked") before reaching flag rank, Chambers had consistently placed the needs of the navy above his personal ambition and despite the premature end of his career, managed to transform and modernize the service he loved.

# 1 / The Naval Academy

Washington Irving Chambers entered the Naval Academy in 1871. He found an institution still in flux with faculty members disputing issues of curriculum, discipline, and more. Despite its twenty-six-year history, the academy had yet to settle into a routine. The Civil War had further complicated matters. New technology, especially the armored, steam-powered warship, forced naval officers to reexamine their profession, and the faculty its curriculum. While the United States had produced some of the most advanced warships in the world during that war, it lost its technological lead in the late 1860s and continued to fall behind through the 1870s as Congress slashed funding and naval officers squabbled over technology and ship design. Those who tolerated steam engines as a necessary evil and possessed little faith in modern ordnance and armor emerged as the initial victors in this struggle. Not surprisingly, they also saw little need for the kind of education offered by the academy, arguing that naval officers could better master the skills of their profession at sea than in classrooms on shore.

A growing number of technology-minded progressives who recognized that officers of a modern navy needed classroom education in engineering and science as well as practical experience at sea opposed their conservative elders and fought for reform. They included Admiral Christopher R. P. Rodgers, who became the eighth superintendent of the academy in 1874, future admirals Robley D. Evans, William T. Sampson, and Winfield Scott Schley, and innovative instructors and reformers Theodorus B. M. Mason,

Bowman H. McCalla, and James Russell Soley. Like civilian progressives, they believed in technological progress, scientific methodology, and its applicability to a wide array of problems. The debate between the old navy conservatives and these rising progressives, interrupted by war, resumed with increasing fury in the postwar years, and greatly affected the Naval Academy in the 1870s.[1]

Despite these officers' efforts, the academy curriculum remained deficient in several areas. It lacked a good course in ordnance until the mid-1880s, because the navy had no modern ordnance. Instructors encouraged marksmanship at the newly built pistol and rifle galleries, but for larger ordnance the midshipmen had only smoothbore, muzzle-loading cannon—obsolete even by the standards of the U.S. Navy.[2] Despite a gradual increase in engineering courses, the curriculum remained rooted in the age of sail. Courses on naval tactics emphasized signaling and memorizing Myer's Signal Code rather than squadron maneuvers.

The ambiguous position of engineers in the navy reflected the struggle to adopt the steam engine. They formed their own corps, with a separate rank structure and its own course through the academy that emphasized technical and practical areas. Other midshipmen received no instruction in steam engineering until their final year of study. Yet, engineers could never rise to command a ship; only line officers could. The conflict between line officers and staff officers, especially the engineers, over control of their service and recognition raged throughout the late nineteenth and early twentieth centuries, further hindering the adoption of new technologies.

At that time, the academy served as the sole source of U.S. naval officers. Candidates competed fiercely for admission, and about a third failed the difficult entrance exam. More than half of the students resigned or were dismissed within their first two years of study. The academy's faculty kept the midshipmen under constant scrutiny, ranked them relative to one another in each subject, and punished them for any misconduct. Class rank at graduation established the new officer's standing in the long line for promotion and dogged him throughout his career. Despite the efforts of reformers, advancement in the nineteenth century remained based strictly on seniority. If his health held out, he could expect to rise to captain and possibly admiral, though he would likely reach that rank just before his mandatory retirement for old age. The handful of officers who graduated from the academy in these years saw themselves as an elite group. Because of the small classes of this era they knew each other very well, perhaps, as one later wrote, "even better than brothers."[3] Friendships begun at the academy often lasted a lifetime. So too, did rivalries.

## Midshipman Chambers

Washington Irving Chambers was born on April 4, 1856, in the small town of Kingston, in Ulster County, New York, a few miles north of Poughkeepsie. Few records of his childhood remain. He maintained a close relationship with his parents, especially his mother who he credited for "all the good and manly impulses of my youth." Chambers, who preferred friends to call him Irving, spent his entire childhood in Kingston. He first applied to the Naval Academy for the 1870 school year, having just reached the minimum age of 14, but proved unable to win his congressman's appointment, which went to a better-connected friend who dropped out of the academy before completing his first year. This cleared the way for Chambers, who received the appointment from his congressional district the following year. Athletic, he easily passed the physical exam, and the entrance examination on his first try. Despite having waited a year, Chambers was one of the youngest members of his class.[4]

Chambers proved unusual in other ways as well. His father, Jacob, was a shoemaker—an occupation rarely found in the academy's register of midshipmen. Only one in seven academy appointees in the nineteenth century were the sons of artisans or small shopkeepers. More than half came from professional or upper-class families that consisted mostly of bankers, lawyers, physicians, and manufacturers. These young men had usually enjoyed considerable educational advantages including private schools and special tutors who helped them cram for the entrance exams. The midshipmen from working-class backgrounds generally came from the more prosperous members of their trade, and this seems the case for Chambers's family. Certainly, his parents could afford a good education for their only son.[5]

Chambers entered the Naval Academy one year after Congress had acted to trim the bloated naval officer corps. Not surprisingly, the brunt of its efforts fell on those with the least political influence, the midshipmen. Instead of graduating from the academy as ensigns, they had to serve a two-year tour of duty at sea before they received their commissions on a space-available basis. In 1873, Congress made commissioning automatic after completing two years at sea. This mollified the midshipmen somewhat, but none appreciated the two-year addition to a glacially slow promotion process.

Life at the academy was regimented, designed to mold a diverse collection of young men into largely interchangeable naval officers. As William F. Fullam later complained, the "individuality and independence" of midshipmen were "constantly discouraged."[6] Instruction included seamanship, navigation, and the skills any naval officer would need, but also prepared them for high society. The faculty expected them to behave as "gentlemen" and always addressed them as mister, the term "boys" being reserved for the academy's African American servants. The midshipmen learned to dance and attended a regular series of balls. Fencing, at which Chambers excelled, remained part of the curriculum, though few officers expected to grab cutlasses and lead boarding parties onto enemy ships.

The midshipmen lived two to a room and alternated as superintendent, the one responsible for sweeping the floor and keeping the room neat, though the academy's servants supplemented their efforts. The faculty scrutinized their housekeeping efforts in regular inspections. Two classroom periods divided their mornings, followed by another one in the afternoon. The midshipmen marched in and out of the dining hall, each section eating at a separate table under its captain. Meals consisted of a repetitive selection of breads, potatoes, seasonal vegetables, beef, pork, and occasionally fish, which encouraged the midshipmen to eat well while off the grounds. Many of them, including Chambers, climbed the fruit trees surrounding the Superintendent's house to supplement their diet. Expenses for uniforms, mess, laundry, and such consumed more than half of the $500 annual pay, and they spent much of the rest in town. When not in class or at drill, they were expected to spend their time studying in their rooms. Only between 9:30 to 10:00 in the evening were they free to roam the halls and visit friends. On weekends, all midshipmen attended the Sunday morning church service. They received leave to visit home in September but celebrated Christmas and other holidays at the academy.[7]

Most new midshipmen arrived in the fall, but some, like Chambers, chose to arrive in June. The early arrivals lived on board the *Santee,* an aging sloop permanently moored at the academy. On board they received an early start learning to sleep in hammocks and other aspects of shipboard life including knotting and splicing and learning to climb the masts and rigging.

Once the rest of their class arrived in the fall, they joined them in the dormitories.

Chambers had to work hard his first year to keep up with his older and often better-educated classmates. Year's end found his grades deficient, below the minimum requirement, in both math and composition, nor were his scores in other subjects much to be proud of. Because of his academic deficiencies, he was not ranked in his class, and could have been dismissed. Chambers convinced the faculty to allow him to repeat his first year so he could improve his grades, a process often allowed for students with slight deficiencies but who showed promise of improvement. It became regular procedure two years later.[8] Chambers formed his closest friendships at the academy among similarly deficient classmates, including William Braunersreuther, Charles A. Gove, and fellow New Yorker James H. Sears, who were all held back either that year or the next.

At least part of Chambers's academic difficulties stemmed from his recreational activities and participation in numerous pranks with his older friends, or "skylarking" as the academy faculty termed his antics. By his second year, Chambers found himself with an increasing number of citations for a host of infractions including visiting after hours, "mimicking the reveille bugle at 1:15 a.m.," organizing late night swimming parties, "not sharing his intentions concerning liberty," absconding with a mast and sail from the monitor *Amphitrite,* and assorted other pranks. He frequently covered for his friends when in charge of his dormitory floor, permitting them to visit after hours—something he did not possess the authority to do.

In his second year, he began experimenting with drinking and smoking, vices he almost definitely picked up from Braunersreuther, Gove, and Sears, who smoked and smuggled in alcoholic beverages. Like much of late nineteenth-century society, the academy faculty condemned tobacco while simultaneously condoning its use. Rear Admiral John L. Worden, for instance, allowed members of the first class to enjoy it, but other midshipmen received a severe tongue-lashing for using it. Worden became famous for his fire and brimstone lectures against the vile weed, all delivered while chewing tobacco. He never managed to stamp out its use, nor did his successors, and midshipmen encountered little difficulty in smuggling the forbidden substances into their rooms.[9]

As a student, Chambers excelled in French and fencing, but faltered in technical subjects, particularly math. A talented gymnast and the best fencer in his class, he demonstrated his skills at the gymnastics exhibitions held several times each year. His forced repetition of his first year helped him catch up academically. By the end of the 1872–73 school year he ranked 22nd out of the 105 members of the new third class, well ahead of his more fun-loving friends Braunersreuther, De Witt Coffman, and Gove, but behind several others of his growing circle of friends including George C. Foulk, Henry T. Mayo, and Templin M. Potts. He had collected 112 demerits, roughly average for his class. Some had amassed more than two hundred and a few over three hundred. Only one, Charles C. Rogers, who ranked second in the class, received none.[10]

The academy's most common punishment, demerits usually ranged from one to ten for an offense. In theory, midshipmen who amassed more than 301 in a year suffered dismissal, but the faculty made numerous exceptions. Punishments could also include extra instruction, extra drill, and even confinement on board the *Santee*. As one midshipman explained in a letter to his father: "a moderate lot of demerits don't do the least harm, but show that you are not quite subdued. As a general thing, you will find that those who run a whole year without them are the outcasts of the institution, who are spiritless and friendless." Too many, though, indicated "a rash harebrained youth."[11] Chambers at times veered close to that category, but he never quite crossed the line. Instead, his occasional antics made him popular with his fellow midshipmen.

The following year, Chambers's class faced the difficult semiannual exams, and as was typical, just over half failed. Chambers ranked 40 out of the 48 survivors who entered the following year, well behind most of his friends. Even Braunersreuther (22) and Gove (24) passed him, and Sears, having forsaken his wild ways, ranked fourth in the class. Among the few behind Chambers were Koroku Katsu and Jiro Kunitomo, two Japanese students who, faced with language difficulties and ignored by most of their classmates, ranked 45 and 46 respectively and struggled in most subjects. The shock of his poor showing spurred Chambers to study harder, and he once again pulled out of the bottom ranks of his class to rank 39th the following year, just short of the merit list (top 38).[12]

Little happened to break the academy routine during Chambers's time there. The midshipmen helped put out a fire in the engineering building. In 1873, they marched in Ulysses S. Grant's second inauguration. Having heard a rumor that despite poor weather, the West Point cadets would march without their overcoats, they decided to do likewise. Word of this spread to the West Pointers who then did decide to march without their overcoats. So, both groups marched through a downpour in only their dress uniforms. Roughly half became ill. This infuriated Admiral Worden, but none of the attending officers had interfered. It had become a matter of honor, on which the midshipmen had learned to place a high premium. Grant visited the academy twice during Chambers's five years there, and on January 10, 1873, the academy held a special ball for him, Commodore Daniel Ammen, and Admiral David Dixon Porter. The midshipmen attended and the party lasted well after midnight. A good dancer, Chambers, enjoyed these events and devoted considerable efforts to impressing the opposite sex.[13]

## Hazing in the 1870s

The practice of hazing developed slowly at the Naval Academy. By 1870, it had become regular and increasingly "brutal, senseless, and physical." Usually, members of the third class hazed the newly arrived fourth (or plebe) class. This consisted of a range of quick indignities. "A plebe might be compelled to eat soap or drink ink . . . shaved with a blunt instrument; ordered to make a face, to stand on his head or . . . to recite 'Mary has a little lamb' over and over again." He might be tossed into the Severn River or trod upon. Those who violated the norms of conduct, such as Alfred Thayer Mahan who reported a classmate for talking in the ranks, were placed in "coventry," shunned by the other midshipmen.[14]

This institution increasingly got out of hand in the 1870s. Victims sometimes resisted, and fistfights and other violence became common. Once, a midshipman drew a knife to defend himself. Sometimes, as in the famous fight between two of Chambers's contemporaries, Bradley A. Fiske and future Nobel physicist Albert A. Michelson, organized and refereed fights ensued. The faculty expected midshipmen to guard their honor, even to the point of violence, and rarely interfered in this process.

Plebes who turned to the faculty for help became targets for more serious hazing. As fourth classman William Green wrote in 1873: "There is no use in appealing to the officers, as the whole class will go for you then." Those officers who opposed hazing seemed powerless to stop it.[15] According to Park Benjamin, several members of Chambers's entering class were "roughly handled." Their treatment was, in fact, so bad that it provoked criticism from both military and civilian authorities including the Board of Visitors, who annually inspected the academy. The three African American midshipmen who attended the academy in these years suffered particularly vicious hazing and abandoned their naval careers.[16]

Under increasing pressure from civilian authorities and the parents of the abused midshipmen, Admiral Worden launched a full investigation. He expelled thirteen midshipmen for having "committed gross inhumanities upon members of the junior class." Numerous others received lesser punishments. As Park Benjamin observed, official condemnation seemed only to fuel the practice and more incidents followed. Despite his warnings, Worden found that hazing continued "under circumstances of great cruelty." Worden had previously faced outraged letters from the parents of the hazed; now they poured in from the parents of the hazers, complaining that he had dismissed their sons for youthful pranks. Worden, though, refused to reverse any of the punishments.[17]

Benjamin's assertion that the worst hazed became the worst hazers may be true, and Chambers may well have been one of the midshipmen "roughly handled" during his first year. Several members of Chambers's class did become active hazers, and the faculty cited Chambers the following year for "hearing or encouraging the hazing of fourth classmen."[18] Either from conscience or due to his anomalous position of repeating his first year, making him a member of the fourth class, but not a plebe, Chambers did not directly haze anyone. Yet, in 1874 he became involved in the most serious hazing incident in the academy's history.

On Sunday, February 8, Chambers's fellow third classman Augustus C. Almy entered the room of fourth classman Thomas G. Harkness and attempted to haze him. After Harkness refused to accede to whatever petty indignities Almy had in mind, Almy became belligerent and "wantonly insulted and unlawfully ordered and threatened" Harkness, who stood his ground and "refused to obey his order or yield to his threats, regarding them, as they were, ungentlemanly insults, and culpable abuses of authority." Frustrated, Almy left in search of reinforcements, but found only disinterest. If he could not handle a fourth classman, that was his problem. He spent the next day convincing classmates to support him, claiming that Harkness had insulted them and cast aspersions on their honor and the honor of their class. That night, Chambers and eighteen others returned with Almy to confront Harkness in his room.[19] They turned off the lights, closed the blinds, and beat Harkness to the ground. Almy, and possibly others, repeatedly kicked him once he was down. Hearing the approach of Lieutenant Commander George W. Coffin, who had come to investigate, they ran, leaving Harkness a bloody heap on the floor.[20]

Already far larger than any previously reported hazing, it did not end there. While Coffin failed to catch any of the midshipmen that night, he could identify some of the twenty perpetrators. Apprehension and punishment of the others was certain. The remainder of the third class, thirty-three in all, gathered in a secret meeting two days later. Faced with the dismissal of nearly half of their class, they decided to act. With only one dissenting vote, that of Clifford J. Bousch, they adopted a resolution claiming that the guilty twenty had acted with the approval of the whole class to uphold its honor. As the act was motivated by honor, they demanded to share in any punishment meted out to the perpetrators, and sent their signed petition to Worden. This was, of course, gross insubordination and a direct challenge to the authority of the superintendent and faculty.

The petition incensed Worden who saw it as an effort to hide the guilty. Investigation unearthed the perpetrators, and Worden expelled Almy, but no others. Harkness repeatedly asked for leniency for his attackers. In exchange, the third class promised to end all hazing. Possibly, Harkness's plea swayed Worden. More likely, he simply could not dismiss that many midshipmen, and the nineteen all seemed equally guilty, though none testified against any of the others. Worden gave them each ten demerits for "making or aiding and abetting a pusillanimous attack on a member of the fourth class," confined them to the academy during the day and the *Santee* at night, and assigned them double drills. Instead of a summer vacation, Worden sent them on a practice cruise. They remained confined to the academy after the cruise, receiving no leave to return home in September. The rest of the third class received what they had asked for, sharing in all the punishments except the double drill.[21]

This incident forced Congress to intervene. On June 23, 1874, it passed a law making every form of hazing, no matter how trivial, a court martial offense. A board of three officers would try the accused. Their recommendation for dismissal, if approved by the superintendent, was final. Any student so dismissed could not be readmitted, so political pressure would no longer save the guilty. Readmitted that October, Almy was one of the few exceptions as his offense predated the law's passage.

Rear Admiral Rodgers became superintendent shortly after this incident and rigorously applied the new law. He forced six midshipmen to resign rather than face courts martial, but hazing continued and the midshipmen refused to testify against one another. In September 1875, a serious outbreak of hazing occurred on the return of third class from their practice cruise. Yet, by the 1880s the situation had calmed down, and no longer provoked mention in the press. Robert E. Coontz (Class of 1885), for example, claimed that by his day there was little brutality to it. The worst case he witnessed was a midshipman who was held upside down while water was poured down his pants legs.[22]

Explanations for hazing, particularly the upsurge in the 1870s, vary and remain unsatisfactory. The level of hazing certainly varied from plebe to plebe. One might be made to stand on his head for a few minutes while another would be kept at it for a considerably longer period despite having repeatedly fainted. For some it was a simple right of passage; for others it was calculated brutality designed to force them to resign. Almy's initial attempt at hazing Harkness was routine and ignored by his classmates, until Almy told them their honor was at stake. Harkness, despite his treatment, insisted on testifying on behalf of his attackers, except for Almy. The guilty nineteen testified against Almy, but not against one another. Having lied to them, Almy had broken their code and was no longer entitled to their protection. The rest of the third class, including such model midshipmen as Charles C. Rogers, insisted on standing by their classmates because the honor of all was at stake. Just as in their rainy march before President Grant, their honor bound them together in a questionable act. While Worden and later Rodgers could decry hazing, one of its results was exactly what the academy faculty sought to create—a small group of officers motivated by honor who saw themselves as a "band of brothers" and stood by each regardless of the consequences. Forty years later, Chambers would still be able to call on academy classmates for support and favors, particularly those who participated in the assault on Harkness.

## Chambers's Summer Cruises

The midshipmen received extensive training in handling sailing vessels. They practiced throughout the year on board the sloop *Dale* and each summer on one of the old sailing warships at the academy. Chambers twice sailed on the twenty-year-old sloop *Constellation.* On board the midshipmen trained extensively in all the complexities of sailing these old ships. The first classmen each had duty in turn as captain of the top, officer of the forecastle, and midshipman of the quarterdeck. Each also took the deck under sail as their final preparation to take their place as naval officers. The third classmen performed much of the work on board. They learned to man the rigging, handle sail, make simple repairs, to man a lead, respond to emergencies, and many other tasks. They slept in hammocks and bathed in salt water, sharing nine washbasins between sixty of them, and ate hardtack and dried fruit. The officers carefully rationed fresh water, passing it out under guard to the crew.[23]

The practice ships sailed along the eastern seaboard, never far from the coast, stopping at various navy yards, installations, and manufacturing centers. The midshipmen thus learned not just ship handling but also ship construction, maintenance, and repair. They became familiar with what passed for new technology in the U.S. Navy at the navy yards, as the equipment on the practice ships was hopelessly obsolete. In 1874 and again on his final cruise, Chambers's class visited the Torpedo Station at Newport. There they listened to detailed lectures on chemistry, electricity, and the manufacture of dynamite. They took a tour of the *Alarm,* the United States' only torpedo boat, and the first classmen fired a few torpedoes. These weapons fascinated Chambers who took detailed notes on their design and operation. This brief stop apparently kindled his lasting interest in torpedoes.[24]

The midshipmen crewed their ship alongside her small group of experienced sailors, their first significant experience with the navy's enlisted men. Sailors received measly pay and few benefits, so the navy attracted few recruits with a deep commitment to the service. This, combined with the vast social gulf that separated the two groups, led to exceptionally harsh treatment of the enlisted ranks. While Congress had outlawed flogging, officers contrived new punishments for their unruly sailors, punishments for which the midshipmen would be responsible once they became officers. At any given time, at least one of the *Constellation*'s crew was being punished. This usually meant restriction to bread and water, though sailors might be confined in irons. The most common charges were insubordination or refusing to obey orders, though fights among the crew occurred regularly, especially as many returned from leave drunk. Numerous sailors deserted from the *Constellation* on these cruises. Some returned weeks later, having merely "overstayed" their leave, but most left for good, and one died trying to swim ashore.[25]

During the 1870s and 1880s, the ships of the U.S. Navy became involved in a series of embarrassing collisions. These excited frequent and derogatory comment in the press, such as a *New York Times* editorial that called for an end to "the disastrous experiment of sending our men-of-war to sea, where they are at all times in danger of being sunk by coal schooners and fishing smacks."[26] On Chambers's 1873 practice cruise, a small schooner collided with the *Constellation,* slightly damaging both ships. Chambers blamed the schooner for the collision, as did the *Constellation*'s captain, Commander Augustus P. Cooke. It was not uncommon for civilian vessels to bump warships and then file suit for damages. Conversely, the U.S. Navy was hardly at the peak of its efficiency. Its ships were clearly responsible for some of these collisions, and it would hardly be surprising for a ship crewed primarily by inexperienced midshipmen to have caused another.

## Graduation

Chambers entered his final year with average grades but was very popular among his classmates. The faculty appointed Chambers and Sears cadet-ensigns, and Foulk to cadet lieutenant commander. A position particularly coveted by first classmen was membership on the hop committee, which arranged the regular dances at the academy and the final celebrations of graduation or "June Week," when Annapolis was in "fiesta and large numbers of young girls arrive to gladden the midshipmen after their year of hard study." During this week, the Board of Visitors made its annual inspection, and the academy treated them and other dignitaries and visitors to drills and exhibitions all capped by a ball after the graduation ceremonies. The midshipmen elected the hop committee from the members of the first class, and in 1876, they chose Chambers and several of his circle of friends including Foulk, Mayo, Potts, and Sears. Chambers entered the year ranked 24th in his class, but dropped four places in standing over the year, probably due to the great dedication with which he pursued his hop committee duties.[27]

Chambers graduated from the Naval Academy on June 20, 1876, 28th in his class of 42. Chambers and twelve others had entered the academy in 1871 and took five years to complete the course. Only twenty-nine of the sixty-nine midshipmen who entered with Chambers in 1871 graduated. Most of his friends graduated well ahead of him. Henry C. Gearing, Foulk, Potts, and Sears all graduated in the top ten.

Between the faculty at the academy and the officers he met on his practice cruises, Chambers had made a number of connections that would help him later in his career. These included reformers Lieutenant Caspar H. Goodrich, Lieutenant Raymond P. Rodgers, and Lieutenant Commander French Ensor Chadwick, who he had met on board the *Constellation,* and the *Constellation*'s 1875 captain, Commander Silas Terry. Chambers impressed both Sampson and Schley, and he would serve under both of them later in his career. These connections proved invaluable for Chambers in aiding his career, as he lacked the political connections of many of his friends—connections that despite protestations to the contrary, officers in these years routinely used to further their careers.

Chambers and his classmates graduated in their nation's centennial year into a navy that had as little room for them as it had for modern ships. An 1876 survey of naval powers failed to even mention the United States, though the fifteen nations it did describe included Turkey, Peru, and Brazil, countries behind the United States in industry and technology. The centennial exhibition that opened that year in Philadelphia displayed the scientific and technological achievements of the United States. Of particular interest to the midshipmen were the breech-loading cannon at its entrance and the enormous 1,400-horse-power Corliss steam engine that powered many of the exhibits, which included mowers, reapers, railroad cars, sewing machines, typewriters, and looms. Those midshipmen not part of the 10 million visitors had probably seen the models and other exposition exhibits carried by the transport *Tallapoosa,* which visited the academy. Clearly, the United States could build modern warships, but it would be a decade before Chambers or any member of his class set foot on a remotely modern ship. Instead, they served on board ships that became a source of amusement to foreign naval officers.[28]

# 2 / Early Cruises

Chambers graduated from the Naval Academy eager for adventure. Over the next few years he developed his skills as a sailor, impressing a succession of captains with his seamanship and bravery. He also became interested in new technology and ship design, tinkering with inventions and sketching ship plans whenever he had a chance.

Like his fellow graduates, Chambers lobbied for a prestigious assignment and worked to get assigned to the same ship as his friends. Recent graduates used whatever connections and political influence they had in arranging this crucial first duty. Chambers proved lucky in this regard when Charles Gove arranged a posting through the influence of a friendly senator to the *Pensacola,* the flagship of Rear Admiral Alexander Murray's South American Squadron. Gove put in a good word for his friends, and Chambers, De Witt Coffman, Henry Gearing, and Charles Pond received orders to the same ship. They were to take passage on a mail steamer from New York to Panama and there await the *Pensacola*'s arrival.[1]

Chambers received his orders at home and left for New York the next day, where he stayed with an aunt. He and his four classmates sailed the following day on the mail steamer *Acapulco* along with Lieutenant Raymond P. Rodgers, the son of Admiral Christopher R. P. Rodgers, who had also been posted to the *Pensacola.* Lieutenant Rodgers chaperoned them on the voyage, keeping the recent graduates out of trouble and from offending the

*Acapulco*'s captain, a sailor of the old school who derided the midshipmen's fancy education. The six naval officers shared three rooms, two per room. Chambers roomed with Rodgers at Rodgers's request. Chambers had impressed Rodgers as a student at the academy, and they became friends on this trip.[2]

The five midshipmen enjoyed the voyage and spent a great deal of time socializing and competing for the favor of the few eligible ladies. Chambers met all the passengers, and spent a great deal of time watching them, recording his precise observations in his diary. He made particularly careful notes about a dentist who he watched fall prey to "the treacherous little god of love," something he would soon do himself.[3] While hardly important in subject matter, his notes show acute observation and attention to detail.

## Gallivanting around Panama

The *Acapulco* arrived in Aspinwall (contemporary Colon), Panama, which was still part of Colombia, just over a week later. Rodgers and the midshipmen then crossed the isthmus by train to Panama City where they would await the *Pensacola.* The trip took a day, and Chambers enjoyed the journey. New places fascinated him and he marveled at the lush, tropical scenery of the long ride. On arrival, they took rooms in the Grand Hotel paying for them out of their own pockets, a common complaint of officers in the cash-strapped navy. Lieutentant Rodgers again chose to room with Chambers.

Chambers and his friends sampled the delights of the town, "paying a great deal of attention to the ladies." Chambers found time to court two of them, one quite seriously. His first love, Sarilla, broke off the relationship, throwing Chambers into a deep, though rather short, depression. He recovered quickly and became enraptured with another young woman, whom he referred to in his journal as his "darling V." He visited her frequently, met her parents, and took pains to reassure them that his intentions were both serious and honorable. He promised V that he would always love her and would return for her. She, in turn, promised to wait for him. As he confessed to his journal: "I pray to God to make me worthy of the angelic being, to prevent my disappointing her, and to give me success in order that we may soon be happy." He seems not, however, to have told his own parents about his intentions. Nor is there any indication that he thought of her once he left Panama for good.[4]

Female companionship satisfied only part of the needs of the eager, young midshipmen. All proved desperate for adventure and short on patience. They hired local guides and set off into the jungle; they explored the old mining district and, over the protests of their guides, entered several abandoned mines. Rumors of bandits only excited them to further explorations. Chambers enjoyed Panama's mild winter climate and calm weather, but he was less than impressed with the local populace, whom he considered "very indolent."[5] Chambers was equally unimpressed with the soldiers of these nations whose poorly maintained equipment was even older than the navy's, and he discussed this at length with Rodgers.

The *Pensacola*'s arrival on November 23 brought only a brief pause to the midshipmen's explorations and adventures. Rodgers and the midshipmen quickly settled on board, the midshipmen sharing one cramped stateroom. Each of the midshipmen stood watch for two days and then received three off, having only to be on board for quarters at 9:30 p.m. This left them plenty of time to visit their numerous "lady acquaintances," and pursue other adventures. The arrival of four more of their classmates further crowded their quarters and encouraged the nine midshipmen to spend as much time as possible on shore. The court martial and dismissal for drunkenness of a lieutenant of the squadron seems not to have affected their own carousing.[6]

The primary mission of the U.S. Navy in those halcyon years was to show the flag and police the seas. It dispersed its ships around the globe where they visited countless ports to support U.S. commerce and diplomacy. Only rarely did they become involved in armed conflict, and when they did it was usually a punitive expedition on shore. The *Pensacola* made a regular circuit of visits at ports on her station and spent more time moored than at sea. This allowed Chambers and other officers to pursue active social lives ashore.

Naval officers received free passes on the Isthmian Railroad, so Chambers and his friends regularly returned to Aspinwall, as did many of the officers of the *Pensacola,* attending dances and other social events there. Despite his professed love for "V," Chambers attended a number of dances. At one, he danced with a number of local ladies who spoke no English. Chambers, despite his recent practice, still had trouble with Spanish, and proved unable to extricate himself from a difficult situation when two of his dance partners felt slighted. He had to get Lieutenant Thomas Phelps, who spoke Spanish fluently, to straighten things out. On his return, he resolved to improve his Spanish and eventually became comfortable with the language.[7]

## Duty On Board the *Pensacola*

Captain John Irwin commanded the 3,000-ton screw sloop *Pensacola,* the flagship of the South American Squadron. Sixteen officers (nine of them midshipmen) served on board, and the flagship boasted forty-five marines, a sixteen-piece band, and several Chinese servants. In addition to the roughly two hundred members of the crew, whose numbers fluctuated wildly due to the vagaries of enlistment and desertion, the ship was also home to a menagerie of pets including dogs, cats, parrots, a pig, and a monkey. Most belonged to Admiral Murray. Commissioned in 1861, the ship boasted a distinguished Civil War record. While hardly the oldest ship in the navy, the *Pensacola,* armed with a collection of Civil War–era muzzle-loading cannon and capable of steaming at only 8 knots, was obsolete for naval warfare. To save coal, Captain Irwin usually relied on the ship's full set of sails to reach his destinations.[8]

Yet, in the 1870s, Chambers could have done a lot worse, and he considered himself fortunate to get this posting. Even the most modern American ships were but quaint antiques compared to European warships. A few years later, George Foulk on board the *Trenton,* the most modern ship in the navy, and the first to be electrified, wrote to Chambers of his disappointment with the ship. He "had hoped to get at least on board a ship of war which might at least be not sneered at in the comparison of our ships with those of foreign navies" and intended to avoid "going to sea in a United States man of war until one is built fit to be called such."[9] Chambers and his classmates would have a long wait.

The midshipmen's duties in running the ship proved light. Instead, the senior officers kept them busy honing their skills for their promotion exams. They had to prove themselves competent in navigation, recordkeeping, and other skills essential to running a warship. All brought with them a sextant or octant, a comparing watch, treatises on navigation and marine surveying, and a blank journal in which to enter professional notes. While at sea they daily computed all courses and distances run and completed other navigational exercises. Each of them determined the ship's position at noon and reported to the captain to check his work. Chambers always received excellent marks. Each also maintained copies of the ship's log and his division's watch, quarter and station bills, and stood junior deck watches. Irwin placed Chambers in charge of the 3rd division and the ship's whaleboat.[10]

The *Pensacola* spent the next several months on an uneventful cruise with long stopovers at several ports before sailing for home in April. On the way, they stopped at Punta Arenas, Costa Rica, and several Mexican ports including San Blas and Acapulco. They recoaled at the U.S. coaling station in Pichilingue Bay—a grand name for a dilapidated shed and its one employee. The crew brought the coal to the ship in a lighter and then hauled it on board in baskets—a difficult and slow process that covered the ship with coal dust that filtered into everything. Chambers began studying the problem of coaling. As he commented at the time, off-loading the coal from a hulk, as the navy did at its European coaling station, would have solved the problem, but Congress would not appropriate funds for better coaling stations until the 1890s.[11]

As at the academy, Chambers's sense of humor continued to get him in trouble. In February, following the *Pensacola*'s return to Panama, he marched the band ashore in full military regalia to serenade the local American consul. While they carried no weapons, it was an insult to Colombia's sovereignty, and angry local officials demanded an apology. On hearing of the incident, Irwin required Chambers to apologize, though Chambers continued to think of it as a fine joke.[12] It would not be his last brush with local officials sensitive to the presence of Americans. In fact, minor incidents between American naval officers and local officials proved common.

Later that month, a *Pensacola* sailor overindulged himself at a local tavern and became involved in a brawl. Nearby, Chambers rounded up several other sailors and broke up the fight. They had just restrained the intoxicated man when the local police arrived. Not waiting to ask questions, the policemen waded in with billy clubs, attacking the intoxicated sailor and those restraining him. Chambers led their retreat out of the bar and managed to get everyone on board the dinghy and back to the ship with only minor injuries. The police, without a suspect in custody, let the matter drop.[13]

Mexico offered more pleasures to the ship's crew and officers, but also more run-ins with the local officials. The *Pensacola* arrived in Acapulco on May 1. When out of uniform, the crew was treated well, but there began an escalating series of incidents between local officials and crewmembers who went ashore in uniform. A local sentry harassed Chambers and his friends, despite having treated them well the previous day when they were out of uniform. Other officers and members of the crew reported similar incidents. Following several other incidents, Captain Irwin demanded the local officials apologize and fire a salute to the U.S. flag, which they did after some delay.[14]

This occasional harassment did not stop the crew from enjoying its frequent leaves on shore. Nor did the possibility that rebel forces might attack the city. Rather, Chambers and his friends hoped to witness a battle. The paymaster's clerk, unable to resist the local entertainment, dipped into ship's funds to satisfy his gambling debts. The unenviable task of straightening out the books fell to Chambers, who assisted the paymaster and later shared the blame for the austerity measures that followed as they were forced to make up for the "loan" by economizing on purchases of rations and stores.[15]

Continuing this slow progress, the *Pensacola* stopped at Mazatlán and other Mexican ports, and arrived in San Francisco in September. Chambers had served on board for ten months. Both Irwin and Lieutenant Commander George H. Wadleigh, the ship's executive officer, commended him as "zealous and capable." Irwin recommended him as a "good deck and drill officer" who was fully "proficient in navigation." His "bearing as an officer and gentleman reflects credit on him and on the institution from which he graduated."[16]

## The *Portsmouth*

Chambers had enjoyed his time on the *Pensacola,* but was eager for new challenges and experiences. He wrote Rear Admiral Ammen, the Chief of the Bureau of Navigation, requesting a transfer to the *Portsmouth,* then outfitting in San Francisco for a voyage around Cape Horn. Chambers argued that participation in this cruise would be "beneficial and instructive . . . from a professional point of view." Ammen declined his request, but Chambers, Braunersreuther, Coffman, and Gove managed to arrange the transfer. Possibly, they arranged an exchange with midshipmen on the *Portsmouth* who wanted to stay home, and Gove may again have used his political influence to secure them an assignment. They reported aboard the *Portsmouth* on October 8 along with classmate Wildemar D. Rose.[17] Clearly, the voyage around Cape Horn was only part of their motivation, if it factored in at all. The *Portsmouth* was an aging, third-rate sloop, but its final destination was

France, famous for its social pleasures. She would carry American exhibits for the Paris Exposition, the latest in a series of technological extravaganzas at which the industrial nations displayed their latest products.

The *Portsmouth,* under Commander Norman H. Farquhar, was an old, full-rigged sloop, built before the age of steam and never modernized. Crowded and poorly lit, a former crewmember considered the ship "as stumpy and ugly a craft as can be imagined." Yet, thanks to an excellent underwater design, supposedly copied from a famous French privateer, the *Portsmouth* was quite fast, and "had little difficulty running down any ship not powered by steam."[18] What it would then do was questionable, as the ship's entire armament down to the rifles in the arms locker was hopelessly obsolete.

There was much to do in fitting out the *Portsmouth,* and the eighty-member crew received little help from the understaffed Mare Island Navy Yard. Chambers made himself useful in every way he could, and quickly impressed his new captain. The midshipmen stood their first watches while the ship was in port, an easy, but important, step in accustoming themselves to the routine in preparation for becoming watch officers.

The *Portsmouth* left San Francisco in October and sailed south, crossing the equator on November 12. This was the first crossing for Chambers and other midshipmen, as well as many of the crew, and the "pollywogs" endured the usual rituals, festivities, and visit from "King Neptune." Continuing south, they crossed Cape Horn and then sailed north along the coast of South America. Chambers enjoyed the long voyage under sail, and "always performed [his duties] cheerfully and intelligently." The long trip, during which the ship never once docked, gave the midshipmen an excellent opportunity to hone their skills under the watchful eye of Lieutenant Clifford Gill, the ship's navigation officer. They calculated their position and took navigational readings each day, which Gill double-checked. Chambers again received excellent marks. On the trip he "held the deck regularly in the day and navigated the ship finding the position daily." Farquhar soon considered him "fully qualified to be navigator of any ship."[19]

They arrived in New York on February 15, 1878, and loaded the exhibits for the exposition. Gove left for other duties, as did half the crew whose enlistments were up. Three weeks later, Commander Frederick McNair relieved Farquhar in command of the *Portsmouth.* Eighteen new apprentices joined the ship, but they remained shorthanded and McNair delayed his departure until the 14th to await more recruits. The *Portsmouth* arrived in Le Havre on April 5 after an uneventful voyage during which Chambers and the other officers were kept busy whipping the new crew into shape. In Le Havre, Chambers's friend Templin Potts joined the ship. He had arrived earlier in the venerable *Constitution,* which had also transported exposition exhibits. The officers received a month's leave and departed the ship a few at a time in rough order of seniority. Chambers left in May, toured France, and visited the exposition.

There was little to do in port but work on board the ship. With many of the officers gone, the midshipmen stood half the watches, and supervised the remaining crew in painting the ship, drying the sails, repairing masts and spars, tightening the ratlines, and other tasks. As the months dragged on and the crew completed the essential tasks, the officers kept them at work to combat boredom and keep them out of trouble. Desertion became a problem, and the number of disciplinary incidents soared among the restless crew. Between these incidents and the almost weekly arrival of the police with another captured deserter, not a day went by without some member of the crew, and often several, confined. Meanwhile, the term of service expired for several crewmembers who left for posts on board nearby merchant ships.

Aside from leave and occasional visits ashore, little happened to break the routine on board. On August 12, Chambers and some of the other officers accepted an invitation to attend a British naval review. Watching with their hosts from the yacht *Dida,* they witnessed a grand procession of the premier naval power of the world. The ships were all more modern than the antiquated *Portsmouth* or any American warship. This came as no surprise to Chambers, but seeing so many at once proved a humbling experience. Shortly after the review, McNair turned over command of the *Portsmouth* to Commander Arent S. Crowninshield, a reformer who would serve on the first Naval Advisory Board.

## The Paris Exposition of 1878

The Paris Exposition was the latest in a series of technological expositions at which the developed nations showed their products in the hopes of furthering commerce. Convinced by concerted lobbying and considerable pressure from the press, Congress funded an American delegation. The United States sent twenty railroad cars of goods including steam engines, mills, pumps, machine tools, Gatling guns, Colt revolvers, Sharps and Remington rifles, torpedoes, railroad machinery, and a host of agricultural products and implements. While it boasted of the quality of American military inventions, the *New York Times* assured readers that the United States limited its weapons research to defensive weapons as "becomes a nation at peace with all mankind and desirous of remaining so."[20]

Americans received few invitations to the many celebrations accompanying the event, but received many awards from the exposition's judges. In fact, the United States received the highest proportion of awards for its number of exhibitors. The *London Times* marveled at "the American inventive genius" that developed "more that is new and practical in mechanism than all Europe combined." Here again, the United States' considerable technological capabilities stood in marked contrast to the sad state of its navy, though the Naval Academy received a gold medal for the "best system of education in the United States." The French inducted a host of American inventors into the Legion of Honor, including Thomas Edison for the phonograph, Elisha Gray for the telephone, and Cyrus McCormick for his agricultural inventions. They also inducted Lieutenant Benjamin H. Buckingham into the Legion of Honor for his work coordinating the U.S. exhibits. Chambers met him at the exhibition, and the two spoke at length about new technology and naval advances.[21]

After an almost six months' stay, the *Portsmouth* sailed for New York on November 1. In the North Atlantic, the ship entered a violent storm that quickly built to a hurricane that lasted from December 9 to 11. Chambers and the other midshipmen repeatedly led the crew up the masts to adjust the sails and make emergency repairs. During one of these efforts, lightning struck repeatedly about the ship. Blinded and disoriented, Chambers was almost blown overboard, but managed to cling to the rigging. The battered ship arrived in New York on December 20, whereupon a number of the crew deserted. The *Portsmouth* continued on to Hampton Roads, where Chambers was detached and traveled home to await new orders.[22]

Chambers's commanding officers again thought well of him and sent in glowing reports on his fitness in anticipation of his promotion exam. McNair noted his excellent "deportment, attention to duty, and professional aptitude," as well as his "desire to improve himself." Crowninshield believed he would make an excellent and "efficient officer." He "found him attentive and zealous in the performance of his duties."[23]

In March, Chambers traveled to Annapolis for his promotion exams, which he passed easily. Commissioned an ensign on April 14, he received a month's leave and then reported to the *Marion.* All the graduates of the Naval Academy of the 1870s faced a long wait for promotion from ensign to lieutenant. The 1879 graduates served seventeen years before becoming junior lieutenants: six as cadet-midshipmen, one as midshipmen, and then nine as ensigns. Chambers was well aware of the long wait before him and it was the reason he, like many junior officers, lobbied for promotion reform that would clear out the dead wood of aging officers above them and allow promotion for merit rather than seniority.[24]

## The *Marion*

The *Marion* was an interesting ship that within its 1,900 tons encapsulated most of the problems of the post–Civil War navy. It was one of the famous ships "repaired" during the Grant administration under the orders of Secretary of the Navy George Robeson. A thrifty Congress authorized little new ship construction during the 1870s, but it did fund repairs of existing ships. So, Robeson ordered ships repaired that should have been scrapped, or built new ships with the same names as the old ones to conceal their true origin. Apart from hiding assorted corrupt practices, the supply and construction contracts also provided numerous jobs for the party faithful. As several people later testified to Congress, ships "had millions of dollars expended upon them" and were "rebuilt in the navy-yards in order to give patronage to enable the Republican party to hold its own in doubtful districts."[25]

During the early 1870s navy yard workers rebuilt the *Marion* from an old sailing sloop. Commissioned in 1875, she was an entirely new ship that shared hardly a timber or fitting with the original. When Chambers joined the ship, Chief Engineer James W. King had just completed his survey of the world's navies. He considered the *Marion* and her five sister-ships to be "of the most value" to the navy after the *Trenton,* the only reasonably modern cruiser in the fleet. The *Marion,* considerably faster than the *Pensacola,* could exceed 12 knots for short periods, but carried the usual collection of muzzle-loading antiques that passed for ordnance in the navy.[26]

Chambers quickly impressed the *Marion*'s captain, Commander Francis M. Bunce, with his "personal gallantry," attention to detail, and technical knowledge. Despite his increasing interest in new technology and innovation,

Chambers worked to perfect his skills as a sailor, and always volunteered for dangerous duty. Once "during a gale at night the weather main topsail sheet and main lift parted." Chambers rushed aloft, and led the crew in emergency repairs, reeving "a hawser in place of the parted lift."[27]

Hazards other than stormy seas threatened the crew. Constant travel from port to port exposed them to numerous diseases. The *Marion* left Valparaíso, Chile, on February 6, 1880, and all appeared normal, but by the time the ship reached Montevideo, Uruguay, on the 19th, a dozen crewmembers had fallen ill, including the ship's doctor. Local officials ordered the *Marion* quarantined off Flores Island where the officers and crew waited for the epidemic to pass. New cases appeared each day, but most recovered, perhaps helped by the fresh vegetables sent from shore. At the epidemic's peak, so many of the crew were ill that barely enough remained to stand regular watches. Two officers and several sailors died, but most recovered by the end of March, and they fumigated the ship with sulfur. The disease had spread to the other ships in the harbor, and cooperating with officials on shore, Bunce and the *Marion* helped enforce the quarantine, repeatedly running down ships that tried to reach shore in violation of quarantine regulations. The *Marion* remained in port until mid-May, and then sailed for the Falkland Islands.

## Ordnance and Innovation

An officer made his reputation in these years through seamanship, and "smartness at drills with sails and spars." Target practice, squadron maneuvers, and other wartime skills counted for little. Many captains never fired their guns at all. The combination of peace, obsolete ordnance, and poorly trained crews made it seem pointless. Commander Bunce at least made an effort at target practice, but discovered that the *Marion*'s guns were completely inaccurate in all but the calmest of seas. He set Chambers to work on a solution, and Chambers made a number of improvements to the gun carriages. While lieutenants Roswell D. Hitchcock, Edwin C. Pendleton, and James R. Selfridge thought his design would fail under stress, they were sufficiently impressed to help Chambers perfect it. The four of them reported on their work and final design to the Bureau of Ordnance.[28]

Chambers's work on gun carriages led him to embrace an even greater challenge: designing first a turret and then an entire ship, a monitor he named the *Hiawatha.* Like all line officers, he had taken only one course in naval architecture at the Naval Academy, but he studied on his own and followed foreign developments closely.

In an age when turrets mounting one gun were still common and double turrets rare in the U.S. Navy, Chambers proposed placing three guns into a single turret. They would be of mixed caliber (two 10-inch and one 15-inch) to keep the size of the turret small enough to fit on the small ships and monitors the United States preferred. He proposed mounting the guns farther back in the turret than usual, which would allow smaller gun ports, and redesigned the breeches of the guns to allow this and to make reloading easier. Chambers's turret would maximize firepower on the navy's small ships, but the United States had no facilities to produce large ordnance. He proposed buying ordnance from Krupp in Germany, as had several of his fellow officers.

At 6,000 tons, his monitor design was comparable to the navy's *Miantonomah* class ships, but carried a much larger armament. In addition to two of his triple turrets, it would have a ram and carry a mixture of torpedoes as well as two 40-foot torpedo boats, which it would deploy before combat. Chambers was particularly interested in torpedoes and worried about defending against them. He provided the *Hiawatha* with a double hull, as numerous engineers of the time proposed, and added a barrier of cork and compressed cotton in between the two hulls, hoping this would absorb some of the force of torpedo detonations. In addition to the standard precautions of watertight doors, torpedo nets, and pumping equipment, Chambers also suggested a series of inflatable rubber bags in the compartments below deck. The crew would inflate these before combat to fill the compartments and keep any water out. Chambers knew little about engines, and simply copied those of the *Miantonomah,* though he increased coal storage to allow a cruising range of 3,300 miles.[29]

The three-gun turrets and torpedoes gave Chambers's design considerable striking power. The ram would be useless in combat, but at the time, many officers advocated them based on experience in the American Civil War and the Battle of Lissa between Italy and Austria. In the United States, their leading advocate was Admiral Ammen. Chambers's ship was likely to please the older, more conservative reformers like Ammen, for it used existing technologies and tactical concepts and reflected the contemporary American emphasis on commerce raiding and coast defense. Chambers's antitorpedo gimmickry aside, the design might have originated with Ammen, who also fancied himself a designer of warships.

Chambers's plans and proposals impressed Captain Montgomery Sicard, the Chief of Bureau of Ordnance and Gunnery, who made copies of them for his files and sent them to the Naval Advisory Board, then meeting to make recommendations on rebuilding the navy. The board's priority, though, lay in replacing the navy's dilapidated cruisers, so it set Chambers's designs aside. The Naval Institute published Chambers's plans in its journal *Proceedings*. Chambers continued to correspond with Sicard, discussing ship design and ordnance with him and sending him additional plans and drawings. The prospect of reform and modernization excited Chambers, and he wanted to be part of the process.[30]

## The Rescue of the *Trinity*

Chambers spent most of his time performing the same routine tasks as any shipboard officer of his day. The *Marion* was hardly a research test bed. Her missions were those of the old navy, cruising the coast of South America, sometimes even entering frigid Antarctic waters to aid American whaling ships. Chambers stood watches and continued to hone his skills as a sailor and navigator. Bunce repeatedly praised Chambers, saying he is "remarkable for attention to his duties and skillful in their performance," and saying that as an officer and a gentleman, "he was all that could be desired."[31] Chambers, though, was unimpressed with Bunce.

Commander Silas W. Terry relieved Bunce as the *Marion*'s captain on September 22, 1881, and set sail for Buenos Aires. After years on station without a refit, the *Marion* was in poor shape, and Terry had to turn back to make repairs. He found the ship's bottom covered with barnacles and many fittings had all but rusted away—a situation that may explain Chambers's soured opinion of Terry's predecessor. The repairs took more than a month, and gave Chambers, who helped supervise the work, an opportunity to demonstrate his initiative and growing technical skills. Shortly after returning to sea, the *Marion* received orders to search for the whaler *Trinity*, from which nothing had been heard in eighteen months.

Initial reports indicated that the *Trinity* had been operating off Tierra del Fuego, but this proved in error. Fortunately, Terry telegraphed back to double-check his orders and determined that the ship was in fact believed lost near Heard's Island in the Indian Ocean. The *Marion* possessed no charts of the area nor were charts locally available. Resorting again to the telegraph, Terry arranged for the necessary charts to be delivered by steamship to Cape Town, South Africa, and then sailed across the Pacific. After picking up the maps and supplies, they proceeded the 3,000 miles to Heard's Island in eighteen days without once using their engines. Lookouts located the *Trinity*'s crew on Heard's Island the night of January 12. The following morning Chambers led one of the two rescue parties ashore. The heavy, rock-strewn surf and freezing temperature hampered the operation, and it took several hours to retrieve all the survivors. The *Marion* returned to Cape Town on February 20 and then sailed for South America, stopping on the way to rescue the stranded British steamship *Poonah*.[32]

## Intelligence Officer

Reform-minded officers steadily gained influence as the normal progression of promotion slowly moved them into prominent positions. In June of 1882, Commodore John Grimes Walker, the new Chief of the Bureau of Navigation and one of the leading reformers of the navy, ordered all ships to appoint intelligence officers. They would help the newly created Office of Naval Intelligence (ONI) gather data on foreign ships and bases. Bunce and many other captains ignored this order, but Terry, perhaps aware of Chambers's bent in this direction, added intelligence gathering to his duties. For the duration of his tour, Chambers sent regular reports on Latin America to the ONI as did his friend and mentor Lieutenant Rodgers.

Chambers proved a good choice for the job as his ship design work kept him conversant with the latest developments. He maintained his interest in torpedoes, and in August of 1882, sent the ONI a detailed report on a new English-built Argentine 21-knot torpedo boat that outclassed anything in the U.S. Navy. Chambers managed to get invited on board, and interviewed several of the Yarrow Company's employees who had sailed her from England. They gave him a complete tour, allowing him to compile a complete report on the ship, including her fittings, machinery, engine, and armament. He even managed to draw up blueprints for the ship, which particularly pleased the ONI. Terry repeatedly commended Chambers for his work as an intelligence officer, and considered him "useful in the highest degree to the service."[33]

As Chambers's tour of duty neared its expiration, the *Marion* sailed up the coast to the United States, reaching Portsmouth, New Hampshire, on December 13, 1882, after an extended stay in Bermuda. Chambers had no interest in leaving his next assignment to the vicissitudes of chance and bureaucratic politics, and his connections among reformers gave him an opportunity to influence his fate. His next assignment had to be on shore, as the Bureau of Navigation required officers to alternate between sea and shore duty in order to guarantee sea experience for all officers. Several people offered Chambers choice assignments, including Marshal Oliver, his drawing instructor at the Naval Academy, who offered him a position on the faculty.[34]

Two offers in particular excited Chambers's interest. Montgomery Sicard, still the Chief of the Bureau of Ordnance, repeatedly offered Chambers a post. Lieutenant Theodorus B. M. Mason, the head of the Office of Naval Intelligence, had read Chambers's reports and wanted him for his staff. Chambers found it hard to choose between the ONI and the Ordnance Bureau, and asked several friends for advice. Buckingham, his friend from the Paris Exposition, recommended that he accept Sicard's offer so he could work on new ordnance. The construction of the navy's first modern, steel warships had finally forced Congress to modernize ordnance manufacture in the United States and fund a modern gun factory at the Washington Navy Yard. As Chambers well knew, though, the United States lagged far behind the European powers. As he wrote the following year, the "art of gun construction in this country, owing to our long neglect, is again almost in its infancy." He thought the United States so far behind that "nothing less than a great effort on the part of the government will again enable our private gun-founders to compete . . . or our guns to become known for their excellence." Believing he would learn more about modern technology and ordnance from foreign governments, Chambers chose the ONI. Mason considered this a major coup and congratulated himself on getting Chambers and his "excellent ideas." It would prove to be the perfect assignment for Chambers.[35]

# 3 / The Greely Relief Expedition

When Chambers arrived at the Office of Naval Intelligence, Mason was still organizing it and establishing a routine. Chambers helped get the filing system in order and catalog the steadily increasing number of reports from shipboard intelligence officers, industry contacts, and other sources. Mason had written: "If you continue in the road which you are now traveling you will never have any trouble about duty." Men like Chambers who made "themselves useful outside of their mere routine duties" never had trouble getting good assignments. This turned out to be prophetic. Mason lost Chambers for much of the following year precisely because he was so desirable. Chambers's experience and high standing with a number of officers led to a temporary transfer to the Bureau of Ordnance, his assignment the Greely Relief Expedition, and then to a survey expedition to Nicaragua. After these special assignments, he returned to the ONI.[1]

## The Greely Expedition

Along with policing the seas, exploration was a traditional mission of the U.S. Navy. It had launched several expeditions to the Arctic over the past decades, and lost several ships there, most recently the steamer *Jeannette.* Commanded by George W. DeLong, the *Jeannette* had left San Francisco in 1879, passed through the Bering Strait, and sailed north. Advancing ice caught and slowly crushed the ship over the course of twenty-one months. Afterward, the crew split into the ship's three small boats and rowed south, but became separated in a dense fog. One boat disappeared, never to be found. DeLong's group died of starvation and exposure. Only the third boat under Chief Engineer George Melville reached civilization. A Senate investigation later faulted the navy for sending a ship unable to withstand the rigors of the Arctic. Ironically, the *Jeannette,* a gift from Arctic enthusiast James Gordon Bennett, had been far more suited to the voyage than any of the navy's other ships.[2]

After the failure of the *Jeannette* expedition, the navy wisely decided to focus its attentions on safer parts of the world—a recognition that its limited budget, aging ships, and unevenly trained personnel were not up to the rigors of Arctic exploration. For better or worse, the army decided it would try its hand at this dangerous venture.

The United States was hardly alone in its interest in Arctic exploration. Many nations had launched expeditions, and experienced their own successes and failures in that inhospitable region. Austrian explorer Karl Weyprecht presided over three International Polar Conferences in 1879, 1880, and 1881, at which the major exploring nations agreed to cooperate in making various meteorological, astronomical, and other observations from a ring of stations circling the North Pole. The stations would also send out teams to gather organic and mineral samples and explore the area. The United States agreed to place and staff two of these polar stations: one at Point Barrow, Alaska, the other on Ellesmere Island, an isolated spot northwest of Greenland along Lady Franklin Bay. The Weather Bureau, part of the broad array of agencies directed by the Chief Signal Officer of the Army would direct the United States' program. The Point Barrow expedition, commanded by Lieutenant P. Henry Ray, completed its two-year mission and returned in good health in 1883. The Lady Franklin Bay expedition would not fare as well.[3]

General William B. Hazen, the head of the Signal Corps, chose Lieutenant Adolphus W. Greely to lead the expedition of twenty soldiers and four officers to Lady Franklin Bay. Greely, fresh off an outpost in the American West, had little Arctic experience. His expedition left the United States on August 25, 1881, on board the whaler *Proteus.* Relief ships would bring more supplies in the summers of 1882 and 1883, and check that the explorers were well. Yet, Greely's orders specified that "if not visited in 1882, Lieutenant

Greely will abandon station not later than September 1, 1883, and will retreat southward by boat, following closely the east coast of Grinnell Land [an island west of Greenland], until the relieving vessel is met or Littleton Island is reached."[4] In the event the relief ships could not reach Greely, they were to wait as long as possible in Smith Sound and then cache supplies for him on Littleton Island and withdraw south ahead of the advancing ice pack.

The *Proteus* made an unexpectedly easy passage north, encountering little difficulty from ice. This gave all involved a false sense of optimism for the future. In fact, only three of the many previous expeditions had made it this far north. The *Proteus* helped Greely's team establish their base at Fort Conger and left them with three years' of supplies. A nearby coal seam would supply their fuel. All looked good for Greely and his men, but the 1882 resupply ship, the *Neptune,* failed to find a passage through the ice and cached supplies for Greely at several sites far south of Fort Conger before returning home.

The following year, army Lieutenant Edward A. Garlington in the *Proteus* commanded a more determined effort to reach Greely. To support his effort, the navy supplied the *Yantic,* an old, wooden steamer that lacked the hull strength to survive the briefest encounter with the ice pack, let alone to force a passage through it. She spent most of the voyage under sail due to mechanical difficulties. The *Proteus,* forced to proceed into dangerous waters alone, was trapped by a sudden advance of the ice in the Kane Sea and crushed. The undisciplined crew fought over the spoils as the ship went down, salvaging little. The civilian captain, Lieutenant Garlington, and Garlington's naval advisor, Lieutenant John C. Colwell, eventually managed to regain control of the crew. They cached what few supplies they salvaged, and rowed south across Melville Bay in the ship's boats toward Upernivik where the *Yantic* rescued them. The *Yantic* sailed home with both crews, while Greely on August 10, oblivious to what had occurred but obedient to his orders, gathered his men and began moving south, abandoning his well-supplied base for a dangerous journey on foot and in small boats through hundreds of miles of Arctic wilderness.[5]

## The Relief Expedition

Secretary of War Robert Todd Lincoln, desperate to avert disaster and save Greely's party, asked Secretary of the Navy William Chandler for help. President Chester A. Arthur convened a joint army-navy board to develop a rescue plan. It met from December 20 to January 22 without reaching a consensus. Garlington wanted to lead an army expedition to rescue Greely. Commander Bowman H. McCalla envisioned a navy operation. Others recommended a compromise—navy ships carrying an army relief party. President Arthur decided on an all-navy rescue operation, though Congress did not authorize funds for the expedition until February 13.

Because the navy had no ships suited for Arctic exploration, it would have to purchase them overseas. The only ships in the world built for this work were the famous Dundee whalers, built in Scotland and made out of several different woods to balance strength and elasticity, and iron reinforced bows to smash through ice. While the Senate wrangled over the wording of the appropriation, Chandler arranged for Lieutenant Commander French Ensor Chadwick, the ONI's attaché in Britain, to purchase two Dundee whalers, the *Thetis* and *Bear.* Eager to improve relations with the United States, Britain donated the *Alert,* a veteran of George Nares's 1875 Arctic expedition, then lying partially dismantled in a London dry dock.

Chandler chose Commander Winfield Scott Schley to lead the rescue expedition. Schley boasted a distinguished Civil War record and extensive duty in Asia. He had served as Commander Lewis A. Kimberly's adjutant during the successful 1871 assault on two Korean forts, and had a reputation for bold leadership and decisiveness. A charter member of the U.S. Naval Institute, he was well acquainted with other reform-minded officers.

Schley had followed the sad tale of the expedition in the newspapers, and had suggested to several friends that "some naval officer" would have "to go up there and bring them back." After several conversations with Chandler, Schley received his orders to assemble the rescue force on February 18. By then, he considered it a forlorn hope. Even if Greely's party could be found, they would likely be found dead just as DeLong's group had been. Despite his reservations, Schley agreed to accept the command as long as he could choose his officers, a process in which President Arthur may have participated.[6]

Schley selected his men carefully. All were volunteers and passed a rigorous medical exam. The seamen and petty officers had to reenlist as no one knew how long the expedition would last. All of its 115 members received an extra $10 a month pay and a bonus of two months' pay on successful return. Schley chose twenty-four officers for the expedition, of whom eight had previous Arctic experience. Many he knew personally, and he had met Chambers and the younger officers while teaching at the Naval Academy. Schley chose the *Thetis,* the most powerfully built and engined of the expedition's ships as his flagship. Commander George W. Coffin commanded the *Alert* and Lieutenant William H. Emory commanded the *Bear.* The expeditions' officers began arriving in New York in late March, and Schley assigned each ship an experienced civilian ice-master and at least one officer with Arctic or Antarctic experience. His own ship included two-time Arctic survivor George Melville and Chambers.

Senate debate on the expedition had been fierce. Many senators believed that Greely's party had already died, a pessimism bolstered by the contemporaneous hearings on the *Jeannette* disaster. Senator Eugene Hale, long a champion of the navy, managed to push through funding, though not without a contentious addition to the bill. Over the objections of Schley, Chandler, and Lincoln, the Senate offered a reward to anyone helping rescue Greely's expedition. Schley argued that this would lead unprepared vessels to rush into dangerous waters: they would get in his way and might need rescue themselves. The *New York Times* wryly commented that the Arctic whalers, the only ones likely to pursue the reward, could take care of themselves; it was the army and navy that kept getting into trouble in the polar regions. Chandler finally acquiesced and issued a $25,000 reward to any civilians who either rescued Greely or ascertained his fate. Many whalers left port early to search for Greely.[7]

Preparations for the expedition took a great deal of time. Chambers and the other officers supervised work on the ships—a process slowed by the throngs of reporters and the curious who observed their outfitting at the New York Navy Yard. Chambers, working closely with the commandant of the yard, spent most of his time supervising the refitting of the *Thetis,* and his speed, efficiency, knowledge of ship design, and organization earned him a commendation from Schley. The small crew complements, necessary to limit supply consumption and minimize the loss of life in event of disaster, meant plenty of work for everyone. All three ships needed extensive work. Crews needed to remove fishing equipment from the *Thetis* and the *Bear,* and the aging *Alert* needed extensive repairs. Schley's men tore out compartments to make room for supplies and overhauled the engines. They added braces to the hulls following the suggestions of Chief Constructor of the Navy Theodore Wilson. Schley stocked up for a long expedition and insisted on the best supplies and equipment. He even arranged to have 2,000 tons of the best Welsh coal shipped to St. Johns, Newfoundland, to await his squadron. Schley's officers also procured or cobbled together a variety of specialized equipment including new ice augers developed by the ever-inventive Bradley Fiske, then a lieutenant with the Bureau of Ordnance, and 600 explosive charges designed to clear passages through the ice. They purchased copies of every book on the Arctic they could find, which they studied when they had time.[8]

To hurry the expedition along, Schley sent out the ships as they became ready. The *Bear* sailed first on April 24. The following day Schley transferred Chambers to the *Alert* to speed up her preparations, and recalled him to the *Thetis* just before departure. In his haste, Chambers forgot his cold weather clothing, but in letters to friends, he confidently stated that he expected to enjoy his trip to the North Pole. Privately he worried about an expedition he saw as disorganized and its ships overcrowded. He presumably knew what he was getting into, as his friend Henry Mayo had served in the *Yantic* the previous year.[9]

The *Thetis*'s engine shaft broke shortly after departure, and the ship spent a day under sail while Melville fixed it. Lookouts spotted the first iceberg on May 7th, and three more the following day. They reached St. John's, Newfoundland, on May 9, finding the *Bear* and the *Loch Garry,* a British steamer leased for the expedition to carry its coal, awaiting them. The U.S. Navy did not have a single vessel suitable for this task. The *Loch Garry* was an ordinary iron steamer of 1,000 tons, entirely unsuited for travel through the Arctic ice, though some of its civilian crew of eighteen had experience in the north. Her commander, Captain Robert Jones, an old, bewhiskered Scot with a weather-beaten face, was an experienced ice navigator. Schley could not get insurance for the ship, and worried that its civilian crew might abandon his expedition. To prevent the latter and ease coordination with the rest of the squadron, he sent Chambers aboard as supercargo with two sailors and subordinated Captain Jones to Chambers. Chambers would keep a regular watch and help guide the ship through the ice. Chambers wanted to remain with the *Thetis,* and considered the assignment a "thankless billet."[10]

After refueling from the *Loch Garry,* Schley ordered the *Bear* to press northward, while the *Thetis* remained in St. John's to gather supplies and information. He questioned the locals, but learned little of use and nothing about Greely. Chambers rounded up supplies, hired several sled dog teams, and purchased new cold weather clothes for himself.

The *Thetis* and *Loch Garry* left St. John's on May 12, the *Loch Garry* following three cable lengths behind the *Thetis.* As soon as they cleared the harbor, a thick fog engulfed them. Lookouts soon spotted floating blocks of ice, which both ships repeatedly dodged. The weather worsened through the day, turning to a gale that lasted through the morning of May 22, when they arrived at the harbor ice of Godhavn. For the first time, the crews had to anchor in ice and had some difficulty with this new task. Thereafter, Schley and Chambers required their respective crews to practice this, so that ice anchoring became a quick task, usually accomplished in three minutes. A new gale packed the harbor with ice, delaying their departure by a day and half. Schley again questioned local people. This time he heard vague rumors of white men trapped on the ice, but nothing that would help locate them.[11]

The *Thetis* and *Loch Garry* left on the 24th, bound for Upernivik. The *Thetis* became stuck in the ice off Hare Island. The *Loch Garry* tried to pull her off, but the line snapped and she barely avoided being trapped herself. Chambers and Jones backed the *Loch Garry* out of danger and both ships dispatched parties who cleared a path with ice augers and explosives. The two ships then continued on their way until they hit solid ice at the North Fiord. The *Thetis* rammed in about 50 yards and stayed there for the night. The *Loch Garry* remained safely away. A gale the next morning almost drove the *Loch Garry* into the ice, and Schley ordered her back to Godhavn to await a change in the wind, though Chambers signaled his willingness to remain. The *Thetis* pushed into the ice pack, a slow and dangerous process. The ice was usually 10 feet thick and sometimes more than 20 feet thick. The explosives and torpedoes Schley had counted on proved ineffective. They loosened the ice, keeping the pressure from building and crushing the ship, but not enough to allow her to continue her voyage.[12]

When the weather cleared, the *Loch Garry* resumed the journey north. Carefully pushing through the clearing ice, she caught up with the *Thetis* on the 28th. By then, Schley and Chambers had gained considerable experience in navigating these waters. Schley later contended: "If a commander does not come to grief in the first week or ten days in the ice, he will have learned much that will help him to avoid ice dangers afterward."[13] Yet, both recognized that they still had much to learn. When the *Wolf* and the *Arctic,* two of the many whalers eager to share in the reward money, joined the *Thetis* and *Loch Garry* a few days later Schley invited their captains on board and quizzed them on the Arctic—a practice he repeated several times during the expedition so his officers could learn from the whalers.

The following morning, the *Arctic* and *Thetis* smashed their way into the ice followed by the *Wolf* with the *Loch Garry* in the rear. Not very maneuverable and slower than the whalers, the *Loch Garry* had trouble keeping to the path cleared by the *Thetis.* Despite their best efforts, the *Wolf* frequently had to turn back and help extricate the *Loch Garry.* The passage that Schley described as "exciting and anxious" as he watched from the crow's nest of the *Thetis* was considerably more so to those on board the ungainly *Loch Garry,* which several times only narrowly avoided disaster. Schley spent twenty hours in the crow's nest guiding his ship while his navigator below struggled to plot their course on outdated charts that sometimes showed them considerably inland. Whalers continued to arrive, and soon eight of them sailed near Schley's squadron, hoping to claim the reward. Schley's growing armada arrived off Upernivik on the morning of the 29th, where they joined the *Bear,* which had arrived on the 27th. Emory had tried to press on but managed to travel only 18 miles before the thick ice pack blocked his advance.[14]

The *Bear* and *Thetis* set out that evening after recruiting native guides and more dog teams and recoaling from the *Loch Garry.* They left *Loch Garry* to await the *Alert,* the last expedition ship to depart New York. Schley needed to press ahead and could not delay to escort the *Loch Garry.* The ice in Melville Bay made it too dangerous for the *Loch Garry* to proceed alone, though Chambers and Jones were again willing to make the attempt. Even escorted by the *Alert,* there was a good chance of the *Loch Garry* foundering, so Schley ordered Chambers to cache 50 tons of coal for the squadron's return trip. While separated, Chambers and Schley communicated intermittently through letters carried by passing whalers.[15]

The *Alert,* under Commander Coffin, reached Upernivik on the 13th, two weeks after Schley had left. The largest of the ice-capable ships, the *Alert,* carried the disassembled sheds and building materials to establish a base camp that a prolonged search would require. While waiting for warmer weather, Chambers transferred coal from the *Loch Garry* to the *Alert,* and stowed an extra quantity on her deck in case the *Loch Garry* failed to make it through. Both ships repeatedly exercised their crews in abandoning ship, underscoring the serious risk that the ungainly *Loch Garry* and the worn-out *Alert* faced venturing north.

They left Upernivik on June 19 and soon encountered heavy ice that greatly slowed their passage north. At the Berry Islands, all leads through the ice closed, and they anchored in the ice, awaiting an opportunity to renew their advance. Instead, on June 24 a heavy gale forced them to cut through 4 feet of ice and dock both ships. The gale ceased the next day and both ships again worked their way north, passing Cape Shackleton and then the Duck Islands where solid ice again stopped them. The *Alert* lacked the engine power to attack the ice as aggressively as the *Bear* and *Thetis.* Despite following the *Alert* as closely as she could, rapidly closing ice frequently trapped the *Loch Garry,* and the *Alert* had to double back and free her. On the worst day the ships "were ramming, pushing, and twisting" their way "through the ice, sometimes in the midst of it with no open water, sometimes in a narrow lane." The *Alert* became stuck in the floe, and "the *Loch Garry* came to the rescue and entered on a ramming campaign with a view of getting the *Alert* out of her imprisonment," but became stuck as well. Both crews resorted to explosives and with a combination of ramming and blasting the *Loch Garry* fought through to the *Alert.* They attached a hawser to the *Alert* and tried to pull her out, but it would not hold. They finally freed the *Alert* through a combination of ramming and blasting with explosives. The two ships advanced 8 miles on the 26th and 8 more on the 27th, but thickening ice stopped and then trapped them, leaving them to await better weather or Schley's return. The *Alert* and *Loch Garry* had made it much farther north than Schley had expected.[16]

While the *Alert* and *Loch Garry* had clawed their way north, the *Thetis* and *Bear* completed the objective of the expedition. Moving through the ice together, they took turns leading, and helped extract each other when ice closed in. They repeatedly came close to being trapped by rapidly closing ice, but managed to continue moving north. On June 21, they reached Littleton Island. Finding the supplies cached by the *Neptune* undisturbed, they pressed on the following day, discovering a cairn marking a deposit of Greely's records with a message that he and his party were on Cape Sabine. The last of these papers, dated October 21, 1883, indicated Greely's force had only forty days of rations remaining. Lieutenant Colwell and a search party from the *Bear* found the survivors weak and starving the following day, huddled in a collapsed tent. Greely had shot one of his men for stealing food, and the survivors had resorted to cannibalism. Of the original party of twenty-seven, only Greely and six others remained, one of whom died on the voyage home.

Returning south, Schley found the *Alert* and *Loch Garry* trapped in the ice on the afternoon of the 30th and freed them. United for the first time, the four ships stood to the south, the *Thetis* leading, the *Loch Garry* second, and the other two following in their wakes ready to assist if necessary. Battered by ice and weather, all the ships had sprung leaks. Leaking and with 5 feet of water in the hold, Emory thought the *Bear* might not make it home.[17] The others were not much better off.

Instead of pack ice, numerous icebergs blocked their passage. Dense fog reduced their speed to only 2 knots, and the ships navigated between the bergs almost blind, constantly sounding their whistles to avoid fouling one another. Near the Duck Islands, rapidly closing ice trapped the *Alert* and *Loch Garry,* and the *Thetis* and *Bear* doubled back and freed them. The squadron reached a large ice floe early the next morning and anchored to it to rest their exhausted crews. The fog cleared near dusk and they resumed their course with the *Thetis* and *Bear* sharing the lead. They reached the Berry Islands on July 2 where thick ice jammed in against the coast forced them into a dangerous, rock-strewn passage that concealed numerous obstacles. The *Bear* hit a submerged rock and it took two hours for the *Alert* and *Thetis* to free her.

After clearing these dangerous waters, Schley sent the *Alert* and *Loch Garry* to Disko, while the *Bear* and *Thetis* left for Upernivik to take on supplies and return the dog teams and native guides. The *Loch Garry* and *Alert* reached Disko the next day, and began repairing and patching their damaged hulls. Chambers and Coffin had their crews transfer the huts and material for the base camp and other supplies to the *Loch Garry* to lighten the load on the *Alert*'s ailing engines.

The *Thetis* and *Bear* arrived at Disko on the 5th, but repairs on the *Alert* delayed the squadron's departure until the 9th. The *Alert*'s engines soon gave out, and the *Loch Garry* took her in tow. While it did not prove necessary, Chambers investigated the possibility of transferring coal from the *Loch Garry* to the *Alert* while underway, and was convinced he could have managed it "without much difficulty."[18] A heavy gale on the 15th forced the *Loch Garry* to drop the line to the *Alert.* Schley ordered the squadron's speed reduced to 2 knots, but the *Alert* fell behind and disappeared in the heavy fog that followed the storm. The *Thetis, Bear,* and *Loch Garry* arrived in St. John's on the 17th. The *Alert* straggled in the following day to find a celebration already in progress. The party moved to the more spacious *Alert,* but none of Greely's party was well enough to take part.

Schley sent the *Loch Garry* home on the 21st with Greely's records, his preliminary report, and three bags of mail from the squadron. They sailed through bad weather the entire way and arrived in New York harbor on the evening of the 26th, empty of coal, high in the water, damaged, and leaking. Sixteen hull plates had buckled and six others had cracked under the strain. The main timbers all showed serious damage and cracking and several of the frame timbers were coming apart.[19]

If Chambers expected a great fanfare, he was disappointed. The *Loch Garry* passed the torpedo boat *Alarm* and the monitor *Passaic* without being recognized. When the *Alarm* ran aground a few minutes later, Chambers gleefully turned the *Loch Garry* about and offered to pull her off, signaling: "we're in the relief squadron yet," though the joke was lost on the *Alarm*'s crew. Members of the press had been tipped off, and interviewed Chambers after the *Loch Garry* docked. Chambers had enjoyed his first command and the mixed crew had functioned well together. Still, the voyage had been arduous, and Chambers showed the strain. Several of the journalists estimated his age as about "40 years old" rather than his actual age of twenty-eight, though "tall and well built with a pleasant countenance." His face was seriously sunburned, his nose swollen and peeling. When asked the usual cliché questions as to his happiness at arriving home, the exhausted Chambers snapped: "We're back and I can't say I'm sorry for it." He quickly relaxed, though, and entertained the reporters with vivid descriptions of Arctic beauty and danger. He complimented Schley's leadership and praised the bravery of his crew and the other members of the expedition.[20]

After seeing to the *Loch Garry,* Chambers rushed north to rejoin the squadron at Portsmouth, New Hampshire, leaving behind a dog he had picked up in the Arctic. The squadron had made good time after leaving St. Johns on the 26th, but delayed its arrival in Portsmouth until just before the welcoming ceremony planned by Acting Rear Admiral Stephen B. Luce and the North Atlantic Squadron. Chambers rejoined the *Thetis* on August 1 when it arrived at Portsmouth. The following day, Luce, Chandler, and General Hazen greeted the expedition's officers on board Luce's flagship, the *Tennessee.* There followed three days of carefully staged celebrations, parades, and receptions with dignitaries and the press. Afterward, the squadron sailed for New York where President Arthur welcomed them back at a reception. The expedition's officers then dispersed to their previous posts. Chambers returned to the Office of Naval Intelligence.[21]

Throughout the months of the Greely Relief Expedition's preparation and voyage, newspapers published a barrage of articles critical of the sad state of the navy. After its return, tales of its and Greely's adventures filled newspapers for weeks. Editorials calling for a larger, or at least more modern navy accompanied many of them. Chambers's friends at the ONI encouraged this by deluging the press with statistics and data. The relief expedition's success exonerated the navy, but press coverage of the army's role in Greely's expedition remained harsh. The press wanted a scapegoat for the disaster and settled on General Hazen who had dispatched Greely with such strange orders. Hazen's efforts to exonerate himself and blame Garlington hardly added to his reputation.[22]

Certainly, the success of the relief expedition allowed the navy to tarnish the reputation of the army, but much more was at stake than bureaucratic infighting. Reform-minded navy officers wanted more than just an increase in naval spending. The success of the Greely Relief Expedition expunged the taint of failed expeditions and other disasters from the navy's record. It also displayed the talents of a new generation of officers, and offered proof not just of the navy's need for new ships, but also that its officers were ready and capable of sailing them into the most dangerous waters of the planet. They were far from the drunks and misfits whose misadventures the press had chronicled through the 1870s. Chandler paraded the expedition's officers before the press as examples of those who would lead the new navy—brave, resourceful, and technically competent, who Schley proclaimed could be "trusted in all emergencies to fulfill the expectation of our beloved people."[23]

Chambers's performance impressed Schley, who singled him out for special praise. Chambers, he reported, "was always most interested and efficient; his judgment and ability were most conspicuous, and to him and to his advice the safety of the *Loch Garry* was mainly due. He enjoyed my highest confidence for his officer-like management of delicate duties." The following year, Schley wrote new Secretary of the Navy William C. Whitney that it was only through Chambers's "competency and professional skill" the *Loch Garry* made it safely through "several hundreds of miles of ice." He regarded "Chambers as one of the most efficient and competent officers of the Navy."[24]

Regardless of the successful rescue, the whole affair showed the problems of military-run scientific missions. Science seemed to take a backseat to heroics and attempts at record setting. The notes of the expedition and its samples proved of limited value. Even before Greely set out for the Arctic, civilian scientists were pushing the military out of primary research. The Interior Department had taken control of the U.S. Geological Survey from the army, and the Department of Agriculture assumed control of the army meteorological program shortly after Greely's return. The army and navy battled these bureaucratic interlopers, but increasingly reduced the priority of these missions as they concentrated on what their officers saw as their primary mission—the preparation for and the fighting of wars.[25]

This proved a slow process, and both services remained interested in exploration, or at least the favorable media attention it garnered. The navy in particular maintained an interest in polar exploration. Aside from Chambers and the other officers of the expedition, the Greely Relief Expedition also held particular importance to Robert Edwin Peary, who Chambers would soon meet. A navy civil engineer, Peary read of the relief expedition's adventures and became obsessed with polar exploration. From 1885, perhaps due to conversations with Chambers, he "single-mindedly planned a rendezvous with the top of the world."[26]

# 4 / The Nicaraguan Survey

Chambers soon found himself in another expedition, this time surveying a canal route. The United States had a long interest in the Caribbean and the construction of a canal through Central America. Over the years, entrepreneurs and engineers had proposed several different routes, though most favored Panama or Nicaragua. The debate over their relative advantages raged throughout the last decades of the nineteenth century. Interest between them waxed and waned, influenced as much by the politics of the region as by engineering difficulties. In general, Americans favored the Nicaraguan route, while Europeans preferred a route through Panama. Inability to settle on a location and design left the door open for many new proposals to link the Atlantic and Pacific. The most popular of these in the United States was the Eads ship railway. Famous engineer James Buchanan Eads offered to build a huge railroad across the isthmus. Ships would be hoisted out of the water at one coast, placed on flatbed cars, transported overland, and then hoisted back into the water to continue their voyage. This system had been used with canal boats, but never on the grandiose scale Eads suggested.

Proposals for canal construction predated the Civil War. Navalists, such as Lieutenant Robert Shufeldt, envisioned an isthmian canal as the linchpin in a globe-spanning network of commercial and naval interests. Only after the Civil War did canal advocates garner public support for their efforts. It was a slow process, hindered by the success of the transcontinental railroad, which many considered a sufficient link between the coasts. Secretary of State William H. Seward shared Shufeldt's vision and negotiated an agreement with Nicaragua for canal construction in 1867, but Seward had outpaced public opinion and nothing came of it.[1]

A growing number of naval officers championed canal construction in the 1870s, particularly Admiral Daniel Ammen, who emerged as their leader. He lobbied for a canal, and convinced the navy to send several expeditions to survey possible routes.[2] Shufeldt led the first of these expeditions and surveyed a route across Tehuantepec, Mexico, in 1870–71. He lobbied for its acceptance in the early 1870s, but later switched his support to the Nicaraguan route. Commander Thomas O. Selfridge led a larger survey that investigated possible routes through Nicaragua in 1871–72, but the rainy season halted his operations. Commander Edward P. Lull, aided by Chief Civil Engineer Aniceto G. Menocal, resumed the survey in December. Lake Nicaragua would aid the construction and operation of the canal, but Lull and Menocal had difficulty finding a route that avoided the unstable soil common to the area and nine active or potentially active volcanoes. Menocal returned in 1874 in a privately financed expedition. Lull continued to gather data on the possible routes and submitted his report to the Interoceanic Canal Commission in 1876. Both Lull and Menocal favored a Nicaraguan route and convinced the commission that Nicaragua offered great advantages, and fewer "difficulties from engineering, commercial, and economic points of view." Most naval officers joined them in supporting the Nicaraguan route.[3]

Various European companies and nations also negotiated for canal concessions, but the unstable politics of Central America and the machinations of Guatemalan dictator Justo Rufino Barrios complicated their efforts. Barrios plotted with foreign powers, offering canal concessions in exchange for support in uniting Central America under his rule. His neighbors, in turn, offered concessions in the hopes of winning foreign support to resist Barrios.[4]

In 1878, a group of French investors led by Ferdinand de Lesseps, the designer of the Suez Canal, received a concession from Colombia to build a canal through Panama. The following year, de Lesseps arranged for the French Geographic Society to host a conference on isthmian canal routes and their respective difficulties. De Lesseps's real purpose was to gain international approval for a canal through Panama and to begin raising funds. Most developed nations sent delegations. Ammen and Menocal led the American delegation, and obstinately argued for the Nicaraguan route. Not surprisingly, the votes went against them, and the conference issued a report favoring de Lesseps's route. De Lesseps organized a construction company and left for Panama to begin work.

De Lesseps's progress failed to discourage the Nicaraguan enthusiasts. After the Paris conference, Ammen retired from the navy to pursue canal building full-time, and incite American concern over the issue. Many Americans feared a European-built canal, believing it would become a base for European commercial interests and renewed imperialism. "What Europe digs with the spade," Congressman John Finerty later warned, "she will maintain with the sword." Shufeldt similarly opposed a foreign-owned canal that would "throw the commerce of the Pacific" into the hands of a European power. Ammen and his supporters argued that even if de Lesseps's managed to build a canal—something that was far from certain—the United States would still have to build its own canal for security and to prevent a French embargo of its commerce. Even President Hayes seemed convinced of the urgency of the situation, and objected to a European-owned canal as a violation of the Monroe Doctrine. "The policy of this country," he told Congress, was an American controlled canal. "The United States cannot consent to the surrender of this control to any European power." Few politicians shared these concerns, but Hayes's speech spurred the canal advocates to redouble their efforts.[5]

In 1879, Ammen and Menocal attracted a group of investors, including former General George B. McClellan, Levi P. Morton, and Seth Ledyard Phelps. Together they organized the Provisional Interoceanic Canal Society (PICS), and convinced former President Grant and other prominent Americans to join. Phelps became the corporation's president and led its fund-raising efforts. Menocal returned to Nicaragua and negotiated a new construction agreement and ninety-nine-year concession. The Nicaraguan Congress allowed Menocal three years for surveys and planning before starting construction. If work did not commence within three years, Nicaragua would withdraw the concession and look for other takers.[6]

On Menocal's return, the PICS reorganized as the Maritime Canal Company of Nicaragua and began fund-raising and congressional lobbying in earnest. Senator John F. Miller of California introduced a bill providing political and financial guarantees to the canal company, and it bounced in and out of several committees for the next two years. Ammen, Menocal, and their supporters lobbied for it furiously, and arranged for favorable reports and testimony from naval officers who glossed over the Nicaraguan route's problems: its great length, the necessity for locks, the lack of natural harbors, and the threat of volcanic devastation. The bill failed by a narrow margin in 1884, foiled in part by lobbying from de Lesseps and Eads. The restrictions of the Clayton-Bulwer treaty, which guaranteed the neutrality of any isthmian canal, influenced several Congressmen. Why build a canal if the United States could not take full advantage of it?[7]

The Maritime Canal Company's other fund-raising efforts also failed, and it faced bankruptcy as the concession's time limit neared. McClellan and Grant, who was dying of throat cancer, tried to organize financial backing through the Grant and Ward banking firm of which Grant was a partner, but that bank collapsed. The company's fund-raising efforts collapsed along with the aging general's health, and its concession lapsed on September 30, 1884.

Still, the company had friends in high places, and Secretary of State Frederick T. Frelinghuysen arranged a new concession in the Frelinghuysen-Zavala Treaty with Nicaragua. President Arthur expressed his support for the agreement in a message to the Senate, and argued that it would open Asian markets to American industry and agriculture.[8] Secretary of the Navy Chandler ordered Menocal to resurvey the eastern portion of the proposed route. Menocal had already resurveyed the short western section of the route that would connect Lake Nicaragua to the Pacific in 1880. Chandler and Menocal hoped to improve on Lull's 1873 route and reduce construction costs. Every dollar saved could make the difference between congressional ratification and failure.

## The Surveying Expedition

The navy assigned three officers to help Menocal: Passed Assistant Surgeon John F. Bransford, Chambers, and Civil Engineer Robert E. Peary. Bransford was there to ensure the health of the expedition in an exceptionally unhealthy part of the world. Menocal, Peary, and Chambers would carry out the work of the survey along with locally hired labor. Peary was Menocal's protégé and would be the expedition's pioneer and chief explorer. Like many engineers in the navy, he graduated from a civilian engineering school and passed the navy's civil engineering exam to receive his commission. Menocal, who had served on Peary's exam board, made him his assistant, and guided Peary's career by arranging choice assignments for him.[9]

Chambers's appointment to the expedition seems to be a result of his intelligence work, knowledge of the area, fluency in Spanish, excellent reputation following the Greely Relief Expedition, and his many connections with reform-minded officers. In Chambers, the expedition received not just an experienced explorer, but a publicist as well. Chambers had already emerged as an ardent spokesman for reform and an advocate of an isthmian canal. Menocal could be certain of his support. Chandler himself may well have recommended Chambers. They had met in the celebrations following the return of the Greely Relief Expedition and Chandler had read his intelligence reports. Regardless, Chambers received confidential instructions from Chandler and sent him regular reports on their progress and on de Lesseps's construction team.[10]

Chambers, Menocal, and Peary left New York on board a mail steamer on December 20, 1884. They traveled first to Aspinwall and then crossed the isthmus on the Panama Railroad. A delay in transporting their supplies allowed them to spend two days inspecting de Lesseps's work. Over the previous few years several American naval officers had visited de Lesseps to monitor his progress—all part of the coordinated intelligence effort managed by the ONI. Chambers's friend Raymond Rodgers thought that de Lesseps would succeed, but most observers lacked his optimism. Shufeldt, who tracked de Lesseps's progress through a variety of sources, expected him to fail. So, too, did Chambers, who reported that de Lesseps was plagued with problems and was proceeding slower than expected. Disease whittled away the work force. Corruption was rampant, and large contracts went only to those "in league with the Canal Officials." Workers dumped excavated soil wherever it was convenient, even in places where rains washed it back into the cuts. Chambers estimated that de Lesseps had completed only 5 percent of the work on the canal. At that rate, it would take him another eighteen years to finish. Lieutenant William W. Kimball made a detailed survey of the Panama route later that year and reached similar conclusions. De Lesseps was in trouble. There was still time for the United States to complete its canal first.[11]

From Panama, the expedition sailed to Nicaragua on board the steam sloop *Lackawanna,* and arrived in Corinto on January 7, 1885. From there, they traveled inland and hired a private steamer to explore Lake Managua, stopping briefly in Managua to pay their respects to President Cardenas and other officials. Cardenas assured them that he would help their expedition any way he could. Continuing into the interior, they reached Grenada on January 13, where they hired guides, porters, and two cooks. Fifteen members strong, they left Grenada, crossed Lake Nicaragua by steamer, and reached their starting point at the confluence of the Rio San Juan and the Sarapiqui River on January 22, where they set up camp.[12]

Menocal had planned that he and Peary would to do the bulk of the surveying while Chambers would be in charge of the camp and handle the logistical details, but Menocal had overestimated his health and stamina. He soon began to have problems in the tropical climate. Chambers "with uniform kindness," repeatedly offered to relieve Menocal "of the hardest part of the work, by running either the transit or the level . . . over the most difficult part of the route." At first Menocal refused, but the sheer quantity of the work and his worsening health and "painful indispositions" forced him to rely on Chambers. By the last month of the expedition, Menocal remained in camp, coordinating detached parties under Chambers and Peary. Chambers also took the expedition's many photographs, having learned photography during his brief time at the ONI.[13]

Several engineers had proposed building a dam at the junction of the San Juan and Sarapiqui Rivers to raise the level of the San Juan, essentially turning it into an extension of Lake Nicaragua. This would considerably shorten the canal. Peary and Menocal explored the area, testing the soil and seeking a site for the dam, while Chambers paddled up the river in a canoe to survey it and check its depth. After three days of careful study they determined that constructing a dam there was unfeasible. This forced them to investigate the more difficult option—digging the canal through the San Francisco River valley.[14]

The expedition packed up the following day and hiked to the valley entrance near Greytown, where they established Camp Chandler. Dense jungle covered the hilly terrain, and even rubber hunters had not entered the valley. The lower elevations were all swamp thickly inhabited by mosquitoes and snakes. The dense vegetation made it impossible to advance even a few feet without using their machetes. It rained constantly, and the explorers were often up to their waists in water and mud as they stumbled forward over uncertain and shifting ground. Some of the vegetation was toxic and splattered caustic fluid in all directions when cut. It blinded the eye of one worker, and everyone suffered from skin irritations. Day after day the expedition slowly worked its way up each of the San Francisco's many tributaries. The work took much longer than expected, slowed, as Chambers wrote, by "many privations, hardships and copious rains." After they broke their ax, they had only hatchets and machetes to clear the dense growth.[15]

The hard work quickly exhausted their porters, and injuries mounted as the survey dragged on. One porter, after spotting a small boat on February 4, demanded his pay from Menocal and ran off to catch a ride back to civilization. Two days later, Chambers shot an enormous iguana that provided a welcome break from their stale rations for those willing to try it. Chambers continued to hunt to supplement their food supply, though he soon realized that there was another hunter in the area. A jaguar trailed the party, raiding its food at night. Chambers and Peary tried to track down the cat, but it eluded them in the dense jungle.[16]

When it became obvious that they would not finish the survey on time, Menocal traveled back to the nearest telegraph station and wired home for permission to remain in the field another month. He took with him half their force of local laborers who had been worn out by the heavy work of the expedition. After receiving the navy's affirmative reply, he arranged for additional provisions to be sent down the river, hired new porters, and hiked back to Camp Chandler.

Chambers and Peary meanwhile continued the slow work of surveying the valley, advancing only a few miles a day. The increasingly dense vegetation hampered their work, and they had to climb trees to get their bearings. Menocal had considered bringing a balloon with the expedition to take sightings from above the jungle's canopy, but the dense jungle would have torn it to shreds. Chambers and Peary were frequently far from camp with little in the way of supplies. Often they bedded down with little more than palm leaves for shelter and rubber blankets for beds. Chambers repeatedly relocated their base camp as they advanced deeper into the valley, moving by foot and in canoes that could barely hold their 800 pounds of equipment. In relocating the camp, Chambers handled "the heaviest part of the work." He not only had "the immediate supervision of the arduous work of overcoming the obstructions, but would, in his zeal, jump into the water when serious obstacles were met with, and by his own personal efforts assist in removing the logs blocking the way, or in lifting canoes bodily over them." Chambers worked well with the hired men and continually inspired them to greater efforts "by word and personal exertions." In contrast, Menocal often lost his temper with the porters and provoked several of them to quit. As the expedition continued, Menocal again had to return to Grenada to hire fresh men.[17]

The expedition finally completed its work and started its journey home on April 26, stopping on the way to observe de Lesseps's progress. They arrived in New York on June 2, and after a short leave, returned to their previous assignments. On July 17, Menocal summoned Peary and Chambers to his Washington Navy Yard office. There, they spent the next three months preparing maps and writing their report. Their route reduced the canal's length by eleven and a half miles, the required excavation by more than 20 miles, and the cost to under $50 million, a savings of almost $17 million. They concluded that a Nicaraguan canal was practical, free from serious engineering difficulties, and "the most economical, convenient and safe route for interoceanic ship communication between the Atlantic and Pacific Oceans." They finished their report on October 15 when the perennially understaffed Office of Naval Intelligence insisted that Chambers return. Between the Greely Relief Expedition and the Nicaraguan survey, he had been gone for a year.[18]

Menocal effusively praised both Chambers and Peary for their "untiring energy and perseverance," and credited them with making the expedition a success. In addition to "important services rendered in connection with the field work," Chambers proved invaluable in the "onerous duties of executive in the camp organization." Without him, the expedition might well have failed. Certainly, Menocal would have been in the field much longer.[19]

The departure of the expedition reinvigorated the canal advocates who again pressed Congress for funds and treaty ratification, but the Democrats blocked these. While the nominal issue was the abrogation of the Clayton-Bulwer treaty, the failure of ratification had as much to do with party politics. The close elections of the 1880s and changing control of the presidency and Congress destroyed the possibility of compromise between the two parties who sought every electoral advantage. Incoming President Grover Cleveland opposed the treaty and withdrew it from consideration, declaring that a canal should be a "trust for mankind" removed from the "domination of a single power." Besides, Cleveland contended, the construction, ownership, and defense of a canal were "beyond the scope of our national polity or present means."[20]

Menocal and his friends remained undaunted. Despite Cleveland's rhetoric, circumstances pointed to an increasing U.S. interest in the isthmus. While Chambers, Menocal, and Peary had explored Nicaragua, rebels in Panama attacked Colombian forces, shut down the isthmian railway, and seized ships and property belonging to Americans. Cleveland dispatched a naval expedition, and 750 marines and sailors occupied Panama City to protect it from the rebels. Clearly, the United States possessed both an interest in the region and the means to police it.

On December 3, 1886, Ammen, Menocal, and several of their supporters organized a second Provisional Canal Association and restarted the whole process. Menocal negotiated a new concession from Nicaragua and supporters launched yet another publicity campaign. Both houses of Congress passed bills wishing the company success, but provided no funds. De Lesseps's company went bankrupt, presenting American canal advocates both an opportunity to build the first canal and a warning of its difficulty. The navy sent another expedition to Nicaragua, which confirmed Menocal's route as the best choice.[21]

Chambers, back at the ONI, remained involved in the canal project and repeatedly wrote to defend it. Like many naval officers, Chambers invested in the company. So, too, did commanders Arent S. Crowninshield and Henry C. Taylor who lobbied for congressional funding of the canal. Chambers wrote many of the new company's marketing pamphlets and briefing materials and explained that the canal was essential to further trade and to redress the mercantile imbalance between the United States and Great Britain. He believed it would lead to the commercial supremacy of the United States from which "sea power would follow."[22]

The canal would be more than an economic boon to the United States. It would also become a center of culture and progress from which the United States would "develop" Nicaragua and aid the people of this "wonderful country" on their road to civilization. It was the United States' duty, Chambers argued, "to demonstrate to the world that our free and liberal institutions are lasting." It was an argument influenced by best-selling author Josiah Strong who called on Americans, as the "chosen people," to do their duty, to uplift the heathen multitudes into "the light of the highest Christian civilization," to offer them the twin benefits of a "pure spiritual Christianity" and the American ideal of "civil liberty." For Chambers, the canal would become a lasting symbol of the emergence of the United States as a great power and its moral superiority over both decadent Europe and impoverished Latin America.[23]

Other naval officers also championed the canal, including commanders Charles H. Stockton and Henry C. Taylor. In arguments that echoed Chambers's points, both argued for the overriding commercial need for a canal, though they emphasized its military necessity more than Chambers. Taylor, much like Chambers, argued that opening a canal through Nicaragua would not only give the United States control of the Pacific, but it would also become a base from which its warships could strike "rapid and effective blows in both oceans." Both saw it as only the beginning of colonial expansion. Once built, the United States would need a larger navy and overseas bases to protect it, making the canal not only militarily useful but also an excellent argument for naval expansion.[24]

Building a canal, though, was no simple task. Menocal's new corporation issued $100 million of stock. Its subsidiary, the Nicaragua Canal Construction Company, began work in late 1889, but fell behind schedule as funds ran out. Efforts to issue more bonds failed in the panic of 1893, and the company collapsed. Despite repeated entreaties, Congress never offered the financial support the project required.

Chambers returned to the Office of Naval Intelligence following the 1885 expedition with a growing circle of influential contacts including many high-ranking officers. His work on the canal and his writings on its importance brought him to the attention of Alfred Thayer Mahan and other officers at the newly created Naval War College. Chambers, still a mere ensign, found himself routinely corresponding with senior officers and the Secretary of the Navy.

# 5 / The Office of Naval Intelligence

The Office of Naval Intelligence owed its existence to the work of reformers both inside and outside the navy. James Garfield came to the presidency in 1881 with a reform agenda and appointed several reformers to his cabinet including Secretary of the Navy William H. Hunt. Dynamic and insightful, Hunt demanded a navy capable of "active and aggressive warfare in the ports and waters of an enemy."[1] During his short tenure, he created the institutions that led the drive for naval reform through the 1880s: the Naval Advisory Board and the Office of Naval Intelligence.

Commodore John Grimes Walker, the Chief of the Bureau of Navigation, convinced Hunt to create the ONI. Like Hunt, Walker was an experienced manager with great respect for and experience with new technology. Walker had worked for the Chicago, Burlington, and Quincy Railroad before returning to the navy, and embraced the drive for efficiency then sweeping American business. He believed it essential to rationalize the navy's convoluted administrative structure, centralize its planning, modernize its fleet and infrastructure, and improve officer training.[2]

Walker expected the ONI to play a key role in the reform and modernization of the navy. It would collect and store information, and systematize "the collection and classification of information," especially that relating "to the strength and resources of foreign navies."[3] The Naval Advisory Board, benefiting from ONI data, would create plans for modern warships and supervise the construction of a modern fleet. Walker supported the new agency and appointed a number of promising officers to it. Without him, it would likely have withered and died, a victim of bureaucratic neglect.

Following Garfield's assassination, Chester Arthur reshuffled the cabinet to reward his political supporters, replacing Hunt with William E. Chandler, a long-time Republican functionary. Chandler chose Lieutenant Theodorus B. M. Mason to lead the ONI. A protégé of Walker and Admiral Christopher R. P. Rodgers, Mason had served as Arthur's naval aide. Strongly influenced by Stephen B. Luce, the navy's leading reformer, he saw the ONI as the first step in creating a naval general staff. Helped by these influential patrons, Mason convinced Chandler to clarify the mission of the ONI. It would not only gather the information necessary for the modernization of the navy but also the information needed to allow the navy to plan strategy and draw up war plans against a variety of opponents. Preparation for war, Luce, Mason, and other reformers argued, should be the primary mission of the navy.[4]

Crowded and understaffed, the ONI made its home in the State, War, and Navy building, doing the best it could with its limited resources. Congress did not appropriate funds for the agency until the 1890s. Walker assigned Mason only three officers to help him in 1882, among them Chambers's classmate Templin M. Potts. That same year, Walker ordered all warships to appoint intelligence officers who would report to the ONI on foreign navies and events. Many captains resented the interference of Washington bureaucracy in their commands and ignored the order.[5]

Mason organized the office on functional lines. Different sections collected data of interest to the different bureaus of the navy. This was far from the best system for creating a coherent strategic vision, but Mason understood that if the ONI failed to prove its worth to the navy's bureaus, it would not outlive Walker's tenure as Chief of the Bureau of Navigation. The ONI had to function effectively within the existing system while it worked to reform it.[6]

Mason's new staff gathered and recataloged all the intelligence data haphazardly collected since the Civil War and then set about gathering new data. Chambers, Rodgers, and other shipboard intelligence officers, and French Ensor Chadwick, the ONI's foreign attaché, studied, mapped, and later photographed foreign coasts, ports, and naval facilities. They compiled the routes and specifications of foreign merchant shipping and the specifications and stations of foreign warships. They "collected blueprints for a torpedo boat, a boiler, a dry dock, a magazine, a gun milling and drilling machine, and a rifling machine," along with numerous drawings of ships, machinery, guns and gun carriages, armor, turrets, and torpedoes, and "notes on experiments with armor, naval gunnery, submarine mines, and torpedoes." They bought and translated foreign books and interviewed foreign officers. By September 1883, they had compiled a list of all the warships under construction in Europe and Latin America.[7]

As its organization jelled, the ONI published a regular series of reports on important topics and distributed its General Information Series to American naval officers. Its first reports covered the operations of the French navy in Tunis, naval operations in the War of the Pacific between Chile, Peru, and Bolivia, and British operations in Egypt in 1882. Its publications, particularly the General Information Series, were far ahead of any comparable foreign naval document. U.S. intelligence officers often traded them to foreign naval officers in exchange for data the ONI needed. The ONI monitored technological exhibitions, naval operations, and naval construction throughout the world. Protected by Walker, it grew. He assigned it three more officers in 1883 (lieutenants William H. Driggs, Robert McLean, and Sidney Staunton) and three in 1884: Lieutenant William H. Beehler, and ensigns Frank R. Heath, and William L. Rodgers, though several others departed.[8]

Despite his expedition-related absences, Chambers settled in well at the ONI and proved an excellent organizer. He "arranged the forms for intelligence reports, arranged the files of drawings and plans, and mounted and arranged the growing collection of photographs." He collected and organized data on foreign ports, and arranged the war maps. He drafted plans for foreign warships, and prepared the original plates for the "Diagrams of Typical War Ships." He translated a number of French publications, including the "Italian Fleet," which appeared in *United Service Magazine.* Chambers also processed the deluge of letters from inventors eager to sell the products of their genius to the navy, winnowing out those that actually showed promise.[9]

Chambers and John Baptiste Bernadou, who joined the staff in 1885, set the tone at Office of Naval Intelligence for the rest of the decade. "They understood rapid technological change," and proved adept at mastering the "details of new ship design, machinery, explosives, and ordnance." Modernization could not occur rapidly enough for them, and they kept up with the pace of technological innovation while many fellow officers fell behind. They "displayed an unusual grasp of the relationship between sea power and national economic expansion and expressed the sentiments of those who welcomed a more vigorous foreign and naval policy."[10]

As its staff grew, the ONI added two new foreign attachés, both friends of Chambers. In 1883, it sent George T. Foulk to Korea to monitor the build-up of Russian, Japanese, and Chinese forces in the region. He became the United States chargé d'affaires in 1886 and worked to save Korea from foreign encroachment. Benjamin Buckingham became the ONI's attaché in Paris in 1885. He reported on events throughout the continent, supplementing the work of Edward Very who reported on European naval developments and sent in drawings of French and British equipment. A successful inventor, Very had served on the Naval Advisory Board before leaving the navy to work for the Hotchkiss Company in France.[11]

## Invention

Encouraged by Mason, Chambers continued his inventing, and worked on a number of projects in addition to his regular duties. Weapons systems, especially torpedoes, remained his primary interest. He designed several guns and gun carriages and sent them to Sicard at the Bureau of Ordnance, who again complimented him for his "ingenious" work. Chambers next designed a rocket-propelled torpedo. Fired from a naval gun, it would allow any ship to fire torpedoes without the need for torpedo tubes. Chambers copied parts of the Whitehead torpedo, which many navies had adopted, but produced a simpler design that he expected would have twice the Whitehead's accurate range of 500 yards.[12]

Despite Sicard's support, Chambers felt ignored by the navy's bureaus. He decided to offer some of his designs to private firms rather than the Ordnance Bureau where they would "gather dust." He offered to sell his torpedo to the West Point Foundry Association, which suggested that Chambers patent it first, since no one had patented a rocket-fired torpedo. Once he had a patent, he should come talk to them in New York. Chambers agreed and offered them a host of his other designs, but he knew not to put all his eggs in one basket. A friend of his in the Argentine navy was working on a similar design, and he suspected others might be as well. He filed his patent application, but continued to offer his torpedo to private firms, including Hotchkiss. He wrote to Chandler offering the navy the rights to his torpedo if it helped him patent it and reimbursed his $500 expenses in designing it. The navy paid his $20 patent application fee, but never reimbursed his expenses or showed any interest in developing his torpedo. Chambers himself had little time for his invention until his return from Nicaragua.[13]

Chambers maintained his interest in ship design, and working at the ONI helped him keep up with the latest developments and to correspond with shipbuilders and naval architects. He developed a network of contacts in the shipbuilding industry including James Howden, who owned a design firm in Glasgow, Scotland. Howden sent him several ship blueprints with detailed descriptions of their machinery, and they developed an excellent working relationship.[14] It is sometimes hard to determine whether Chambers contacted businesses to gather information for himself or the ONI, but the two were not mutually exclusive. Information that helped Chambers with his inventions would also help the navy modernize.

## Spokesman for Reform

For a decade, the U.S. Naval Institute had worked for naval reform and modernization, publishing articles on naval developments in its journal *Proceedings*. In 1880, it inaugurated an essay contest with a prize for the best essay. Chambers entered the 1884 contest on the topic of "The Reconstruction and Increase of the Navy." He won and received a gold medal and $100. He read his paper at the Naval Institute's annual meting after returning from the Greely Relief Expedition.

In his wide-ranging essay, Chambers covered virtually every aspect of naval policy. He built on the work of previous prize essayists—all of them junior officers—who had proposed modernizing the navy, expanding the merchant marine, and increasing the nation's naval presence to enforce the Monroe Doctrine.[15] Chambers offered a much bolder vision. Following in the tradition of Luce and Shufeldt, he argued that history showed the necessity of a strong navy for national prosperity. International rivalry and arms races were normal. War was inevitable, "a necessary evil" that could not be avoided. The nation needed to rearm. The peacetime navy should foremost be a nucleus for wartime expansion and preparing for war should become its primary mission.

Aside from preparing for war and the old missions of showing the flag and policing the seas, Chambers argued the navy should adopt two new missions: (1) gathering intelligence on the military progress of other nations, and (2) enforcing the neutrality laws "to prevent other powers from doing it for us." The former was an obvious justification of the mission of the ONI, the latter a call for the vigorous enforcement of the Monroe Doctrine. If the United States did not police the Caribbean, European powers would use the constant turmoil there to justify intervention. Chambers expected the United States to build an isthmian canal and wanted Europeans kept well away from it.

Chambers attacked the navy's bureau system and its administration. The convoluted and overlapping duties of the bureaus kept them working at cross-purposes, often putting more effort into winning bureaucratic battles than rebuilding the fleet. Like Luce, he advocated a naval general staff modeled on the German General Staff that incorporated the ONI as a key component. Its chief would be the Secretary of the Navy's assistant, absorbing the duties of the Chief of the Bureau of Navigation and overseeing the bureaus. The general staff would guide strategy and war planning and study the "broad principles of naval warfare."[16]

Like many of his fellow officers, Chambers admired the Royal Navy and wanted the U.S. Navy to emulate it. Yet, only Britain had the bases and infrastructure in the Americas to support a war against the United States. With that in mind, Chambers used a potential war with Britain to determine the needs of the navy. In this prospective war Chambers listed four missions for it in order of importance: (1) preventing Britain from establishing an effective blockade or bombarding coastal installations; (2) intercepting its convoys, troop transports, and supplies en route to North America; (3) the destruction of its commerce; (4) joint army-navy expeditions against Canada and other British colonies and bases.

The first and third described the existing policy of the United States—coast defense and commerce raiding; the second and fourth offered something rarely discussed following the Civil War—squadron level engagement of enemy forces. Chambers accepted that the United States would never be strong enough to challenge the Royal Navy in a grand, open water battle like Trafalgar. Neither would it be able to blockade the British Isles, to lay siege "to the heart" of Britain "by offensive operations against the arteries leading to it," which he believed was the most effective way to defeat Britain. Still, he was unwilling to surrender control of the seas and suggested the United

States blockade Vancouver and the St. Lawrence Seaway. If one could not blockade the mother country, her nearest and largest colonies would have to suffice.[17]

The navy had neither the ships nor infrastructure for even this limited effort. Chambers addressed this in the heart of his paper, outlining a building program for a modern yet politically acceptable fleet. Chambers believed in consistent technological progress and addressed it throughout his essay. Armored ships were "indispensable to raise a blockade." The increasing range of naval artillery would make ramming attacks impossible and limit the effectiveness of torpedoes in open water. Over the next decade, he wanted the United States to build nine battleships, seven small and seven large ironclads, thirty-eight gunboats, and twenty torpedo boats. Unlike many of his contemporaries, Chambers began his discussion with strategy and then proceeded to develop a fleet to support it. Far too many of his fellow officers advocated new technologies and larger warships simply because they existed or could be built, and gave little thought to how they fit into strategy.

Laid down one per year, each of Chambers's battleships would incorporate the latest technological developments. In the event of war, they would attack enemy convoys, blockade its coast, and engage its battle line. The large ironclads, at 7,000 tons displacement and a 3,000-mile cruising range, were similar to the small battleships the United States would soon build: the *Maine* and the *Texas.* Chambers carefully used the neutral term "ironclad" in describing them to allow his readers to draw their own conclusions. Those who advocated battleships would see them as such, while those opposed to blue water expansion would think he meant monitors. The large ironclads would support the battleships in offensive operations, the small ironclads and torpedo boats would defend the coast, and the rest of the fleet would attack enemy commerce. As historian Robert Seager points out, the navy encouraged the views of Chambers and other reformers to circulate to undermine its official (and congressionally preferred) strategy of commerce raiding and coast defense.[18] Chambers expected commerce raiding to do little more than distract enemy warships. The clash of major warships would win wars.

In peacetime, Chambers expected the navy to disperse its battleships among its foreign squadrons. Each would have a covey of gunboats assigned to it to allow it to project its power into shallow waters and up rivers. Individual gunboats would show the flag in less important regions. A modern fleet, Chambers argued, would better execute traditional policy.

Chambers's critics pounced on the hole in his proposed fleet. He did not recommend any cruisers in the 3,000- to 5,000-ton range such as the *Atlanta, Boston,* and *Chicago*—a ship type the Naval Advisory Board continued to recommend. Chambers argued that these cruisers were too large for effective commerce raiding, but too small and weak to engage armored warships. They were a waste of money. As he said, "no ship should be built which does not designedly occupy her place in the great scheme of preparation for war for national defense." As the fleet expanded there would be a need for balance, but it still had several dozen wooden cruisers and was building steel replacements. It was large and small ships that the navy lacked. The one bit of rhetoric his critics unanimously approved, and which became a standard piece of language in congressional appropriations, was the principle that "no ship should be built that is not superior, or at least fully equal, to those of any other nation, of the same type." This was a lofty goal that harkened back to the famous American frigates of the War of 1812 that could out-sail anything they could not outfight and outfight what they could not out-sail. Three years earlier, the first Naval Advisory Board had made a similar plea for the nation to "win back from Europe our former prestige as the best ship-builders in the world." In an age of rapid technological change and competing tactical principles, though, superiority was difficult to judge. Congress eventually settled on paying bonuses for faster and faster ships, speed being an easily measured characteristic.[19] Like many naval officers, Chambers believed that the fortunes of the navy and the merchant marine were linked. The rehabilitation of one required the rehabilitation of the other. The U.S. merchant marine had declined steadily for almost three decades. To reverse that trend, Chambers recommended government subsidies for mail steamers and "those industries on which we must depend for finished ships." These needed government "encouragement" to expand and multiply so that they could meet wartime demands. Government inspectors would monitor this expansion and prevent a repetition of the corruption of the 1870s.[20]

Chambers repeatedly emphasized officers' educational needs. The "life of a successful naval officer," he declared, "is from necessity a life more of study than of work." The government should fund basic science, invest in research facilities, such as a model tank to test hull forms, and support inventors like him with annual prizes. Genius needed to be cultivated "for purposes of national defense." The navy needed warriors whose usefulness depended "not only on personal valor, but on high scientific attainments and constant application in the use of complicated instruments of modern warfare." It needed officers who were competent, trained professionals.[21]

Several important reformers praised Chambers's paper. Caspar Goodrich defended it as "able and suggestive." Chambers's friend Foulk commended his ideas and called him "the Man for the Profession." Mason, who probably read drafts of Chambers's essay, was his most vocal defender and reinforced several of Chambers's points. He argued for administrative improvements and a general staff, and emphasized that the navy could not improvise a modern fleet for war. It needed to build it during peace. The discussion of Chambers's paper revealed the consensus among reformers for battleships, an enlarged role for the navy, war planning, and the creation of a general staff.[22]

Following the Nicaraguan survey, Chambers returned to the ONI in October 1885 to find it on a sound footing. While Mason, Potts, and two others had left, five new officers replaced them. Slow growth had brought the ONI's staff to ten officers and a few clerks. It assigned another attaché to Europe, and the Bureau of Navigation cracked down and required all ships to have intelligence officers by the end of the year. The ONI continued to supply the intelligence needs of the Secretary of the Navy and the bureaus. It deluged Congress with naval statistics and worked to publicize the navy's needs to the press. It continued to publish its reports, which now included a monthly intelligence bulletin and an annual report on naval progress. In 1888, it issued its mammoth *Coaling, Docking, and Repair Facilities of the Ports of the World,* the result of almost a decade of work.

Raymond Rodgers, who had replaced Mason as the head of the ONI in April 1885, surpassed his predecessor in pushing reforms. He collected under him an articulate and aggressive staff that was perhaps the "most remarkable" ever to serve the ONI. He brought in John C. Colwell, who had served on the Greely Relief Expedition, Seaton Schroeder, and other officers who went on to have distinguished careers. Chambers continued to compile data and draft the plans of foreign warships, and wrote a series of articles for the General Information Series. He assisted Lieutenant Frederick Singer in compiling data on ship construction, design, equipment, and boats and helped Schroeder prepare a report on the Isthmus of Panama. Chambers enjoyed his work at the ONI and Rodgers helped get his tour extended an extra year.[23]

New Secretary of the Navy William C. Whitney advocated naval modernization and supported the ONI. He further clarified its mission to encompass collecting and classifying information on "all subjects connected with war, or which can have a bearing upon naval action, and to prepare plans of campaign covering all contingencies of active naval operations." Beginning in 1886 the Annual Report of the Secretary of the Navy contained intelligence summaries supplied by the ONI. Whitney expected the office to play an important part in efforts to revitalize the navy and end the corruption that plagued its administration. ONI officers continued to distinguish themselves in writing and supplied Luce and Mahan at the Naval War College with maps, charts, and other data for their strategic studies. The ONI had integrated itself into the administrative infrastructure of the navy.[24]

## Torpedoes

Following his return to the ONI, Chambers resumed work on his inventions. He hired the law firm of Munson & Phillips, which specialized in patents, and received a patent for his torpedo on March 17, 1885. Unfortunately, this was his only good news. He could not find anyone to buy his invention, and his expenses and legal fees mounted. His mother was in debt and needed his help to pay off her creditors. The Hotchkiss Company seemed his best prospect, and Very assured him the company was interested, but Hotchkiss had taken ill and showed no signs of recovering. The company, in disarray, could not consider any new devices.

Hoping to stimulate interest in his torpedo, Chambers applied vainly for patents in foreign countries. As his frustrations mounted, Very suggested he give up on profiting from invention. He wished him luck, "but having had lots of experience with [the Very pistol] which really has paid me fairly well, I can only say that I am down on those kinds of responsibilities. Naval people are not well calculated to do that kind of business. . . . I hope that you are an exception."[25]

Chambers was not. Between his work at the ONI and his absences for the Greely and Nicaraguan expeditions, he had little time to work on his inventions, let alone market them to an arms industry overwhelmed with submissions from inventors. In July, Chambers heard that Minneapolis-based inventor Asa Weeks had contested his patent. In a formal defense, Chambers proved that his work predated Weeks's, and Weeks relented after failing to convince Chambers to pool his efforts with him.[26]

While Chambers's naval career continued to go well, and he was promoted to lieutenant (j.g.), his efforts at invention proved an endless frustration. His experience with torpedoes served him well in the navy, and he repeatedly published reports on them in ONI bulletins. He became the resident torpedo expert, but his efforts to patent and sell his devices soured him on the process of invention. He never realized a profit from his work on torpedoes. He impressed prospective buyers and the navy, but never enough to fund his efforts. Setting his inventions aside, he returned to his efforts to design warships.[27]

## New Ships

The U.S. Navy continued to modernize its fleet, building new ships and scrapping old, but it was a slow process. Congress had authorized the famous "ABCD" ships in 1883. In 1885, Secretary Whitney united Democrats and Republicans, and Congress authorized funds for the gunboats *Yorktown* and *Petrel* and the cruisers *Newark* and *Charleston.* In 1886, Congress committed itself to naval modernization with an appropriation that dwarfed those of the previous few years and showed an interest in experimenting with new ship types. To clear out limited dry dock space, it authorized $3,178,046 to complete four of the five monitors (*Amphitrite, Monadnock, Puritan, Terror*), which had awaited funds since 1874. It authorized the British-designed protected cruiser *Baltimore,* the American-designed dynamite gun cruiser *Vesuvius,* and a sorely needed torpedo boat. In a significant policy departure, Congress authorized the construction of the navy's first ocean-going armored warships. These would eventually become the second-rate battleships *Maine* and the larger *Texas,* though before her completion the navy classified the *Maine* as an armored cruiser. The Naval Advisory Board would judge a competition to select the designs and award the winners $15,000.

The cash prize sparked Chambers's interest. Several times the amount of his annual salary, it would more than pay off his and his mother's debts. Tapping his network of friends and contacts, he learned everything he could about the contest. His main informant was Charles Henige, a protégé of Naval Constructor Francis Bowles, the U.S. Navy's first scientifically trained constructor. Like Bowles, Henige was well educated, and thought little of most of those involved in ship design and construction in the United States. He had worked as a draftsman for the Naval Advisory Board for three years and later for the ONI where he and Chambers became friends. Henige warned Chambers that the strict competition criteria would produce few entries, and mostly from foreign firms.[28]

Undaunted, Chambers set to work, calling on his friends and contacts when he needed help, particularly Howden. He completed designs for both categories that he named the *Iowa* (6,000 tons) and the *Ohio* (6,300 tons). Both would have carried an impressive armament for the day: four 10-inch, four 6-inch, and a variety of smaller guns. Howden complimented Chambers's work and helped him incorporate his new engines. He expected the *Iowa* to achieve a top speed of 18 knots—fast for an armored ship of the time. Henige helped Chambers draw up the plans for both ships. Chambers's designs compared favorably to the entries of several prestigious British firms, which is not surprising since Chambers had Howden's help and the resources of the ONI to gather information. As data came in, he modified his designs accordingly.[29]

Competitors submitted fifteen different designs to the contest. Most were for the smaller of the two ships. The Naval Advisory Board chose the British Barrow firm's design for the future *Texas,* but it failed to reach a decision on the entries for the smaller ship. The board believed Chambers's entry and those of three foreign firms were "excellent," each with "many good features," but refused to decide among them or classify them in order of preference. It made no award.

The foreign firms, Barrow, H. A. Grandjead, and Thames, accepted this decision with good grace, but Chambers was furious. Once again, he felt slighted by the navy bureaucracy and this time a lot of money was at stake. He believed the navy had planned on using its own design all along and had not seriously considered his work.[30] One of the rejected designs was by Naval Constructor Samuel H. Pook, a personal enemy of Henige. Chambers and Henige both believed that the Bureau of Construction had intrigued through Pook to have its own design selected even though it did not meet the competition's strict criteria.

Knowing that the navy would ignore a protest from him alone, Chambers worked to interest the other contestants in a combined protest. He contacted William E. Stillings, a New York lawyer and family friend, and asked him to make inquiries for him. Stillings contacted Edward Cahill, the middleman between Whitney and Tammany Hall, and began laying the groundwork to push Chambers's case. Cahill promised to investigate the situation and plead Chambers's case to Whitney. Stillings found two other disgruntled designers, who vowed they would never submit designs under the current system. The decision had infuriated Howden as well, and he helped Chambers intrigue with Thames and some of the other British firms. While upset by the decision, Chambers's fellow competitors proved unwilling to make a fuss. The $15,000 that seemed a princely sum to Chambers was negligible to multimillion-dollar firms. Meanwhile, Chambers continued to do his job at the ONI. Ironically, it fell upon him to arrange for Lieutenant James D. J. Kelley, the navy's press liaison, to publicize the design recommended by the board.[31]

Chambers planned to take his case to the public, but changed his mind. Perhaps one of his friends dissuaded him. In a letter he never sent to the *Army and Navy Journal,* he ruthlessly criticized the design process inside the navy and claimed that the contest had been a sham. The Naval Advisory Board never intended to pay the prize money. He had heard rumors that the Construction Bureau's design, "a slight modification of that of the Brazilian ship *Riachuelo,*" had been favored all along despite its ineligibility to compete and obsolescence. "So tarnished has the reputation of the [Navy] Department become that it is doubtful whether any plans would have been received had" it not offered $15,000.[32]

In the end, Chambers simply fired off a letter to Secretary Whitney, demanding that the Naval Advisory Board do its job and choose a winner. He defended his design, repeated his criticisms of the contest, and continued to argue that the Construction Bureau design had been favored all along. Whitney politely commended Chambers, but supported the board's decision. It was not obligated to choose a winner. The bureau design was not entered in the competition, could not be chosen, and would not be built. Chambers wrote one last defense of his design and then wisely withdrew. He defended his actions arguing that he had "an absorbing interest in the progress of the Navy" and that his "sincere desire to see the best plans adopted, irrespective of personal considerations" had guided him throughout the competition. He thanked Whitney for commending him and took the opportunity to push for modernization. He recommended the navy build a model tank to test hull forms, and asked Whitney to send him to Europe to study those in use there. Chambers did not get a trip to Europe, but his career survived a confrontation with the Secretary of the Navy undamaged. A design for the *Maine* emerged out of a synthesis of the competing designs. Congress did not fund a model tank until 1896.[33]

Chambers's design efforts brought him to the attention of high-ranking officers, and several of them offered him assignments. Rear Admiral Bancroft Gherardi, the commandant of the New York Navy Yard, wanted Chambers to help with the construction of the *Maine,* and considered him the best-qualified person for the job. His friend Henige tipped him off that Commander Robley Evans, who would supervise the *Maine*'s construction, wanted Chambers on his team. His work had also impressed Captain Francis Ramsay, the chief judge of the design competition. The navy would normally have sent Chambers back to sea in the normal pattern of rotation, but with Gherardi and Evans supporting his request, he extended his time on shore yet again, this time as the Assistant Superintendent of the *Maine.* Chambers, like his friend Foulk, intended to stay on shore and work to modernize the fleet. He hoped his experience in building some of the navy's new ships would translate into an appointment to one of them. Henige encouraged Chambers, noting that with his reputation he could probably get ten years of shore duty if he wanted it. He also noted that Chambers's appointment would "make our friend [Pook] feel a little sick." Chambers, probably willingly, had been drawn into the thick of the battle between line officers and the bureaus and between the younger, scientifically trained constructors like Bowles and Richard Gatewood and their conservative elders. His appointment was a slap in the face to the Bureau of Construction, which would normally have assigned one of its naval constructors to supervise construction.[34]

The United States was capable of producing modern ships and by the early 1890s no longer depended on foreign steel or designs. New factories, new plants, and the newly created program in naval architecture at the Massachusetts Institute of Technology, all pushed by reformers at the ONI, solved these deficiencies. Chambers expected to benefit as the process of reform and modernization continued. He had found favor among the highest-ranking officers of the navy and enjoyed a network of friends to support his efforts. Rodgers regretted losing Chambers and promised in the future "to be of any service to you which may be in my power." The future looked very good to Lieutenant Chambers.[35]

# 6 / The New York Navy Yard

Following the Civil War, Republican Party bosses used employment at the nation's navy yards to reward their supporters. Most of the 5,000 jobs went to its faithful members, as did most federal employment during this heyday of the spoils system. "Workmen were chosen not only because they belonged to the party of the administration," observers declared, "but because they belonged to the faction of this or that boss of the local political machine." To provide work for the party faithful, the navy repaired its aging ships over and over again, kept open unneeded facilities, and purchased stores to the point that it had enough sail to equip the entire British navy.[1] This corruption provoked congressional investigations when Democrats gained control of the House, but reform came slowly, and the Democrats proved similarly corrupt.

Naval officers accepted the spoils system as the price of doing their jobs. They had political ties and needed to maintain them. Well-placed friends in Congress helped them gain choice assignments and could save an officer's career from almost any disaster. Few challenged the spoils system, and those who did focused less on the influence of politicians and more on the role of the navy's disparate bureaus in the corrupt system.

The yards reflected the navy's inefficient bureau system in microcosm. Each of the navy's eight bureaus (Provisions and Clothing, Ordnance, Construction and Repair, Yards and Docks, Steam Engineering, Navigation,

Equipment and Recruiting, and Medicine and Surgery) jealously guarded its respective prerogatives; refused to "yield authority to secure coordination"; competed for money, power, and patronage; and pursued its own ends with little regard for the service as a whole. Each bureau maintained separate facilities in each yard, and purchased supplies and hired civilian workers without consulting its fellows. A bureau's facilities were "independent establishments, little principalities . . . each owing allegiance to its own sovereign, the chief of the bureau to which it belongs." Patronage flowed through these bureaus and made an inefficient system worse. The yards were "overloaded with tradition and customs," and "cumbrous organizations" obstructed work. Technical responsibility disappeared "in the elaborately graded multitude of semitechnical and semimilitary officials." Instead of smoothness, there was friction; "instead of promptness, delay and procrastination; instead of thrift, extravagance; instead of unity of action, a mass of discordant interests."[2]

The yard commandant had direct authority over only a handful of officers, office clerks, and messengers. Most of a yard's employees worked for one of the bureaus, the majority for either Steam Engineering or Construction and Repair. One commandant later wrote in frustration that he had "little charge or authority over its organization, mechanical work, the keeping of its rolls or other books connected therewith, the employment and discharge of men, or its expenditures and supplies."[3] He was a captain without subordinates.

During the 1880s and 1890s, it became increasingly important for both political parties to at least appear to work for civil service reform. The 1883 Pendleton Act initiated merit-based hiring for a small number of government jobs and gave reformers an opening to fight corruption. It slowly chipped away at the spoils system since the losing party in an election often extended civil service protection to government jobs held by its members. This prevented their termination without cause, and steadily expanded the number of jobs governed by civil service regulations. Journalists, who increasingly focused on any hint of scandal and decried the sad state of the navy, helped the reformers underline the need for qualified workers in an age of rapid technological change.

Secretary of the Navy Chandler, partly due to congressional obstruction and partly due to his own commitment to the spoils system, changed little during his tenure. His successor William C. Whitney proved more ambitious, though members of his own party impeded his efforts. Whitney reorganized the bureaus, eliminating some duplication, and forced the major navy yards to specialize: Washington in ordnance, Boston in equipment, and San Francisco, Norfolk, and New York in shipbuilding and repairs. Yet, despite his desire for reform, Whitney pulled out all the stops to aid his party in the 1888 presidential campaign. The New York Navy Yard, the nation's largest, hired over 1,000 men just before the election, and terminated their positions shortly thereafter. Whitney also "diverted funds on the eve of election" from shipbuilding to clothing contracts to reward party supporters.[4]

## Chambers at the Yard

Chambers's post in New York brought him close to home and allowed him to visit family and friends regularly. He arrived at the yard on May 15, 1888, well aware of its problems from personal experience and letters from friends. Little had changed since the Pendleton Act passed. Chambers's friends specifically warned him about Samuel Pook, one of the design competition contestants. Pook had guided the preliminary work on the *Maine* and was completing the wooden shed in which the *Maine* would be built. His reputation for graft and corruption was legendary, a characteristic shared by several of the older naval constructors. According to Charles Henige, who had worked with many of them, "all of the full constructors are more politicians than shipbuilders." They "do not care whether the government receives any equivalent for the money expended and all they aim at is to make themselves solid with the politicians." If an opportunity arose, none of them would hesitate to "play into their own pockets." Chambers plunged into this highly political environment in the midst of the 1888 election and Whitney's effort to win votes through patronage. Despite Whitney's earlier efforts at reform, Chambers concluded that politicians would "run things just the same as before."[5]

The spoils system was hardly the yard's only problem. Despite some recent renovation, the facility was both inadequately and primitively equipped for its many tasks. Aging, barely serviceable ships clogged its docks and tied up workmen. Construction of new ships overwhelmed the yard's limited resources of trained manpower, and interfered with its other tasks as the primary port of the North Atlantic Squadron.

Work on the *Maine* and his efforts to improve the yard kept Chambers busy, but he maintained his interest in ship design on which he advised Raymond Rodgers and the ONI. Rodgers in turn sent him plans for American and foreign warships, and the two consulted on recent developments. Sicard, too, maintained a high opinion of Chambers and kept him informed of new developments. Perennially short of cash, Chambers supplemented his income as a legal consultant on maritime collisions and as a consultant for the *New York Herald,* in which he published a few articles on the navy.[6]

Work at the yard proved very different from Chambers's previous assignments. He had to work closely not only with the naval constructors and other staff officers but also the civilian workforce. Chambers had plenty of experience maintaining order among unruly seamen, but at the yard he had to enforce order on civilians without benefit of stringent naval regulations and rules of justice. He particularly worried that "workmen accustomed to regard their employment as a reward for political services" would become "disgruntled" and cause trouble. Shortly after arriving, Chambers joined Commander Francis M. Green and Lieutenant Commander Abraham B. H. Lillie on a special board that investigated a series of assaults and violent incidents at the yard. More often than not, the workers' refusal to testify against one another stymied its efforts. Two weeks after the board settled its first case, two apprentices picked a fight with the leading blacksmith. Helped by his senior apprentice, the blacksmith pummeled his attackers senseless and sent them on their way. Like the blacksmith, most foremen preferred to enforce their authority with their fists. They wanted no interference from those in uniform.[7]

## The ABCDs and the *Maine*

A variety of problems accompanied the construction of the navy's first new ships, the cruisers *Atlanta, Boston,* and *Chicago,* and the dispatch boat *Dolphin* (the ABCDs). Authorized by Congress in 1883, then Secretary of the Navy Chandler awarded their contracts to John Roach, a Republican contributor implicated in the "repairs" scandals of the Grant administration. Roach submitted the lowest bid for the ships—a bid so low that it ignited suspicions of corruption.[8] Not surprisingly, cost overruns became a problem. In a controversial decision, Whitney seized the ABCDs from Roach's shipyards, forcing Roach into bankruptcy, and ordered them completed in the navy yards. The *Atlanta, Chicago,* and the newer *Yorktown* all neared completion at the yard when Chambers arrived.

The builders and work crews of these ships experienced numerous problems adapting to new technology and construction techniques. Much of the ships' equipment had to be sent back to manufacturers for repairs and modifications, as did the guns and gun parts from the Washington Navy Yard. Commander Chadwick reported numerous leaks on board the *Yorktown.* About the only pieces of equipment that worked correctly on arrival were the electric shell hoists installed by the Sprague Electric Railway, a company founded by former naval officer Frank Sprague.[9]

Chambers helped oversee the completion of these ships and spent most of his time working on the *Maine.* As the election neared, they received more workers and authorization to pay overtime. Skilled workers, who were in short supply, put in double shifts, rushing to complete the ships in time for the inauguration and a planned naval demonstration. Chambers's technological expertise repeatedly proved useful. Working with the Edison Company, he helped install the new electric lights on the ships, and he helped Commander Charles O'Neil, the yard's ordnance inspector, redesign the *Chicago*'s faulty gun sights.[10]

Chambers arrived eager to work on the navy's first battleship, but he also understood the precariousness of his position. Staff officers from the Bureaus of Construction and Steam Engineering had previously controlled ship construction. The navy had sent Chambers into their domain with an obviously subversive assignment—to bring the influence of line officers to bear on that process. Chambers worried about friction between line and staff at the yard, but even more about tensions between the older and younger officers regardless of their line or staff affiliations. He expected that the latter would get little credit if things went well, but all the blame for any problems.[11]

The struggle between the older, traditionally trained constructors and the younger, scientifically trained constructors was heating up in the Bureau of Construction and Repair. Starting in 1879 the navy sent promising engineers to study modern naval construction and engineering in Britain and France, among them Francis T. Bowles and Richard Gatewood. These officers slowly transformed the naval construction corps as promotion moved them into positions of influence. They displaced older constructors who lacked scientific training and whose experience was largely with wooden ships. By the late 1880s, scientifically trained constructors believed they had proven themselves and began demanding greater influence in ship design. The Chief of the Bureau of Construction and Repair, Admiral Theodore D. Wilson, opposed them at every turn, and "made things bad for all the young, scientific constructors." He ignored their successes and seized on their mistakes to discredit them. Many officers, like Henige, were eager to see "W[ilson] in a tight place," and hoped the problems at the New York yard would cause him political embarrassment.[12]

Chambers worked well with the younger constructors, especially Assistant Naval Constructor John B. Hoover, but not their conservative seniors. This clash between the progressives and their hidebound, frequently politically oriented elders caused no end of problems and combined with obsolete methods and waste to slow work on the *Maine*. Thanks to Pook, the *Maine* would be the last U.S. warship built in a shiphouse, since steel ships did not need shelter from the elements. Building a shiphouse, though, was simple work and well suited to the limited skills of politically affiliated workers. This waste appalled Chambers and his compatriots and they set out to stop it, knowing full well that if they "interfered in any way with the politicians," there would be trouble, especially as it was an election year."[13]

Problems plagued the *Maine*, like the ABCDs. Many of the drawings for the *Maine* and the *Texas* proved faulty and had to be redone. The Pittsburgh Steel Casting Company miscast the *Maine*'s sternpost. Other parts proved faulty as well and had to be sent back to their manufacturers. The traditionally trained constructors made a series of mistakes, but frequently managed to cast the blame on others. Obsolete equipment, archaic methods, and personnel problems slowed work. Completing the *Maine* efficiently required solving these problems first.[14]

Chambers prowled the yard, looking for ways to improve its efficiency. Encouraged by Henige, he launched a campaign against corruption in the yard and managed to expose a number of shady dealings. Pook retired early in 1889, possibly to avoid charges resulting from the growing evidence against him, but Chambers proved unable to link Wilson to corruption. Henige was disappointed, but not surprised. "That you have not succeeded in cornering our friend W[ilson] is not a surprise to me, he and his cooperators have been in the business so long that they know how to cover their tracks and I almost think that it is time wasted to attempt to show him up in his true light."[15] Nonetheless, Chambers continued his efforts, though

Wilson was by then trying to have Chambers removed from work on the *Maine.*

Despite Whitney's efforts, the Democrats lost the 1888 election. Like Whitney, new Secretary of the Navy Benjamin Franklin Tracy espoused reform but encountered difficulty implementing it. Shortly before the new administration took office, Commodore Francis M. Ramsay replaced Admiral Bancroft Gherardi as yard commander. This proved a boon for Chambers, for while Gherardi had approved of Chambers's reforming zeal, he gave him little support. Ramsay, who appreciated Chambers's ideas and hard work and often invited him to have dinner with his family, would.

## Tracy, Ramsay, and the Spoils System

Yard workers shared the same desires to improve their lot as their compatriots in private industry and like them chose to organize and collectively bargain. Skilled artisans remained in short supply in the yards, and they struck repeatedly and successfully for higher wages. In January, riveters assigned to the *Maine* stopped work until the navy met their demands for a raise from \$2.40 to \$3.00 per day. Short of skilled labor and under pressure to complete the new ships rapidly, the navy had no choice but to raise wages. Perhaps inspired by the riveters, the clerks and draftsmen who were paid daily petitioned to receive the paid vacation that their salaried coworkers received. Rather than striking, they hired a lawyer to sue the navy. Over the next few years, the government reclassified more and more workers as salaried rather than per diem, the result of the combined pressure of workers from below, legislation like the Pendleton Act from above, and the new navy's need for a better-trained workforce.[16]

The complexity of the new steel ships forced changes in hiring practices at the yards. While the spoils system could fill simple jobs such as watchmen and janitors, the navy needed experienced mechanics, welders, and other specialists. Ramsay found two different hiring policies in force at the yard. The yards could fill positions that required specialized training, such as mechanics. The bureaucracy in Washington filled all other positions. The Secretary of the Navy had to approve a worker's dismissal, and Tracy repeatedly overruled yard commandants and reinstated workers. He could also bypass merit hiring. Tracy routinely recommended workers to yard commandants and the yard commandants invariably complied. Tracy ordered preferential treatment for veterans, overwhelmingly Republican in these years, and Ramsay hired many, some too disabled to perform much work.[17]

Tracy tried to please both the reformers and the spoilsmen who expected him to replace Whitney's appointees with Republicans. While Congress was committed to a larger, more efficient navy, it would not give up the benefits of the spoils system to achieve it. Tracy knew he would eventually have to commit firmly to reform, but circumstances forced his hand sooner than he expected. In his first weeks in office, he announced he would visit the New York yard. He intended this as a routine inspection, but the press seized on a rumor that he would announce major reforms at the navy's most corrupt facility. Fearing scandal, Tracy set in motion a series of reforms that would slowly throttle the spoils system. He visited the yard on April 4, 1889, and in a closed meeting that night talked with many of its officers, including Chambers and his coagitator Lieutenant Allen Paul. They let Tracy know how bad things had become, and how corruption, the spoils system, and machine politics slowed the growth of the navy. Tracy had to choose between the stalwarts of his party and the efficiency of the fleet.[18]

A few weeks after Tracy's visit, the yard hosted a celebration for the centennial of the U.S. government and the inauguration of President Benjamin Harrison who attended the festivities. The senior admiral of the navy, David Dixon Porter, presided over the gala. Chambers helped with the preparations and during the event ferried guests in the tug *Catalpa.* The highlight of the event, a naval procession, showed how much the navy had changed in the six years since Congress funded the ABCDs. The *Atlanta, Boston, Chicago* and *Yorktown,* rushed to completion for the gala, led a procession of aging vessels past Ellis Island for all to see. The stark contrast between the modern steel vessels and their obsolete ancestors was obvious to all. Chambers helped tow the aging ships back to their berths and then paraded as part of a naval brigade on shore. Harrison and other dignitaries concluded the event with speeches calling for the continued rejuvenation of the navy, though none addressed the state of the yard or the spoils system.[19]

Over the next few months, Tracy reversed several of his policies and increasingly delegated hiring authority to officers at the yard. By May, prospective apprentices had to demonstrate their abilities and pass an examination. By June, Ramsay could tell job applicants, and even influential politicians, that he and the Navy Department no longer directly intervened in hiring. This was now "solely up to the foremen." While an important step, it did not immediately solve the problem. The foremen had received their jobs through the spoils system and most remained beholden to local politicians. The Navy Department in Washington continued to choose new foremen. These rules only applied to skilled workers. The Washington bureaucracy still hired clerks, watchmen, storekeepers, and others not directly involved in ship construction.[20]

It would be another year before Tracy took more decisive action, and like his predecessors, he accomplished the most in his last months in office after his party had lost an election. In 1890, Tracy dismissed all the yard foremen and appointed a board that created tests and procedures to choose new foremen. The examinations were "practical in character, having reference exclusively to the requirements of the position to be filled," and aimed at "ascertaining the applicant's knowledge of his business, and his possession of the qualities that will enable him to get good work out of men." The board did not list any educational requirements, and former navy yard employees and military veterans who passed the test received preferential placement. The tests cannot have been that difficult since the board rejected only eighty-one of 1,111 applicants as unqualified. The overwhelming majority of yard foremen passed the tests and retained their jobs.[21]

Tracy still managed to weed out some Democrats. Of the ninety-six senior workers in June 1891 at the Portsmouth yard, only five had been hired under Whitney. Other yards showed a similar pattern, but this failed to satisfy Tracy's detractors who complained that Democrats still held jobs in the yards. A Brooklyn ward captain called Tracy "a fraud on the Party" and asked if "the 800 or 900 Democrats" he retained in the yards would vote the Republican ticket? Yet, other Republicans applauded his efforts. Theodore Roosevelt and the New York Civil Service Association congratulated him for reducing the costs of the New York yard by 25 percent.[22]

While Tracy's slow attack on the spoils system improved the yard's efficiency, much remained to be done. Ramsay focused his attention first on cleaning up the bureaucracy in his immediate sphere of influence, and issued a series of orders beginning March 1889 to get a handle on the situation. He ordered department heads to determine the value of all property, the number of its civilian employees, and their pay. In April, he solicited the department heads for suggestions on improving management and worker supervision. In May, he ordered them to report on absenteeism. In June, he issued a series of orders to reduce paperwork and implemented new requirements to standardize forms, reports, and reporting periods. This reduced the clerical workforce and allowed Ramsay to get a better understanding of yard operations.[23]

Ramsay slowly built his picture of the collection of petty dictatorships under his command and began to focus on individual problems. Perhaps the most contentious of them was the issue of pay for the yard's civilian employees. This involved not only salaries, though low pay continued to provoke occasional strikes, but also how workers were scheduled, who paid them, and the simple mechanics of getting their pay to them. Different bureaus had different payroll procedures, paid their workers at different rates, and classified jobs differently. While foremen gradually received more input in hiring, their involvement in paying their employees caused nothing but trouble. When Chambers arrived at the yard, foremen paid their workers themselves. Some occasionally disappeared with the money, while others extracted contributions for their political bosses.[24]

The yard paid many workers on a daily basis, which complicated the administration of any pay system. At Chambers's suggestion, Ramsay took the foremen out of the system. Instead, time clerks went to the work sites and paid the workers. Unfortunately, this also caused problems. Because the clerks did not know most of the workers personally, they required proof of identity, which some of them lacked. When the pay clerks arrived, all work stopped until each man had received his pay. Men working in the inaccessible parts of ships (inside double bottoms, or inside the boilers for instance) did not get paid. They could arrange to have another worker pick up their pay for them, but this caused its own problems. It further complicated matters that the yard also paid employees who worked elsewhere, such as Lieutenant William W. Kimball's ordnance inspectors at the Hotchkiss plant in Hartford. Ramsay sent them their pay, but did not control its disbursement.[25]

The ONI sent Ramsay and Chambers several reports on the payroll policies of foreign navies, but it would eventually be from private industry, not foreign navies, that the navy adopted its payroll system. Kimball and other officers learned about administration while assigned to private industry and brought time clocks, improved record-keeping systems, and a modern administrative vision into the navy.

Personnel problems were hardly the reformers' only targets. If anything, they were incidental. They gave priority to building modern warships over introducing fair labor practices. Again, Ramsay arrived interested in implementing some reforms, but it was Chambers and Paul who pushed him to act. Chambers took the initiative in investigating the state of the yard and its equipment. For the most part, it was in terrible shape. Workshops, docks, and equipment were old and worn-out. There was no financial plan for the yard, or any plan for its operation or its future. The waste was enormous, and Chambers determined to eliminate it.

Chambers proceeded slowly, suggesting occasional improvements and saving a few dollars when opportunities presented themselves. All the while, he awaited the opportunity to act decisively. That came when Chadwick, who had come to the same conclusions as Chambers, returned to visit and tour the yard. Chadwick, possibly at Chambers's instigation, asked the yard's senior civil engineer, H. Smith Craven, if anyone had developed a comprehensive plan for modernization. Craven's negative reply gave Chambers, who had already drawn up such a plan, his opening, and he presented it to Craven later that day. Probably feeling trapped, Craven approved it. Chambers then brought it to Ramsay's attention, and suggested the creation of a board to "further progressive improvements" in the yard because "economy and efficiency" demanded it. He expected the board to "find a disgraceful state of affairs" that the civil engineers would blame on the interference of line officers.[26]

Chambers's plan touched on every facet of the yard's operation and proposed major changes. The yard needed a new building slip, new wharves, a modern railway landing, a completely new coaling wharf and shed, additional dry docks to handle all the new construction, and new derricks and cranes since the current ones could not lift the guns of the new ships. The current railway pattern in the yard reinforced the isolation of the various bureaus, and Chambers offered a completely new layout. His new infrastructure better linked the yard's workshops, docks, and storerooms to each other and their sources of raw materials. It broke down the barriers that separated the little principalities of the yard and brought the "intelligent control over the whole organization" he had recommended five years before. The yard commandants would finally be in command. Chambers anticipated financial objections to his plan, and predicted that savings from eliminating waste and inefficiency would pay for most improvements. Everything would be "carried out progressively, economically, and surely."[27]

Ramsay concurred with Chambers's recommendation and appointed Lieutenant Hobart L. Tremain, Commander William H. Whiting, and Chief Engineer James W. Whittaker to oversee improvements at the yard and inventory everything in it. Tracy supported this effort and sent several civil engineers to the yard who confirmed what Chambers had reported. Large parts of the yard were dilapidated and falling apart. The old granite dry dock needed repairs, and work on the new timber dry dock was behind schedule. Most yard equipment was worn-out or obsolete. Many buildings had deteriorated, and some were in imminent danger of collapse. Even new buildings showed problems due to poor workmanship. The combination of poor funding and the spoils system had left the yard in terrible shape.[28]

## Ramsay's Aide

Chambers's reform campaign inevitably made enemies. As Henige had warned him: "Politics have always run the New York yard." A constructor "who cannot get along with the politicians is not likely to remain there long, especially if he is one of the scientific ones for whom the great Chief has no special love." Chambers did his best and accomplished the most during the last months of the outgoing Cleveland administrations and the first months of Tracy's tenure while the new Secretary of the Navy learned his job. Wilson, however, continued to intrigue against Chambers and in June 1889, convinced Tracy to remove Chambers and Paul—who had overreached themselves in trying to eliminate corruption in supply purchasing—from the *Maine*'s construction team. In a stern letter, Tracy ordered Ramsay to relieve them "from any duty in connection with the building of the Armored Cruiser *Maine*." Tracy also quashed their latest proposal, deeming it "unnecessary to have kept any accounts relative to expenditure of materials and labor in the work of building the Armored Cruiser *Maine*" other than those that "have heretofore been customary." Ramsay, who had approved of their efforts, if not political acumen, made them his aides and they continued to work for reform.[29]

Removed from day-to-day work on the *Maine*, Chambers had even more time for his favorite pursuit—observing new technology at work. New gadgets and machines fascinated him, and he built on his experience from the ONI in assessing new inventions. His weakness as an inventor lay in his inability to follow a project through to completion. Much better at conceptualization and the initial work, he proved an astute observer and was excellent at weeding out the handful of promising inventions and technologies from the morass of useless, and frequently crackpot, gadgets offered to the yard. He routinely made recommendations to Ramsay on what to accept and what to reject of the many inventions offered them, and served with Hoover and Commander Charles O'Neil on a board to assess new technology. They tested everything from beveling machines to electric welding torches. Ramsay also put Chambers in charge of securing coal for the yard, getting the best prices he could, and cleaning up its storage and distribution system. Coal suppliers deluged Chambers with offers. He examined numerous different pieces of machinery and coal delivery systems, but unable to find what he wanted for sale, he designed a coal shed and other equipment capable of discharging 100 tons of coal in an hour, and started its construction before leaving the yard.[30]

Chambers enjoyed his time at the yard and worked well with his superiors. Both Gherardi and Ramsay praised his work. The former wrote that Chambers's "knowledge of naval construction and attention to his duties were of great help to me" and desired "to call the Department's favorable attention to him." Ramsay declared that Chambers "exhibited a high order of intelligence and was of great assistance to me in the performance of my duties especially in matters pertaining to the construction of vessels and to improvement of the Navy Yard." Ramsay, who soon left to head the Bureau of Navigation, tried to get Chambers posted to the newly commissioned cruiser *Baltimore,* but the assignment went to a better-connected officer. Instead, Ramsay arranged his assignment as the senior watch officer of the new gunboat *Petrel.*[31]

When Chambers and Ramsay left the yard, it showed the signs of their work. They had streamlined its administration, improved recordkeeping, and trimmed both the budget and the workforce while improving efficiency. The plans drafted by Chambers and refined by Ramsay continued to guide the facility's improvements. As more funds became available in 1891 and 1892, workers replaced unsafe buildings and added new dry docks, cranes, and other equipment—all as Chambers recommended. Spoils in hiring remained a problem, but it was during Chambers's time at the yard that the basis for its eventual elimination emerged. In the following years, the government extended testing and merit-based hiring to more positions, particularly after elections. Eventually the Pendleton Act covered all jobs, limiting them to those who passed examinations of their qualifications.

Despite the problems with the ABCDs, it still proved cheaper to build new ships in private yards. Only four of the seventy-three warships Congress authorized between 1883 and 1897 were built entirely in navy yards, three of them in New York. Construction on all four began during Whitney's term, whose experience with John Roach had soured his opinion of private builders. But the navy yards were not the answer. The *Maine* would not be completed until 1895, and work on the other yard-built ships also proceeded slowly. It proved easier to find honest private shipbuilders than to modernize and eliminate corruption from the navy yards. Yard commanders and department heads remained under "constant pressure . . . from local politicians" and members of Congress to provide for their protégés.[32] Navy yards retained their primary function of maintenance, repair, and outfitting of ships, and occasionally completed work on ships, but this became less common. The nation would rely on private industry to build the new navy.

# 7 / The *Petrel* and the *Atlanta*

When Commodore John G. Walker's unprecedented eight-year term as Chief of the Bureau of Navigation came to an end in 1889, he convinced Secretary of the Navy Tracy to promote him to admiral and place him in command of four of the navy's new ships, the cruisers *Atlanta, Boston, Chicago,* and the gunboat *Yorktown.* Tracy sent this "Squadron of Evolution" on a European cruise to train its handpicked officers and crew to handle these new ships. Walker drilled the ships' captains in maneuvering as a squadron, something the navy had not attempted since the 1873 *Virginius* Affair with Spain. Walker and other reformers wanted the navy to discard its doctrine of commerce raiding and single-ship actions. Instead, they advocated squadron and fleet engagements of an enemy's main forces, as Chambers had recommended five years earlier. "For a generation of officers accustomed to moving from port to port at their own pace, indoctrination in formation steaming was a necessary first step in modernization." Keeping station and following signals required a "complete reorientation of attitude" among ship captains and a new signaling system. The squadron's voyage displayed the achievements of the navy's reformers and signaled the United States' intention to reclaim its place as a naval power.[1]

Walker's squadron stood out of Boston on December 7, 1889, crossed the Atlantic and entered the Mediterranean. It slowly circumnavigated the sea, stopping at most major ports. Walker practiced a variety of maneuvers, trained his crews, practiced landing operations, and engaged in target practice on a small island near Corfu. Walker also used the voyage to study European naval developments. His ships were already dated by European standards, and many visiting foreign officers poked fun at them, but in so doing frequently revealed important characteristics of their own warships. Walker encouraged these visits and assigned each of his ships specific intelligence responsibilities. His officers visited European warships and toured naval facilities, compiling data for the ONI. The squadron spent 1890 in Europe and returned to the United States at the end of the year to join the North Atlantic Squadron for maneuvers that disseminated its accumulated knowledge.[2]

## The *Petrel*

By 1889, new ships joined the fleet regularly, among them the *Petrel,* which Chambers joined on December 16, 1889, shortly after her commissioning. Built by Columbian Iron Works of Baltimore, the *Petrel* was a modern, steel gunboat with four 6-inch guns, and a variety of smaller guns—a rather heavy armament for such a small ship that earned the nickname "baby battleship." Half the *Yorktown*'s size, the *Petrel* was the least impressive of the navy's new ships, and one of the few that failed to secure its builders a bonus for exceeding its contract specified speed. Her obsolete single-screw, back-acting compound engines could manage only 11 knots. Yet, the *Petrel* was the fastest and best-armed ship on which Chambers had served. Too slow to keep up with the Squadron of Evolution, the navy assigned the *Petrel* to the North Atlantic Squadron along with the new dispatch boat *Dolphin* and a variety of older ships.[3]

Happy to get an officer of Chamber's experience, the *Petrel*'s commander, Lieutenant Commander Willard H. Brownson, appointed him the ship's intelligence officer. Chambers worked well with his wardroom mates, especially the executive officer, Lieutenant Newton E. Mason. Lieutenant Jesse M. Roper, the *Petrel*'s navigator, was frequently ill, so Chambers took over his duties, often navigating the ship. These collateral duties kept Chambers too busy to work on any of his extracurricular projects.[4]

The *Petrel* carried a crew of 121 that included twenty apprentices and ten marines. Four ensigns, an engineer, a paymaster, and a surgeon rounded out the ship's officers. On the cramped gunboat, only the captain had his own cabin. The ship's ten officers bunked together in the wardroom. The crew slept in hammocks on the berth deck, as they would have in older warships. Most of the crew were American citizens, products of the navy's new recruiting and training system. Fleet modernization and the navy's improving public image helped it attract better-motivated men. This accounted for a marked change in discipline. Infractions were both less common and less serious than those Chambers witnessed a decade earlier, and the officers meted out less severe punishments. Confinement to the berth deck and extra duty were the norm, rather than confinement in irons. In November, Brownson simply dismissed five chronic malefactors from the navy.[5] Service in the new navy was an easily revoked privilege.

Like their compatriots in the Squadron of Evolution, the officers and crew of the *Petrel* had to accustom themselves to their new ship. While the navy's old ships had rarely burned coal, the *Petrel* did so routinely, consuming about one and a half tons per day. The *Petrel* cruised along the East Coast for several months training and drilling in a strange mixture of the new and the old. The crew practiced with modern ordnance, coaled and stoked the engines by electric light, raised and lowered the ship's boats with electric hoists, but also took to the rigging, learning to trim and adjust the sails in the worst of weather, and practiced with cutlasses kept racked on deck for boarding actions. The navy encouraged target practice, but rationed ammunition. Ships invariably fired at short ranges. The *Petrel*'s 6-inch guns had a range of 6 miles (limited to 5 miles by poorly designed gun sponsons), but Brownson invariably ordered target practice at ranges less than 1,000 yards.[6]

The North Atlantic Squadron expanded steadily in these years as the navy assigned it most of the new ships. Admiral Stephen B. Luce, who had taken command of the Squadron in 1888, substantially changed its routine. It "ceased to spend the summers at the principal New England watering places and the winters in New Orleans." Instead, Luce kept his ships drilling and practicing tactical maneuvers. He frequently surprised officers with orders to get under way immediately, put landing parties ashore, or to prepare to repel a torpedo attack. On several occasions, he ordered ships run aground in soft mud and required the youngest officers of the Squadron to get them clear. Rear Admiral Bancroft Gherardi took command of the squadron the following year and continued to drill regularly.[7]

The *Petrel* joined the squadron for maneuvers in June 1890, which differed little from those of the Squadron of Evolution the year before. Officers practiced keeping station, reading and responding to signals, and executed simple maneuvers. At the end of June they anchored off Portland and practiced landing operations, sending marines and sailors ashore. The maneuvers continued through the summer, interspersed with target practice and more landing operations. The squadron returned to New York in late August, and the officers and crew received leave.

The navy then sent the *Petrel* to the Caribbean for the traditional peregrinations from port to port that marked a century of U.S. naval activity. Except for the newness of the ship and the greater attention to drill and training, this cruise differed little from Chambers's cruises a decade before. The *Petrel* arrived off San Juan, Puerto Rico, on December 12, and spent the winter visiting various Caribbean ports. Each visit brought the usual social activities and festivities by the officers with local officials and business people, and the usual bacchanals of the crew in waterfront taverns. In March, they rescued the survivors of a civilian shipwreck on Roncador Reef off Nicaragua, and then worked their way home, arriving in New York before the month's end.[8]

## The *Atlanta*

Chambers passed his promotion exams in June and became a full lieutenant. With his new rank, Chambers also wanted a posting to a larger ship, and Mason and Brownson supported his efforts. Mason rated him excellent as a watch and division officer, while Brownson, who rated him excellent in every category, considered him "thoroughly competent," and wrote that he would be "glad to have him under his command in all circumstances."[9] With their help, Chambers arranged a posting to the protected cruiser *Atlanta,* then under Captain John W. Philip. Chambers's friend, Lieutenant Commander Theodorus B. M. Mason, was the executive officer. The *Atlanta* was still part of the Squadron of Evolution, which then included the *Chicago, Boston,* and the gunboat *Bennington.* Chambers joined the *Atlanta* at Hampton Roads in October. The long voyage to Europe had revealed many faults in the *Atlanta*'s design, and Chambers helped supervise many upgrades to the ship before the squadron sailed.

Armed with two 8-inch and two 6-inch guns, the *Atlanta* carried a crew of 297 and displaced 3,200 tons, the same as the *Boston,* though much smaller than the squadron's flagship, the 4,500-ton *Chicago.* Like the *Petrel,* the *Atlanta, Boston,* and *Chicago* carried a full outfit of sails in addition to their engines. The *Atlanta*'s only armor was a curved deck over the engine compartment—the feature from which the term protected cruiser derived.

On Saturday, October 12, 1891, a major storm appeared off the coast of New York and threatened to sink the *Despatch,* an aging steamer that desperately signaled for help. The navy ordered the *Atlanta,* the only ship in port powerful enough to risk the weather, to the rescue. The *Atlanta,* though, was not ready for sea, and the yard foreman told Captain Philip that it would take at least thirty-six hours to get the *Atlanta* ready because the yard's civilian employees had left for the weekend. Philip rushed to his ship and set his officers and crew to work. True to their motto of "always ready" they left port in fifteen hours and sailed into the worst storm Philip had seen in his four decades of naval service.

Shortly after the *Atlanta*'s departure, word arrived that the *Despatch* had "gone to pieces" in the heavy seas, rendering a rescue pointless. The tug *Catalpa* sailed to recall the *Atlanta,* but proved too slow. Despite the hasty repairs and worn machinery (the engine air pumps operated at only half power), the *Atlanta* maintained a speed of 12 knots and sped to rescue a ship no longer afloat. Like the *Despatch,* the *Atlanta* was trapped by the storm and unable to return to port. Winds reached near hurricane force and waves in excess of 60 feet high crashed over the ship leaving the funnels encrusted with salt. Philip abandoned the rescue effort and concentrated on keeping his own ship afloat, spending most of the next sixty hours on the bridge.[10]

As hours passed, the storm wore down the *Atlanta*'s crew and exposed the ship's weaknesses. Water seeped in around anchor chains. A hawse pipe tore loose and water poured in to the forward compartments. The sailor normally stationed there succumbed to seasickness and abandoned his post, leaving open a hatch through which the sea poured. No one noticed a problem until many of the forward compartments had flooded. While the *Atlanta* had excellent electric pumps in the engine room, there were none in the forward part of the ship. The crew brought in hand pumps and slowly moved forward. Without electricity, they worked by lantern light. Tiring, but winning their battle against the sea, they pumped the first two compartments dry. A crewman then opened the next compartment—the forward paint room—and stuck his lantern in to ascertain its condition. The lantern detonated the paint fumes and the explosion tore through the exhausted work crew leaving six of them injured and two near death. Damage to the ship from the explosion was minimal. A fresh crew completed pumping out the forward compartments. The storm abated, and the *Atlanta* returned to port Thursday evening.[11]

On December 9, Captain Francis J. Higginson took command of the *Atlanta,* and Mason departed her for a new assignment. The Squadron of Evolution sailed for St. Thomas the next day, often cruising separately, and using a mixture of sail and steam depending on the winds and the whims of their captains, a pattern they repeated as they worked their way around South America. When lookouts spotted an old wreck on Chambers's watch, he convinced Higginson to use it for target practice. Higginson ordered the *Atlanta* to close on the wreck and all guns to open fire. Firing at ranges between 200 and 900 yards, they poured over a hundred rounds into the wreck, leaving the wooden sloop riddled with holes but still afloat. Chambers led a crew over in the ships' boats and sank it with explosives to remove it as a hazard to navigation.[12]

Chambers read avidly during the long cruise, having stocked up on books before leaving New York. He pursued his interest in new technology, tinkering with several inventions and continuing to design ships in his spare time. With Higginson's permission, he completely redesigned the *Atlanta*'s boat hoists to allow the rapid and easy hoisting of several boats at once. This brought Chambers to the attention of the Bureau of Equipment, which solicited his input in a study of ship's boats. The United States Transportation Company continued to correspond with Chambers about coal handling equipment, and he gave them his advice freely. He also continued to write occasionally for the *New York Herald,* and sent the newspaper regular reports on news from foreign ports. He maintained his contacts with the Nicaragua Canal Company and wrote to several newspapers, including the *Herald,* to refute attacks on the company. Charles Scribner's Sons approached Chambers to write a book for them on the Nicaraguan Canal, but he apparently declined.[13]

At Montevideo, Admiral Walker transferred his flag to the recently arrived cruiser *Philadelphia* and led his now enlarged squadron in a series of maneuvers that lasted through February. After shore leave at Ensenada, Argentina, they sailed for Maldonado, Uruguay. There on the night of April 21 Chambers led a small crew that helped free the grounded Italian bark *Giuseppe,* for which Admiral Walker commended him for "a difficult job well done." A few days later, the squadron sailed, and retraced its path to the United States, arriving at New York in July where it remained through October. In September, the navy merged the Squadron of Evolution into the North Atlantic Squadron. During these months, Chambers made numerous modifications and changes to the *Atlanta*'s equipment. He adjusted the gun sights and improved a variety of electrical systems. In September, Walker transferred him to the *Chicago* to supervise similar upgrades. Walker sailed the *Chicago* to Newport for the opening session of the Naval War College. There, Chambers and other officers from the squadron listened to Captain Alfred Thayer Mahan's opening address in which he defended the college and explained its purpose.[14]

Mahan had offered Chambers a position on the first permanent faculty of the Naval War College. Uncertain at first, Chambers considered Mahan's work too theoretical and criticized him for ignoring the importance of technological change. In a series of letters, Mahan convinced him of the importance of the college. Chambers attended Mahan's inaugural address, met with him afterward, and at Higginson's urging accepted Mahan's offer. As Higginson wrote, "there are plenty of officers who can drill a division, but very few who can write a good lecture." He would miss Chambers, but would "give him up for the good of the service." Chambers began his work for the Naval War College while on board the *Chicago,* awaiting his transfer.[15]

Unlike many of his fellow officers, Chambers had managed to return to sea in modern warships. While new technology fascinated him, Chambers also relished the challenges of seamanship and command at sea. His proven abilities as line officer would later shield him from criticism from conservative officers who were often suspicious of technically competent officers. Despite his fascination with new technology, Chambers insisted on its practicality and applicability to real and immediate problems, and that new technology must be pursued with practical or strategic purpose. He would apply his ideas at the Naval War College.

# 8 / The Naval War College

Beset by problems obtaining funding, bureaucratic squabbles, and dissonance between competing visions for its purpose and curriculum, the Naval War College faced the greatest challenge to its existence when Chambers arrived in Newport. It needed to find a secure place in the navy's bureaucracy to fulfill Stephen B. Luce's vision of a place where officers would study "their proper profession: war." Its opponents had spent the last few years doing everything they could to destroy it. Few members of Congress actively supported the college. Even Senator Eugene Hale, an ardent navalist, questioned the need for the college. Other politicians questioned its location near the summer homes of Cornelius Vanderbilt and other members of the nation's wealthy elite who flocked to Newport to play "tennis in bathing suits" and indulge in "other enjoyments not usually associated with surf bathing." Were naval officers at Newport to further their educations or their social contacts?[1]

The college remained without a permanent faculty or even a president after Secretary of the Navy William C. Whitney sent Luce's handpicked successor Alfred Thayer Mahan to Puget Sound. Whoever was available read Mahan's lectures on strategy to the 1888 and 1889 classes—a practice that continued in the future and provoked Francis M. Ramsay to ask why the navy needed to send officers to Newport to have Mahan's books read to them? Could they not read them for themselves while at sea? After becoming chief of the Bureau of Navigation, Ramsay refused to assign any students to the college in 1890 or 1891. Captain Francis M. Bunce, who commanded the Apprentice Training School on nearby Goat Island, lobbied to have the college absorbed into his command. Ramsay, in turn, tried to use the college to absorb the Torpedo Station. Other officers thought the Torpedo Station should absorb the college.[2]

At possibly its darkest moment, a presidential election reversed the college's fortunes. Whitney's successor, Benjamin Franklin Tracy, fell under the spell of the reformers and accepted the Mahanian vision for the fleet. In his first annual report, Tracy called for a significant modernization of the fleet and the construction of twenty battleships. He argued that the United States "must have a fleet of battle-ships that will beat off the enemy's fleet on its approach." That fleet "must be able to divert an enemy's force from our coast by threatening its own." Its operations, "though defensive in principle," would be most effective by taking the offensive.[3] Congress appropriated funds for three 10,000-ton "sea-going coastline battleships" the following year.

Urged by Luce, Tracy reassigned Mahan as president of the college in 1892, placed the Torpedo School under his command, and forced Ramsay to release funds for the college. Mahan arrived in Newport in July and knew that he had to quickly establish the college as a permanent fixture within the navy. He needed to regularize the curriculum, recruit a permanent faculty, and attract a better class of students. Failure would doom the college.

Mahan recruited noted reformer Commander Charles H. Stockton, who had served with him on the Puget Sound site selection committee, and Lieutenant James Sears, Chambers's Naval Academy cohort, who had reported for the Office of Naval Intelligence on the Chilean Civil War. For his last faculty position Mahan wanted an officer with solid technical qualifications, but who also shared his strategic vision—an officer who would embody his dual command of the Naval War College and the Torpedo Station. Preserving the college meant accommodating those demanding courses in practical subjects. Mahan, aware of Chambers from his Prize Essay and writings on the Nicaraguan canal, believed he was the perfect candidate. They held virtually identical views on naval expansion, commerce, the isthmian canal, and more.[4]

As mentioned, it took some convincing before Chambers agreed to join the faculty. Chambers argued that the world had entered "a mechanical age."

It was useless for Mahan "to kick against the bricks." He could not turn back the clock. Chambers worried that in his zeal to create a science of strategy, Mahan was ignoring the means to carry it out. He agreed that the study of naval strategy was important, but it should focus on modern ships and weaponry. "One of the chief points in the study of Naval Strategy should be to shape a course of Naval Construction Policy." Mahan wanted to rise above these petty details to get at great principles. Chambers argued that ignoring the technical details that underlay the construction of a modern navy would make it impossible to create a strategy for that fleet. In the modern world, strategy and technology were necessarily linked.[5]

Mahan, impressed with Chambers's critique, redoubled his efforts to recruit him. He responded that technology was important, but "trust in machinery" had been "pushed beyond reason." The "human factor" was everyday "more and more relegated to a position hopelessly inferior." While it was impossible to halt this trend, Mahan hoped "to deflect it somewhat." Otherwise, he feared the art of war would disappear under a "deluge of machinery." He had no problem with Chambers inserting technical details in his lectures as long as he emphasized strategic principles. Otherwise, he feared the college would lose its focus and become just another technical school. He assured Chambers the college would continue to grow, fueled by "the success of my own work, abroad and at home." This success proved the college was on the right track, though its success would "result not from the predominance of my views or your views, but from the fair collision of opinion among men connected with it." There was no "divergence of thought" between them that necessitated them "remaining apart." Chambers agreed to join the faculty.[6]

## The 1892 Session

While Chambers arranged for his transfer, Mahan prepared for the 1892 session scheduled to begin on September 7. Along with funds, Tracy forced Ramsay to send twenty-four students to the college, though this number included Chambers who found himself listed as both a student and a faculty member. The other twenty-three students included some of the least promising officers in the navy. Mahan believed, probably correctly, that Ramsay had deliberately sent the worst officers he could find, hoping to sabotage the program. One of the few exceptions in this unpromising lot was another of

Chambers's friends from the Naval Academy, Lieutenant Henry T. Mayo.[7] Ramsay also delayed the paperwork of both faculty and students, forcing many of them, including Chambers, to work around him.

The session followed the pattern established in the 1880s with lectures on naval strategy and history as well as practical and technical subjects. Stockton and Mahan lectured on strategy and naval history, repeatedly emphasizing that preparation for war needed to be mental as well as physical. Naval officers needed to "imbibe the experience of the past" to craft a strategy for the future. The students probably evinced more interest in what Sears had to say. He discussed the only recent naval conflict, the Pacific War between Chile and Peru, and described the effect of new weapons on naval warfare. These included the sinking of the armored cruiser *Blanco Encalada* by torpedo boats. Chambers lectured on developments in Central America and the importance of an isthmian canal, preferably through Nicaragua. Mahan brought in sixteen visiting lecturers to supplement the faculty, among them his brother Fred, an army major, who lectured on coast defense. The navy desperately wanted to pass this task to the army so it could build a high seas fleet and concentrate on blue water operations.[8]

Despite Mahan's strong defense of the importance of strategy as the "queen of military science," most of the lectures focused on practical and technical subjects such as the mechanical and logistical problems of the new navy. One quarter of them dealt with tactical issues and modern weaponry. Commander Purnell F. Harrington discussed ram tactics. Lieutenant John F. Meigs covered gun tactics. Both described ramming as a normal feature of naval combat. Ensign Albert P. Niblack covered recent developments in naval signaling and their use in recent maneuvers by the Squadron of Evolution and the North Atlantic Squadron. Lieutenant Thomas C. McLean and other officers from the Torpedo Station stopped by to explain the mechanics of various torpedoes. Commander Theodore E. Jewell suggested how they might be used in combat, but explained that little had been done to develop torpedo tactics. Two of the rising stars in the Construction Bureau, Naval Constructors Joseph J. Woodward and David W. Taylor, lectured on ship construction and explained how to conduct speed trials. Passed Assistant Engineer Ira N. Hollis supplemented their lectures with a detailed treatment on recent developments in steam engineering. Lieutenant Joseph B. Murdock did the same for electricity. Lieutenant Commander Albert R. Cowden explained developments in armor including the new Harvey, steel-hardening process.[9]

Students spent the afternoons in individual study and reading the few assigned textbooks. They read Mahan, of course, and Antoine Henri Jomini on whom so much of Mahan's work drew and whom he routinely praised to his students. They also read the works of British admirals John and Philip Colomb who made many of the same points as Mahan. The primary mission of a navy was to engage the enemy fleet on the high seas, and strategic principles endured despite technological change. A few works on recent conflicts rounded out the reading list.[10]

The course ended with a war game of a prospective British invasion of the United States. It pitted a British force of twenty battleships, forty cruisers, and forty torpedo boats against an optimistically large American force of ten battleships, six monitors, twenty-five cruisers, thirty converted merchant cruisers, twenty-five torpedo boats, and thirty converted yachts. It was a scenario remarkably similar to that outlined in Chambers's Prize Essay and probably owed much to his input. Retired Lieutenant William McCarty Little refereed the game using his newly revised rules. His system of war-gaming would become a regular part of the curriculum in 1894.[11]

At the conclusion of the session, Chambers took the opportunity to propose marriage to Isabella Reynolds. They had met as children when Isabella's family moved to Kingston from New Brunswick, and became friends. Chambers apparently began courting her while stationed at the New York Navy Yard. They were married in a small ceremony on December 2, 1892. After a brief honeymoon, they returned to Newport. Their only child, Irving Reynolds Chambers, was born there the following year.[12]

## Torpedoes, Technology, and Strategy

Encouraged by Mahan, Chambers renewed his interest in torpedoes and followed technological developments in a variety of fields. Mahan expected him to become the college's primary lecturer on torpedoes and routinely referred to him as "our torpedo man." Chambers resumed his correspondence with Edward Very and consulted regularly with the officers of the Torpedo Station. He helped test the new Hotchkiss torpedoes and suggested a number of improvements to them. He working with the Torpedo Station to develop torpedo-boat tactics and helped improve their signaling system so these attacks could be coordinated. Chambers also worked with Mahan to integrate torpedo boats into his battleship-dominated conception of strategy. Mahan's own musings on the subject, among his least impressive work, simply suggested that navies would employ torpedo boats much as they had fireships in the era of sail. "Like fire-ships, small torpedo-cruisers" would "complicate the evolutions of the fleet with which they are associated." They would be a threat primarily to anchored warships and might force them to scatter as the Spanish Armada had when attacked by British fireships. Mahan believed that increasing artillery range would doom the torpedo boat as it had the fireship, making it impossible for it to close into range of its target. This was a natural result of his suspicion of technology combined with his excessive focus on battleships. In Mahan's world, good men on poor ships usually beat poor men sailing better ships. Mahan's examination of the British navy showed this was true of the age of sail, but Chambers argued that in the industrial age the pace of technological advance was such that courage, experience, and training often could not bridge the gap between good ships and poor ships.[13]

Chambers had much higher expectations of what torpedo boats could accomplish and a better grasp of technological innovation. In his never-delivered lectures, he sharply criticized the United States for not embracing them sooner. In the War of 1812, the navy should have adopted Robert Fulton's harbor defense plans and used mines and torpedoes extensively. Chambers believed Mahan's comparison with fireships dramatically understated the case. Torpedo boats were faster and more maneuverable than fireships. Like fireships, torpedo boats could attack battleships in port before they could mass on the high seas for a modern Trafalgar. Chambers argued that torpedo boats, unlike fireships, could also operate effectively on the high seas. He was among a handful of officers who pushed for the development of smaller torpedo boats that larger warships would launch and rearm in battle. Regardless of their size, torpedo boats would be a necessary part of any fleet. Any fleet intent on massing for battle would have to defend against torpedo attack.

Even if Mahan was right, and Chambers doubted this, torpedo boats would remain useful in confined and shallow waters. They would not disappear. Chambers rarely fell prey to favoring one weapons system over another. He wanted an integrated fleet that possessed a variety of arms and ship types. The only weapon he consistently criticized was the ram, which still had numerous adherents in the United States. As Chambers repeatedly argued, torpedoes, as well as modern, rapid-firing guns, made ramming attacks little more than suicide. A torpedo was essentially a ram able to operate free from its ship and subsumed its function.[14]

Chambers had worried about the vulnerability of ships to torpedoes as far back as 1882. He closely watched tests on torpedo nets at the Naval Torpedo Station, but these were only useful in protecting ships in port. Even then, their effectiveness seemed doubtful against volleys of torpedoes. Used aggressively, torpedo boats had the potential to upset Mahan's battleship-laden apple cart. Even more threatening were submarines. Chambers observed several of the tests of John Holland's early boats, and wondered in his notes if someday command of the sea would pass to them. Unless someone corrected the battleships' vulnerability to torpedoes, it certainly seemed possible, but he kept these musings to himself.[15]

Sparked by his association with Mahan and a renewed correspondence with Henige, Chambers returned to his efforts at ship design. This time, he worked on battleships, trying to improve their waterline armor and maximize their firepower. Chambers accepted Mahan's argument that concentration was key to victory, and sought to achieve it on an individual ship. He pursued the subject only halfheartedly, but returned to it later in his career.

Chambers's studies at the college and his association with Mahan clarified and focused his understanding of strategy. Like his mentor, he came to believe "that naval strategy had its broad and indefeasible principles" and that the study of the past was "an essential foundation to an intelligent preparation for the present and future." Yet, Mahan's strategic principles did not cover everything. In his lectures, Chambers emphasized the importance of public opinion on the conduct of wars and campaigns. Mahan's goal of engaging the enemy's fleet was "but a means to an end," and a potentially costly one. The gap in Mahan's work that most drew his attention was technology. British Admiral Philip Colomb had commented that, "very little technological knowledge is needed to understand that the methods of strategy may change but that its principles remain immutable. With tactics the case is very different: the history of military tactics is the history of weapons successively employed and a similar evolution may be traced in naval tactics."[16]

The question for Chambers was: when did technology change so much that it forced strategy to change as well? Certainly, the transition from oared galleys to full-rigged sailing ships had opened new strategic opportunities. He believed the steamship, torpedo, submarine, and modern ordnance would do the same. Chambers made his goal at the Naval War College to integrate an appreciation of technology into Mahanian strategy. He argued that the study of strategy and the development of technology were interdependent. There "is no royal road to the study of either independently." By studying them together, he hoped to sift out general principles, and use these principles "to seize first advantage of new improvements" and "wisely direct" the improvement of the navy."[17]

## The Bureaucrats Strike Back

After the 1892 session ended, Mahan's faculty prepared for what they hoped would be an even better session the following year. They modified the curriculum, prepared lesson plans, and wrote several new lectures. Chambers made a number of maps and diagrams for classroom use. Working closely together, they planned a course of study based on the needs of the navy rather than the vicissitudes of teacher availability. They planned for an expanded college with four departments: (1) the Art of War upon the Sea, (2) the Art of War Applied to Coast Defense and Attack, (3) Naval History and Maritime Interests, and (4) the Torpedo Course.[18]

In the midst of their work, Grover Cleveland won the presidential election and Democrats regained control of both houses of Congress. The new administration retained Ramsay as Chief of the Bureau of Navigation, and appointed Hilary Herbert to be the new Secretary of the Navy. Long the senior Democrat on the House Naval Affairs Committee, Herbert was one of the most outspoken proponents of naval modernization, but he also championed economy and efficiency. He had repeatedly voted against funding the Naval War College and had supported efforts to consolidate it with other Newport installations. It seemed likely he would renew these efforts. The time was ripe for the college's enemies to attack.

While the new administration sorted itself out, Bunce and Ramsay united their efforts at consolidation. They had a great deal of support within the navy. The Phythian Board in 1891, for example, had suggested merging the three Newport installations into an enlarged Naval War College composed of four divisions: Art of War, Torpedoes, Gunnery, and Apprentice Training. Bunce and Ramsay had a different scheme in mind, but they capitalized on the support for consolidation in general. They built support for their case in the press, and argued that consolidation was a matter of administrative and economic efficiency and would save the government thousands of dollars. To get journalists' attention, they spread rumors about the goings on at Newport. These included the old stories of college officers socializing with debutantes and bathing beauties, but also several new ones. The most salacious was that sodomy had become rampant among the apprentice seamen on the training ships. Bunce argued, with questionable logic, that moving them ashore would solve the problem.[19]

The *New York Times* ran a series of articles critical of the college that summer. It favored relocating the college to Annapolis and giving its new building to Bunce's apprentices. The college, it complained, met "for only a few months of the year" and was merely a school for those few Annapolis graduates "who indicate a wish to take a post-graduate course." The mission of the Training School was much more important. Reporters described the crowded conditions of the apprentices in exaggerated detail. The state of the marines, who slept in tents year-round, was even worse. The officers of the Training School roomed together in the training ship *Richmond*'s wardroom. Only Bunce slept in comfort ashore. The *Times* condemned these conditions as "a disgrace of government" and demanded that something be done. Assistant Secretary of the Navy William McAdoo visited Newport and came to similar conclusions. Like Herbert, he had opposed its funding as a member of Congress, decrying the "great misfortune that our military schools should be established in connection with watering places characterized in certain seasons of the year as scenes of social display and dissipation." Bunce, pleased with the news coverage, expected to win. He vowed to friends that: "in six months my boys [the apprentices] will be eating their grub in the lecture room of the War College." As momentum built, Ramsay and Bunce took their case for "financial efficiency" to Congress.[20]

Ramsay used his powers as Chief of the Bureau of Navigation to attack the college. In his most famous action, he ordered Mahan back to sea, insisting that even Mahan must abide by the normal requirement of rotation. Mahan and the college's supporters pleaded for an exception, but Ramsay refused, replying that it was "not the job of naval officers to write books." Luce, by then retired, lobbied his friends to stop Mahan's second expulsion, but they could do nothing. Mahan returned to sea in command of the *Chicago* and left for Europe on a cruise that more resembled a book tour than a naval exercise. Herbert honored his choice of successor, and Commander Henry Clay Taylor, an expert tactician, became the college's president.

Ramsay did not stop with Mahan. Whenever possible, he found extra work for members of the college faculty. He valued Chambers's opinion on ship design from their time together at the New York Navy Yard, and sent him to observe the sea trials of a number of new ships in Narragansett Bay. On several occasions, he sent him much farther afield. In January, he appointed Chambers to the preliminary trial board of the *Bancroft,* a new steel gunboat designed as a training ship at the Naval Academy. In June he ordered Chambers to take charge of the old sloop *Fortune,* sail her to New London, and there help with the speed trials of the new armored cruiser *New York.* In July, and then again in August, he sent him to sit on naval examining boards.[21]

Throughout the summer, the college's faculty continued its preparatory work, but they could almost see the vultures circling their building. All four of them were very concerned about the hostility of the press toward their institution. In August, rumor reached them that Ramsay would again refuse to send them students. Frustrated, Chambers wrote Mahan asking for advice. He believed emphatically in the college's mission and was eager to champion its cause. How, he asked, should he proceed to defend the college?

Mahan kept in touch with events at Newport and orchestrated the defense of the college. He intrigued with friends to get college supporter Captain Robley D. Evans appointed to head the Bureau of Navigation. He encouraged Chambers to fight on for the cause, "to go down with his colors flying." If, after "every proper effort, you are beaten by the folly and indifference of second-rate superiors you have no more cause for mortification than a man who is cut down at his post because the rest have run away from his support."[22] Chambers would soon get his chance to prove his worth to the prophet of the new navy.

Under pressure from multiple directions, Secretary of the Navy Herbert decided to visit Newport that summer and investigate the situation himself. He traveled on board the *Dolphin,* whose captain, former naval intelligence attaché Lieutenant Benjamin H. Buckingham, supported the college and admired Mahan. He presented a copy of Mahan's *Influence of Sea Power upon History* to Herbert who read it during the voyage. Impressed, Herbert wrote to Mahan that if the college had "produced nothing more than this book it is worth all the expense incurred for it." This did not mean that the college had to remain at its present location. Herbert remained interested in consolidation, especially as the assault in the press continued. In October, the *New York Times* suggested that the navy close the college since it fulfilled "no useful purpose." Taylor traveled to Washington to lobby for the college and to speak with Herbert again, but met with little success. The momentum in favor of consolidation seemed unstoppable.[23]

In November, Ramsay ordered Chambers and Sears to report to the Apprentice Training School. In addition to their duties at the Naval War College, which were minimal since Ramsay had sent no students, they would each command a division of apprentices. Bunce had won his case for increasing the efficiency of the Newport establishment, but he had not reckoned with the personalities of the officers he sought to borrow.

Chambers, who had previously accepted special assignments from Ramsay without complaint, decided to act. This was not temporary duty at a speed trial or the inspection of a new ship, but a permanent assignment under a different commander—an officer who threatened the college. Chambers may not have been thinking clearly when he sent a letter to Ramsay the next day and enclosed a copy to the Secretary of the Navy. Certainly, he recalled Mahan's encouragement "to go down with his colors flying." Chambers informed Herbert and Ramsay that he could not work at the Training School in addition to the college. Further, he pointed out that he could not report to two different commanding officers. One was quite sufficient. He asked the navy to relieve him of the "arduous" position at the Training School. Worried that they might simply transfer him to the Training Station, he concluded by stating that if they did not allow him to continue teaching at the college, he would accept "any duty other than training apprentices." Sears wrote a similar letter.[24] The two friends, who had cooperated in a series of practical jokes as midshipmen, now played a much more serious game.

When confronted with Chambers, Secretary Whitney had handled the matter calmly, commending and mollifying him. Hilary Herbert, however, was not Whitney. A former Confederate colonel, he was accustomed to having his orders obeyed. An irate Herbert wrote Taylor demanding Sears and Chambers be court-martialed for insubordination. Already facing the budget ax and possible amalgamation with its neighbors, the last thing the college needed was to have half its faculty brought up on charges. Taylor replied that while Chambers and Sears may have acted rashly, their objection was legitimate—two commanding officers was one too many. He tried to calm Herbert down, but the secretary remained unconvinced. Once he heard about the letter, Bunce joined in and accused Chambers and Sears of conspiring in an "unlawful combination" to undermine his authority. He, too, pressed for their courts-martial.[25]

Instead of fearing for their careers, Chambers and Sears welcomed the possibility of a court-martial. It would give them an opportunity to fight back against the college's enemies and expose their underhanded maneuverings. Both expected to win if things went that far. Sears in particular was eager to take Bunce down a notch. How, he wondered, "could a man of his age and experience be so imbecile." Chambers, too, must have wondered how a man he had served under and respected could have turned into such a fierce enemy. While Chambers and Sears were eager to escalate the war of words, Taylor prudently ordered them to keep their mouths shut.[26]

Taylor renewed his own efforts to save the college. After his failed trip to Washington in October, he turned to the public. Speaking to virtually any business, political, or civic group that would listen, he defended the college as necessary for naval modernization. He sent regular press releases to the major newspapers defending it. Luce called on his political contacts to rally to the college, and Mahan continued his machinations, capitalizing on his international fame to save his beloved school. Slowly the tide turned in favor of the college, but too slowly to suit Chambers and Sears.[27]

In December, Ramsay appeared before the House Naval Affairs Committee. In a private meeting, he urged its members to discontinue the appropriation for the college. Bunce renewed his demands for the college's building. Despite the arrival of the *Richmond* and *Lancaster* as training ships, he claimed he needed more space for the apprentices, and Ramsay helped him get it. On December 8, Ramsay ordered Chambers and Sears to turn over their quarters at the college to officers from the Training School. If Bunce could not have them, he would have their quarters. The order arrived without warning and demanded instant compliance. Stockton told Chambers and Sears they could "box things neatly" once they were moved out of their quarters and into tents. He apologized for the windy weather, but assured them that he and Taylor would "do what we can to help you with our limited means." Chambers and Sears passed the next few days shivering outside in tents, waiting to hear if they would be court-martialed.[28]

Mahan, who had encouraged his subordinates in their actions, now had to save them from the incensed Secretary of the Navy. He complained to his sister that Chambers and Sears had "erred by being too precipitate." They should have waited "until every argument had been exhausted with the Secretary [of the Navy]. Had he then persisted, an application for detachment was perfectly correct." Perhaps, but Mahan knew he was partly to blame for the rash action of his former subordinates. He, too, wrote Herbert in their defense. Between them, Mahan and Taylor managed to save the careers of Chambers and Sears, but their time at the college ended. Herbert insisted on their removal from the faculty.[29]

The past year had proved a watershed in the history of the Naval War College. Aside from establishing the curriculum on a sound footing, Chambers, Mahan, Sears, Stockton, Taylor, and their supporters defeated the last serious attempt to destroy the college. On March 14, 1894, the navy merged the Naval Training School, Naval War College, and the Torpedo Station into one command under Bunce. While on the surface a defeat, Mahan's fame shielded the college from direct attacks and it was able to develop unmolested. In 1895, Evans replaced Ramsay as Chief of the Bureau of Navigation, ending the threat from that direction.[30] Twenty-five students attended the four-month 1894 session, the longest in the college's ten-year history. Unfortunately, Chambers was not there to see it.

Exiled from the college, Chambers scrambled for an assignment to his liking before Ramsay sent him to a far distant station. Henige suggested that he join the Naval Academy's faculty, since the new superintendent, noted reformer Captain Robert L. Pythian, wanted him. Phythian, however, had chaired the board that recommended consolidating the Newport installations, so Chambers wanted nothing to do with him. Instead, he accepted a post at the Bureau of Ordnance, which had tried to recruit him for a decade, since he held its new chief, Captain William T. Sampson, in high regard. Chambers continued to follow events at the Naval War College. He consulted with Taylor regularly and helped plan the 1894 and 1895 curriculum and war games.[31]

In 1894, Taylor implemented the curriculum and lectures that Mahan, Stockton, Chambers, and Sears had planned for 1893. The lectures covered the usual topics of history, naval strategy and tactics, coast defense, and weapons systems. Stockton lectured on the importance of the Nicaraguan canal using Chambers's notes. Many of the lectures straddled their topic with one foot in the present and the other rooted firmly in the past. Taylor and Stockton compiled synopses of these lectures into a handbook for students that included their often-conservative criticisms. They argued, for instance, that boarding actions were still possible, as were ramming attacks. They presented the ram as more important than the torpedo and denigrated torpedoes in general.[32] Had Chambers and Sears been able to make their points in person, they might have helped their elders produce a more forward-looking document.

Chambers again deliberately chose the role of martyr and provoked a serious dispute with the Secretary of the Navy and senior officers. The seriousness of this dispute finally sank in to him during his last days at the college. It would be many years before he again directly criticized his superiors. Until then, Chambers proved a model officer and loyal subordinate.

1. Ensign W. I. Chambers (4th from left) and the crew of the *Loch Garry*. Naval Historical Center.

2. Chambers and the crew of the *Alert*. From left to right: Chambers, Ensign Charles S. McClain, Lieutenant Charles J. Badger, Lieutenant Henry J. Hunt, Commander George W. Coffin, Ice Pilot Gifford, Passed Assistant Engineer William H. Nauman, Ensign Albert A. Ackerman, Passed Assistant Surgeon Francis S. Nash. Naval Historical Center.

3. Officers of the Greely Relief Expedition and the survivors from Greely's party. Seated, from left to right are: Private Francis Long, Sergeant David L. Brainard, Lieutenant Adolphus Greely, Private Henry Bierderbick, Private Julius Frederick, Private Maurice Connell. Second Row (left to right): Ensign Albert A. Ackerman, Lieutenant Uriel Sebree, Ensign Charles H. Harlow, Commander George W. Coffin, Lieutenant William H. Emory, Chief Engineer John Lowe, Commodore William S. Schley, Passed Assistant Surgeon Howard E. Ames, Chief Engineer George W. Melville. Seated on upper deck: Lieutenant Samuel C. Lemly, Passed Assistant Surgeon Edward H. Green. Standing on upper deck: Lieutenant Freeman H. Crosby, Lieutenant John C. Colwell, Ensign Charles S. McClain, Lieutenant Henry J. Hunt, Lieutenant Nathaniel R. Usher, Lieutenant Charles J. Badger, Passed Assistant Engineer William H. Nauman, Ensign Lovell K. Reynolds, Lieutenant Emory H. Taunt. Top left: Passed Assistant Surgeon Francis S. Nash and Ensign Washington I. Chambers. Naval Historical Center.

4. Captain Washington I. Chambers in 1910. Naval Historical Center.

5. The Curtiss A-1 at Hammondsport (June 1911) shortly before delivery to the navy. Present, left to right, are: civilian pilots Witmer and Cooper, Dr. Alfred F. Zahm, Lieutenant John W. McClaskey, USMC (retired), Jim Curtiss (mechanic), Glenn H. Curtiss, Lieutenant Theodore G. Ellyson, Captain Washington I. Chambers, Lieutenant John H. Towers, Bill Pickens, and an unidentified Curtiss mechanic. Naval Historical Center.

6. The Curtiss A-1 at Hammondsport (June 1911) shortly before delivery to the navy. Present left to right are: unidentified Curtiss mechanic, Dr. Alfred F. Zahm, Lieutenant John W. McClaskey, USMC (retired), Jim Lamont, Glenn Curtiss, Captain Washington I. Chambers, Lieutenant John H. Towers, Lieutenant Theodore G. Ellyson, and Bill Pickens. Naval Historical Center.

7. Eugene B. Ely taking off from the cruiser *Birmingham* on November 14, 1910. Naval Historical Center.

8. Eugene B. Ely landing on the cruiser *Pennsylvania* on January 18, 1911. Naval Historical Center.

9. Captain Washington I. Chambers (holding the life preserver) and Lieutenant Theodore G. Ellyson in the Curtiss A-2 at Hammondsport for its trial in September 1911. Naval Historical Center.

10. Curtiss plane being hoisted aboard the *Pennsylvania* in San Diego Harbor, February 11, 1911. National Archives (80G1051558).

11. Eugene Ely landing on the *Pennsylvania*, January 18, 1911. National Archives (80G1051561).

# 9 / The *Minneapolis* and the Bureau of Ordnance

By the mid-1890s, the navy had made great strides in rearmament. The navy's first battleships, the small and already dated *Maine* and *Texas,* joined the fleet in 1895, and the more modern *Oregon, Indiana,* and *Massachusetts* a year later. Thereafter Congress authorized new battleships roughly every other year. The navy concentrated most of its armored warships in the North Atlantic Squadron, which by 1897 included all five of the navy's battleships and two armored cruisers, which held regular maneuvers while cruising along the eastern seaboard. The navy scattered its new unarmored warships throughout its squadrons, and those on foreign station continued the old practice of individual ship cruising, but each squadron assembled at least once each year for intensive drill, target practice, and maneuvers. In terms of both equipment and training, the U.S. Navy was a capable force for the first time in twenty-five years.

While the fleet grew, the United States embraced a more confrontational foreign policy. In 1889, a hurricane averted a showdown with Germany over Samoa by sweeping the gunboats of both nations onto a reef. In 1891, the navy mobilized for war following an assault on the crew of the cruiser *Baltimore* in Chile. Two years later, sailors and marines from the cruiser *Boston* helped American settlers seize control of Hawaii. The Cleveland administration changed foreign policy only slightly. Despite his refusal to annex Hawaii, Cleveland was interested in expanding American influence overseas. In

1894, he ordered the navy to break the blockade imposed by rebels in the Brazilian Civil War. In 1895, he successfully supported Venezuela in its boundary dispute with Great Britain over Guiana. These successes vindicated naval expansion and proved the navy's utility in diplomacy. Naval rearmament supported an increasingly aggressive foreign policy that would lead to war with Spain before the close of the decade.[1]

The greatest obstacle to the navy's modernization in the 1880s and 1890s was the lack of domestic industry specializing in steel ship construction. It required more than a decade for American factories to gear up to produce modern ordnance and armor. Steelmakers had great difficulty meeting the navy's stringent quality requirements and keeping pace with advances introduced in Europe. Many manufacturers refused to bid on the growing number of naval contracts due to the high start-up costs. This was especially true for armor and heavy ordnance, items for which there would never be a civilian market. Armor manufacturers were at the mercy of a government that would one year appropriate funds for several armored warships and the next year for none at all. In the 1890s, a series of scandals involving overpricing and poor workmanship wracked this burgeoning industry. Chambers had already encountered these problems while working on the *Maine.* The 1890s found him in the middle of these disputes as they reached their climax.

The navy negotiated its first armor contract with Bethlehem Steel in 1886. When Bethlehem ran into production problems, the navy negotiated a second contract with Carnegie Steel. Both firms proved slow to deliver their goods, quick to levy additional fees, and charged considerably more than their European counterparts. The navy was being overcharged, but could do nothing about it. It needed armor, and Congress required its domestic manufacture. Both companies claimed that the high quality demanded by the navy and the high rejection rate of its inspectors forced up the price. Government officials and the navy accepted this explanation until 1895 when the press discovered that Bethlehem, which was then selling armor to the navy for $625 per ton, had contracted with Russia at the absurdly low price of $250 per ton. In December, the Senate launched a full investigation of armor prices.[2]

## Bureau of Ordnance Inspector

Chambers finished his remaining fourteen months of shore duty as an ordnance inspector for the Bureau of Ordnance, where he reported on March 16,

1894. Captain William T. Sampson sent him back to Newport for his first assignment, this time to the Torpedo Station. Given his long familiarity with torpedoes and his recent work and friendships with the officers there, it was an obvious choice. At the station, Chambers supervised the test firing of several different torpedo types from the *Cushing*, the navy's first modern torpedo boat, and became close friends with the *Cushing*'s commander, Lieutenant Frank F. Fletcher. Together they developed several minor improvements to the reliability and accuracy of the navy's torpedoes and launching mechanisms. They might have accomplished more, but Chambers soon had to leave.[3]

In May, Secretary of the Navy Hilary Herbert became convinced of problems at the Pennsylvania Steel Casting and Machine Company, which made parts for several of the navy's ships. He arranged with Sampson to have Chambers sent to its plant in Chester as an inspector. Chambers's assignment was part of a general increase in inspectors as the navy tried to cope with the growing number of problems with manufacturers. In part, this was due to the increasing number of orders as rearmament accelerated, but Herbert and others suspected some companies of deliberately shipping substandard goods to inflate their profits.

Chambers noticed problems his first day at Pennsylvania Steel Casting. He took notes and began discreetly gathering evidence that would be "convincing and irrefutable." Inspectors at other companies had blown the whistle at the first sign of trouble, but without sufficient evidence to proceed to court, these companies escaped with warnings. Chambers wanted a conviction.[4]

The company's fraudulent practices increased over time. At first, it simply mixed in a few substandard castings into large lots of good castings in the hopes of slipping them past Chambers. It sent those he caught through again in a second try to slip them past. When these efforts failed, the company eradicated the serial numbers on the rejected castings, stamped new numbers on them, and tried to pass them through yet again. Unable to sneak items past Chambers, or at least as many as they would have liked, company officials counterfeited his official stamp. They stamped several rejects as passed, and sent them on to the gun factory at the Washington Navy Yard. Chambers caught a company foreman red-handed with the counterfeited stamp. The company's president, Mortimer H. Bickly, claimed he had known nothing about any of these shenanigans and blamed his foremen for the repeated efforts at fraud. Due to Chambers's investigation, the navy began testing gun castings and forgings twice by independent inspectors after they passed government inspectors. Along with other inspectors, Chambers continued to push for higher standards and tougher inspections of the steel industry.[5]

In November, Sampson sent Chambers to monitor the Midvale Steel Company, headquartered in Philadelphia. Midvale specialized in gun forgings, and was the only company in the United States other than Bethlehem that manufactured high-caliber naval artillery. From Philadelphia Chambers also oversaw the work at a number of smaller plants in the region. This kept him constantly traveling between different factories, often at his own expense—a hardship since the navy proved slow to reimburse him. In between inspections, Chambers also testified in a number of government lawsuits against manufacturers, the most important of which came in December when he testified as the star witness against Pennsylvania Steel Casting.[6]

Chambers's time on shore was due to expire in the spring, but Sampson intervened with Secretary Herbert to keep him at the Bureau of Ordnance. The navy continued to experience problems finding parts for its new ships and was forced to order parts and fittings wherever it could. New cases continued to go to trial and Congress demanded increased scrutiny of industry. The Bureau of Ordnance, overwhelmed with work, needed officers of Chambers's ability more than ever. Sampson managed only a short delay in his transfer. On June 13, the navy ordered Chambers to the cruiser *Minneapolis.*[7]

## The *Minneapolis*

Authorized in 1891 and commissioned in December 1894, the 7,375-ton *Minneapolis* and her sister ship *Columbia* were the ultimate development of the protected cruiser by the United States. In response to congressional pressure for faster and faster ships, her designers sacrificed everything for speed and endurance. They envisioned the two ships as modern *Alabamas,* commerce raiders that could stay at sea indefinitely, relying on their sails for cruising and refueling from prizes as needed. Chief Engineer of the Navy George Melville himself designed their innovative, triple-screw, three-engine plants. The cruisers usually used only two engines to save fuel, employing the third for maximum speed. They could easily overtake any merchant ship afloat and outrun any warship that posed them serious danger. In the summer of

1895, the *Columbia* proved the design in a race, crossing the Atlantic Ocean in just under seven days at an average speed of 18 knots.

Despite their great speed, the ships received harsh criticism from line officers. Lieutenant Albert P. Niblack complained repeatedly about the "craze for speed" that had produced such a poorly armed warship. With a main armament of just one 8-inch and two 6-inch guns, the *Columbia* and *Minneapolis* were poorly armed for ships of their size. Their eight 4-inch and dozen smaller guns would be of little help against a normally armed cruiser, and while both also had four torpedo tubes, few officers had any training or faith in these weapons.[8]

Captain George H. Wadleigh, who had been the executive officer on the *Pensacola* on Chambers's first cruise, commanded the *Minneapolis,* which along with the armored cruiser *New York* and the protected cruisers *Columbia, Montgomery,* and *Raleigh,* formed part of the North Atlantic Squadron. The War College's old nemesis, Admiral Frances M. Bunce, flew his flag in the *New York.* The squadron sailed in August for a routine cruise along the coast. In September, Bunce led it through a series of drills, simple maneuvers, and target practice off Fishers Island near Long Island, New York, that culminated in landing a brigade of marines and sailors. Afterward, Bunce ordered Wadleigh to organize a board of three officers to consider changes and additions to the Fleet Drill Manual and their system of signaling to allow more elaborate maneuvers.

Wadleigh placed Chambers in charge of the board and assigned two of the *Minneapolis*'s other officers, lieutenants James H. Oliver and Joseph B. Murdock, to help him. Together they developed a complex set of maneuvers that involved changing from line to column and back again several times, each time echeloned in a different order. While not particularly useful in combat, they gave the squadron's officers much needed practice in maneuvering and maintaining proper intervals between their ships. While working on these plans, Chambers also designed a new sighting device, which proved slightly superior to the old one in tests. After more maneuvers, the squadron resumed its peregrinations along the coast.[9]

The North Atlantic Squadron, a well-honed tool, regularly received favorable mention in the press. The same could not be said of the small European Squadron. In October, the navy recalled its commander, Rear Admiral William A. Kirkland, following a succession of impolitic actions. In particular, he appeared slow to respond to the needs of American missionaries in the Ottoman Empire. President Cleveland sent Commodore Thomas O. Selfridge Jr. to replace Kirkland with orders to personally oversee their safety. A week of anti-Christian rioting had just left several thousand Armenians dead. The situation escalated while Selfridge traveled to Europe on board a commercial steamer. Fresh riots broke out in November and mobs burned and looted Christian churches, schools, and homes. The missionaries' supporters in the United States demanded that Cleveland take strong action.[10]

Selfridge joined his small squadron of only two cruisers, the *San Francisco* and *Marblehead,* at Le Harve and sailed east, arriving in Alexandretta, Syria, at the end of November. Despite Selfridge's optimistic reports, Cleveland ordered the *Minneapolis* to join the European Squadron. The *Minneapolis* left Hampton Roads on November 27 and arrived at Gibraltar on December 13. The *Minneapolis* had been quite sluggish on the voyage, so Wadleigh ordered Chambers to lead a crew of divers to inspect her bottom. They found the hull seriously incrusted, foul, and corroded. The ship needed to be dry-docked and the hull cleaned, but they had neither the time nor the facilities. Chambers and his crew cleaned the propellers, and the *Minneapolis* continued on her way to Smyrna to join the varied collection of foreign warships that assembled after the riots. These included warships from every major European power that ranged in size from French torpedo boats to the Austrian battleship *Tegetthoff.*[11]

Shortly after the *Minneapolis* arrived, the navy ordered Selfridge to concentrate his squadron at Alexandretta and evacuate the missionaries if rioting resumed. The expected renewal of violence never came, but tensions simmered throughout the spring. In January 1896, the squadron returned to Smyrna, and the *Cincinnati* arrived, bringing Selfridge's squadron to four cruisers. This allowed the admiral to rotate his ships to Italy for maintenance, and he sent the *Marblehead* to Naples for a much-needed overhaul.

The *Minneapolis* continued to have problems working up to speed. Wadleigh, worried about the condition of the hull, put Chambers in charge of a board of officers to monitor the situation. He and his team checked for leaks at each of her stops, and Chambers led a crew in diving suits that inspected the hull. Covered with a thick mat of growth, it was difficult to monitor its condition, but it was clearly getting worse. In April, Chambers reported that the corrosion of the ship's hull had become critical. The ship needed to be dry-docked as soon as practical to be scraped, patched, and completely repainted. On the *Marblehead*'s return, Selfridge sent the *Minneapolis* to Genoa for repairs where Chambers supervised all work on the hull. He determined that careless work in the United States had caused the problems. Workers had left large surfaces unpainted and numerous joins in the hull poorly sealed. Impressed with his work, Wadleigh placed him in charge of all future dockyard work on the *Minneapolis*.[12]

After the overhaul, Selfridge transferred his flag to the *Minneapolis* and sailed for Kronstadt, Russia, to represent the United States at the coronation of Czar Nicholas II. After a brief stop in London they arrived at Kronstadt on May 13. Selfridge and his senior officers traveled to Moscow by train, leaving the rest of the officers and crew to sample the dubious delights of Kronstadt. He remained in Moscow for a month, attending a succession of ceremonies, and rejoined the *Minneapolis* in mid-June to resume their voyage with stops in Denmark, Sweden, and Norway where Selfridge dined with the royal families. After leaving Denmark, he assigned Chambers, Oliver, and Murdock to examine target practice. Their report questioned the current scoring system and recommended practice at longer ranges. Selfridge adopted some of their suggestions and conducted a brief target practice. He sent their report to the Bureau of Ordnance where it languished. The *Minneapolis* then returned to the eastern Mediterranean following reports of renewed violence.[13]

Throughout 1896, relations between Spain and the United States worsened as Spain struggled to suppress a Cuban rebellion. Selfridge worried that if war broke out, the Spanish fleet would trap and destroy his squadron in the Mediterranean. In the event of war, Selfridge decided to counter Spanish superiority in firepower with a massed torpedo attack. On January 1, he ordered his ships to train officers to fire torpedoes and to fire at least two per month. Many American cruisers carried torpedoes, but few had fired them. Only two years before, the *Detroit* had become the first American cruiser to fire one. One of the few officers in the squadron with any torpedo experience, Chambers trained the officers and crew of the *Minneapolis* and helped develop their plan of attack. Fortunately, they never had to execute it.[14]

In May, following several calm months in the Ottoman Empire, the navy ordered the *Minneapolis* back to the North Atlantic Squadron to participate in the navy's largest maneuvers in twenty-five years. Following these, Secretary of the Navy John D. Long ordered the *Minneapolis* and *Columbia* placed out of commission as an economy measure. The same engines that made them among the fastest ships of their size also made them expensive to operate. Decommissioning them would also free up crews for the new battleships joining the fleet.[15]

There were far better candidates in the fleet for decommissioning. On July 1, while undergoing a routine engine trial at the New York Navy Yard, one of the *Puritan*'s boilers exploded, scalding several crewmembers and crippling the ship. The *Puritan* was one of five double-turret monitors that had languished uncompleted through the 1870s and 1880s. The navy completed them more to clear up space in the crowded navy yards than to have them available for service. Following the explosion, the press denounced them as obsolete menaces. Two weeks later, Bunce appointed a board, composed of Chief Engineer Edward Farmer, the head of steam engineering at the yard, George Cowin, the *Puritan*'s chief engineer, and Chambers to investigate the explosion. They were appalled by what they found. One set of rubber seal rings connecting the boilers had ruptured, causing the explosion, but the rings on all the boilers showed severe deterioration—any of them might have ruptured. The rings were just part of the problem. Fragments from the destroyed boiler showed metal fatigue and corrosion. Many parts crumbled in Chambers's hands. Had the rings not failed, the boiler itself might have ruptured causing even more damage. The explosion resulted from poor maintenance on a ship that despite its recent commissioning, was actually quite old.[16] The investigators tendered their report to Bunce, and Chambers departed for a brief leave.

## The Armor Factory Board

The navy continued to experience problems with private industry. In December 1896, navy inspectors declared several of Carnegie's armor plates for the battleships *Kearsarge* and *Kentucky* defective. Over the next few months, they also unearthed defects in the work of other companies. The steel industry's representatives continued to complain about the navy's high standards. While a few inspectors did admit that the navy demanded a higher quality than "that used in any foreign navy," the perception remained that the steel industry as a whole was out to defraud the government.[17] The primary issue, though, became price rather than quality.

In April 1897, Congress declared that it would pay a maximum of only $300 per ton of armor instead of the current price in the United States of

$575 per ton. Secretary of the Navy Long asked Congress to compromise at $400, but was rebuffed. Congress had Bethlehem's contract with Russia as proof of the steel industry's perfidy. At that time, only the Italian navy, which paid $600 per ton, paid more for its armor than the United States. Krupp charged the German Navy only $530 per ton. Le Creusot in France was the cheapest at $475 per ton.[18] Clearly American firms were overcharging, but the price Congress offered was ridiculous.

That summer, not a single firm bid on the armor contracts for the battleships *Alabama, Illinois,* and *Wisconsin.* The steel industry refused to produce armor at a price Congress would pay. Both Congress and the navy explored alternatives to private industry. Carnegie offered to sell the government his plant, a plant built with government subsidies, but this only further infuriated Congress. In August, Congress ordered the navy to investigate the practicality of building a government-owned armor factory and report by the end of the year.[19]

Assistant Secretary of the Navy Theodore Roosevelt quickly established the Armor Factory Board and appointed some of the navy's best technical officers as its members. He chose Commodore John A. Howell, the inventor of the Howell torpedo, to be its president. Along with him served Civil Engineer Mordecai T. Endicott, Lieutenant Frank F. Fletcher, Captain Alexander H. McCormick, and Chief Engineer James H. Perry. He assigned Chambers to be the board's recorder. Roosevelt attended many of the board's meetings and pressed its officers to reach a conclusion quickly.

The board had to determine the practicality of building and then operating a government armor factory "of sufficient capacity to meet the probable requirements" of future naval appropriations. When the members of the board asked Roosevelt what Congress meant by this vague guideline, he told them to design a plant able to produce armor for two battleships per year, about 6,000 tons of armor per year. The board members needed to determine what machinery and specialized equipment the plant would need, how the plant should be laid out, how much land and how many buildings it would need, and finally what raw materials were required for armor production and from what companies they should be purchased. Of particular concern was whether the government should buy steel ingots from private industry or build a steel plant to make its own. The latter would considerably increase the cost of the armor plant, but presumably reduce their materials cost.

The board members spent a week planning their approach and then set out to examine steel plants. A tour of Carnegie's armor plant in Munhall, Pennsylvania, several Bethlehem plants, and the Illinois Steel Company convinced them that they needed more information. Making armor was a complicated process involving many reheatings and temperings, and the technology changed frequently. They needed an expert to advise them, and settled on famed steelmaker John Fritz, who was about to retire from Bethlehem Steel. Secretary of the Navy Long opposed his appointment to the board because of his close connections to the industry, and some board members suspected that Long wanted to appoint a political crony to the position. At its next meeting, Roosevelt confronted Howell about the board's choice. Howell answered evasively, trying to give Roosevelt the option of inserting his own choice. The rest of the board followed Howell's lead and were equally evasive. Frustrated, Roosevelt turned to Chambers, who was taking notes, and asked his opinion. After recovering from his shock, Chambers stammered out that John Fritz was the best person then available. Roosevelt snapped his teeth together with an audible click and then declared: "we will take John Fritz." He wished the committee a good morning and then left the room to confront Long. A few days later, he ordered them to hire Fritz.[20]

Accompanied by its new advisor, the board left to inspect a number of smaller plants in Maryland, Alabama, Tennessee, and North Carolina. They also took a second look at Carnegie's and Bethlehem's operations. At the plants, they interviewed a wide selection of people from the lowest paid steelworkers to upper management. When they finished, they had visited every major steel plant in the country and many of the smaller ones. Chambers, kept busy recording their findings and compiling data, also fended off local politicians who descended on the board at its various stops, hoping to have the factory built in their districts.

The board delivered its report in December. It concluded that a plant capable of producing 6,000 tons per year would cost $3.75 million to build and would have to include a separate steel factory, since the best armor required new steel before it had cooled. The government plant would face many of the same problems as privately owned facilities. Like them, it required special equipment and tools not needed for any other work and would need a steady stream of orders to keep costs down. The failure of Congress to appropriate funds for armor in any given year would force the plant to shut down with the consequent loss of trained workers. Many of these would be highly skilled and hard to replace. Even with a steady stream of orders, the board still expected it to cost more than $300 per ton to produce armor, plus the cost of the plant itself. Despite the cost, the press expected Long to ask for bids to build a plant within the next few months.[21]

As the Armor Factory Board did its work, tensions increased between the United States and Spain. Anti-Spanish rioting broke out in Havana and the United States sent the *Maine* to observe the situation. A daily barrage in the "Yellow Press" convinced Americans that Spanish soldiers had committed unspeakable atrocities. The cry for war grew louder every day, and the question soon became when, not if, the United States would go to war over the last jewel in Spain's colonial crown. As tensions increased, Congress reconsidered its intransigence and authorized the navy to pay up to $400 a ton for armor. Long quickly negotiated new armor contracts with both Carnegie and Bethlehem at that price, and Congress forgot the Armor Factory Board's report.[22]

## The Torpedo Station

Desperate to see action in the upcoming war, Chambers scrambled for a shipboard assignment along with his fellow officers. As usual, the best assignments went to those best connected. Chambers faced a double obstacle. Not only did he lack high political connections, but also the navy needed officers with his technical skills at home to prepare for war and sustain the fleet. Advised by his friend Lieutenant Commander Thomas C. McLean, who commanded the Torpedo Station, Chambers decided to parlay his torpedo expertise to get command of one of the new torpedo boats being rushed to completion. After overseeing their construction, he hoped to command one. With McLean's help, he convinced the Chief of the Bureau of Navigation, Rear Admiral Arent S. Crowninshield, to transfer him to the Torpedo Station at the end of June.[23]

On February 9, 1898, a New York newspaper published Spanish envoy Enrique Dupuy DeLome's private letter to his superiors in which he disparaged President McKinley and questioned his willingness to go to war. Six days later, the *Maine* exploded in Havana harbor. On February 25, according to plan, Roosevelt sent out orders repositioning the fleet and ordered it to prepare for war. When the navy's investigators concluded that the *Maine* had met with foul play, popular sentiment for war became overwhelming. McKinley ordered the navy to blockade Cuba on April 21, and four days later asked Congress to declare war. On the 30th, Commodore George Dewey's Asiatic Squadron entered Manila Bay and reduced the defending Spanish ships to smoking hulks. Still at the Torpedo Station, Chambers was well on his way to missing the war.

Despite its pioneering use of spar torpedoes in the Civil War, the U.S. Navy proved slow to embrace this weapon due to low budgets and technological conservatism. The pioneering work took place in Europe and inventors there solved the major technical problems. Englishman Robert Whitehead, who managed an engineering firm in Fiume, developed the first automobile torpedo in partnership with Austrian Johann Luppis in 1868. Their prototype had a range of only 200 yards and was not particularly accurate, but was a great advance over the spar torpedoes it quickly eclipsed. The Russians successfully used Whitehead torpedoes in the 1876 Russo-Turkish War, and every European power began building torpedo boats, setting off an arms race in small craft. By 1880, Whitehead was the world's premiere manufacturer of torpedoes, having sold 1,500 torpedoes to several different nations. His success sparked numerous competitors. The most successful of them was Louis Schwartzkopf, a German who may have stolen a set of Whitehead's plans. Soon, most of the torpedoes sold around the world were either Whiteheads or Schwartzkopfs.[24]

In the United States, Captain John A. Howell began experimenting with automobile torpedoes in 1870. His final design, patented in 1884, was ingenious. Powered by a heavy flywheel wound by a steam turbine before launch, it outperformed contemporary Whitehead and Schwartzkopf models and unlike them left no trail of air bubbles. Howell sold his rights to the Hotchkiss Company in 1884 and this firm improved his design. Unfortunately, the Howell torpedo faced a serious problem. The same flywheel that made the Howell accurate and almost wakeless constrained its speed and range. New Schwartzkopf and Whitehead torpedoes proved faster, and they continued to get faster every year. By the mid-1890s, Whitehead's newest designs outclassed all others in speed and range. In 1892, the U.S. Navy accepted the superiority of his design and contracted with the E. W. Bliss Company to manufacture Whitehead torpedoes under license. The navy shifted production to the Newport Torpedo Station a few years later.[25]

Despite trying a variety of complicated gadgets, Whitehead could not solve the problem of returning a torpedo to its proper course after it had deviated due to the action of wind or wave. In the mid-1880s, Chambers had tried to leapfrog the problem, quite literally, with his rocket torpedo. Minimizing the torpedo's time in the water minimized its deviation from course. Austrian Ludwig Obry solved this problem in 1895 by linking a gyroscope to a torpedo. This increased torpedo accuracy from hundreds to thousands of yards. Obry patented his invention the following year and then sold his rights to Whitehead. Whitehead linked the gyroscope to an air pressure valve connected to a torpedo's rudder. This system would theoretically reduce torpedo deviation to only half a degree over a 7,000-yard run, though the Whitehead torpedo's maximum range of just over 1,000 yards made this impossible to test. In 1897, the Newport Torpedo Station began installing Obry gyroscopes in all of its torpedoes.[26]

The United States was also behind other nations in developing torpedo boats. The *Alarm* and *Lightning,* commissioned in the mid-1870s and built to carry spar torpedoes, were hopelessly obsolete. The navy did not acquire a modern torpedo boat until 1887 when the Torpedo Station purchased the *Stiletto* from the Herreshoff Manufacturing Company for $25,000. Previously the Herreshoff family yacht, this was the first U.S. torpedo boat fitted with automobile torpedoes. The Herreshoff Company went on to build most of the navy's early torpedo boats. The first of these, and the navy's first steel torpedo boat, was the *Cushing,* commissioned in April 1890. By the end of that year, the world's seven largest navies together possessed more than 800 torpedo boats. The U.S. Navy had only two. On the eve of war with Spain, the navy had only a half dozen torpedo boats in commission with thirteen more under construction. In March, the navy's attaché in France, Lieutenant John C. Colwell, purchased a *Schischau* class torpedo boat and a dozen Schwartzkopf torpedoes and dispatched them to the United States. Congress authorized thirteen more torpedo boats after declaring war.[27] The United States entered the war seriously short of the shallow draft vessels needed to support ground operations in Cuba and the Philippines.

Chambers arrived at the Torpedo Station to find a frenzy of activity as its officers and a growing number of civilian employees rushed to ready ships and weapons for war. They built new wharves along with new buildings. New parts, materials, and machinery arrived almost every day, but the station found itself desperately short of the materials it needed, especially gun cotton and other explosives. Workers had just finished repairing its powder factory, which an explosion had leveled the previous July.

Chambers's first task was to prepare mines, which the navy expected to use to block Spanish harbors in Cuba. The needed explosive material did not arrive until just before war broke out, but Chambers drew up the plans for them and built forty mines in ten days. He then supervised the manufacture of the special projectiles for the *Vesuvius*'s dynamite guns. Like virtually everyone else at the station, he worked day and night preparing munitions, trying to make up for years of neglect in a few months. Chambers fitted out several torpedo boats, but the commands went to other officers. He was too important to let go.[28] Had the war lasted longer, the navy might have granted Chambers's wish, but Spain requested an armistice that July following the destruction of its Cuban squadron and defeats on land.

After the war, the station returned to research and development. For the first time in his career, Chambers was in a position to guide the development of new weapons. He threw himself into his work with a passion. While on board the *Minneapolis* he had produced conceptual sketches for several different torpedo boats, but at the station, he spent most of his time improving torpedoes. He devised a new launching mechanism for them, improved their accuracy, and redesigned the warhead, which too often failed to explode. His greatest achievement was a complete redesign of the Obry gyroscope and the addition of a new mechanism that allowed a torpedo to run a predetermined course within a 260-degree arc of fire. His mechanism, actuated by a heavy clock spring, worked successfully in 150 consecutive tests. Later models allowed torpedoes to correct their course after firing so that torpedoes fired from different tubes assumed the same, parallel course. His work impressed Admiral Charles O'Neil, the Chief of the Bureau of Ordnance, who placed Chambers in charge of all experimental work on torpedoes and mines at the end of 1898.[29]

The following March, the *Stiletto* ran aground while carrying powder and primers for the Naval Proving Ground. Severely damaged and only able to make 4 knots, she was in danger of sinking and an explosion seemed likely. McLean gave Chambers the tug *Leyden* and put him in charge of the delicate rescue operation. Chambers soon returned with the damaged ship in tow.[30] Shortly afterward, the navy promoted him to lieutenant commander and he commanded the torpedo boat *Dupont* in exercises. He spent the rest of his tour designing and tinkering with various inventions and helping overhaul and repair captured Spanish torpedoes and torpedo boats.

As the time neared for Chambers to return to sea, he sought assignment to a battleship, supporting his request with excellent recommendations from his recent commanders. All had rated his performance in all categories as "excellent." Wadleigh had been particularly effusive in his praise, saying that Chambers's knowledge made him "invaluable in a ship of modern construction." Like McLean, he would "specifically select him" for hazardous or independent duty. Chambers's well-rounded experience was marred only by his lack of combat experience. Congress had advanced many of his friends several positions in seniority due to their wartime service: his friend from the ONI, John Baptiste Bernadou, advanced ten numbers up the promotion list; French Ensor Chadwick and Raymond Rodgers both moved up five. In a system where seniority and connections meant everything, Chambers had fallen behind. While at the Torpedo Station, though, he became friends with Lieutenant Lloyd Chandler, the son of the Senator and former Secretary of the Navy. With their help, Chambers managed an assignment to the *Texas* as navigation officer. The navy's oldest battleship was still prestigious duty, and service on board a battleship, any battleship, was essential for his career.[31]

# 10 / Policing an Empire

Victory in the Spanish-American War forced the navy to restructure its squadrons to police the nation's new empire. The navy stationed additional ships in the Caribbean and expanded their patrol routes to include Puerto Rico. As president, Theodore Roosevelt brought a global vision of the nation's foreign interests and with it an increased emphasis on naval expansion. This created more opportunities for ambitious officers such as Chambers, who soon found himself in parts of this new empire.

## The *Texas*

Designed by British naval architect William John of the Barrow Company, the *Texas* had won the design contest Chambers had entered more than a decade before. Delayed by technical problems and the armor shortage, the *Texas* did not join the fleet until 1895. Already obsolete, a major refit the following year added new watertight doors and replaced many fittings. The Bureau of Steam Engineering rebuilt the engines, and the Bureau of Ordnance upgraded the hydraulics on the two 12-inch guns, moved the magazines away from the engines, and removed the torpedo tubes since they could not be fired without endangering the ship. Despite this work, the *Texas* paled in comparison to the navy's newer battleships and armored cruisers. The crowded, unheated living quarters were too close to the engines to cool and kept the crew sweltering in the summer. The *Texas,* which had a reputation as a "hoo doo" ship, also had the highest desertion rate of any battleship in the navy. Yard workers damaged the keel in a recent dry-docking, and many on board expected the navy to decommission the *Texas* soon.[1]

Commanded by Captain Charles D. Sigsbee, who had commanded the *Maine* at the time of her loss, the *Texas* was part of Rear Admiral Norman H. Farquhar's North Atlantic Squadron, which sailed on October 3, and conducted routine maneuvers for two days that concluded with target practice off Hampton Roads. Chambers noticed that Admiral Farquhar had problems coordinating the movements of the squadron. The navy had made great efforts to ensure that each of its battleships and armored cruisers was the most technologically advanced ship it could build at the time. This had produced a fleet with ships of markedly different size and design, many powered by different engines. The different turning radii and speeds of warships made complicated maneuvers difficult, especially in close formations and lines of battle. Chambers learned that no one had bothered to calculate the different turning radii of the ships and cobbled together a crude gadget that would give him the data to calculate the *Texas*'s turning radius and other maneuvering characteristics. It worked successfully in tests and Farquhar had Chambers distribute the device throughout the squadron. From there, it spread throughout the navy.

Chambers also worked on a number of inventions. He kept in touch with his friends at the Torpedo Station and suggested a number of torpedo and gyroscope improvements that performed well in tests. He designed a binnacle hood and lamp, which Lieutenant Commander Samuel W. B. Diehl at the Bureau of Equipment liked and recommended for adoption on the navy's new ships.[2]

Following the maneuvers, the squadron cruised along the Atlantic coast. Only the usual port visits to major cities for participation in local celebrations to garner publicity for the navy broke its routine of training and drill. Chief of the Bureau of Navigation Rear Admiral Crowninshield complained, without effect, that these disrupted training, but politicians insisted on these naval displays, especially during the campaign season. The frequent stops made desertion easy and the *Texas* steadily lost crewmembers.

Following maneuvers in December, the navy ordered Admiral Farquhar to take the *Texas, Dolphin, Machias,* and *New York* to Cuba. In Havana, the *Texas* took on board the remains of the *Maine*'s crew killed by the explosion the previous year, an assignment that Sigsbee asked for. The squadron delivered the bodies to Newport News for burial and returned to New York in time to celebrate the New Year. Three weeks later, Captain William C. Gibson replaced Sigsbee who departed to become the Chief Intelligence Officer of the Navy.

After taking on some new recruits, the squadron sailed on January 28 for a routine cruise through the Caribbean and Gulf of Mexico that was punctuated by the discovery that several recent recruits from New York's Bowery District had smuggled liquor aboard. When the *Texas* docked at Galveston, they pulled off their greatest coup, smuggling aboard several barrels of whiskey. On May 10, petty officers caught two of the smugglers guarding their trove. Both were court-martialed and confined, and the whiskey confiscated. Officers considered the matter closed until May 15, when they reached Bermuda and Captain Gibson ordered the crew to refinish the ship's woodwork with a fresh coat of shellac. A dozen members of the whiskey ring made off with several buckets of shellac. Mixing it with hot water and straining it through rags, they isolated the alcohol, which they mixed with sugar and lime and drank in large quantities. That night ten of these intoxicated sailors assaulted the ship's master at arms and tried to free their incarcerated shipmates. Chambers led several petty officers and sober sailors, subdued the drunken ten, and tossed them in the brig with their friends. This was the first group assault on authority on board any U.S. battleship, though as Captain Gibson acknowledged to the press, such incidents had been commonplace in the days of wooden ships. Despite substantial efforts to improve the quality of its enlisted force, the navy still had work to do.[3]

Commander Morris R. S. MacKenzie took command of the *Texas* on June 3, and announced that she would be decommissioned before the end of the year. All the officers scrambled for new postings. Chambers tried to arrange a transfer within the North Atlantic Squadron, and several of the squadron's captains requested him. Instead, the navy transferred him briefly to the armored cruiser *New York* and then to the gunboat *Annapolis,* outfitting for a voyage to the Philippines, as her executive officer.[4]

## To the Philippines

The 1,000-ton *Annapolis* was a relatively new ship, commissioned in 1897. Designed to replace the navy's old wooden gunboats, she better resembled them than any of the navy's new steel warships. The ship carried a full three-masted barkentine rig of 11,000 feet of sail in addition to a single screw engine capable of only 13 knots. Of shallow draft and armed with six 4-inch guns and a variety of smaller guns, including Gatling guns, the *Annapolis* proved useful supporting operations on shore.

Chambers reported on board in November along with the ship's chief engineer, Lieutenant John F. Luby, and her new commander, Lieutenant Commander Karl Rohrer. The ship was in the midst of an extensive refit. Construction crews were still on board, and Chambers supervised the last stages of their work. They sailed on Sunday, December 30, with the three ships that completed their squadron: the converted yacht *Frolic,* and the tugs *Wompatuck* and *Piscataqua,* purchased by the navy for the Spanish-American War. All four sailed short of their full complement.

The *Annapolis* shepherded her consorts along on a slow voyage made slower by constant mechanical problems and stops for repairs. The squadron arrived at Algiers on February 6 and stayed for two weeks while the *Piscataqua*'s crew repaired a leaky boiler. The *Frolic*'s engines failed on the way to Port Said, and the squadron paused at Malta for repairs. They passed through the Suez Canal in March and arrived at Colombo, Ceylon, on March 24. They arrived in Manila on April 24 after a voyage of almost four months. Rohrer kept the crew busy with drills throughout the voyage, particularly emphasizing small arms.[5]

## The Philippines

The navy enlarged its long-neglected Asiatic Squadron following the Spanish-American War and split it into two commands. One continued to patrol the Chinese coast, while the other, commanded by Admiral Frederick Rodgers, supported army and marine operations in the Philippines. Fighting between American and Filipino soldiers had broken out the night of February 4, 1899. Over the next year, American forces smashed the Filipino army in a series of conventional battles. The Filipinos then resorted to guerilla warfare at which they proved more adept. General Arthur MacArthur launched an aggressive campaign against them, hounding their forces in the field while scattering garrisons throughout the islands' cities and towns to break their network of sympathizers and informants. In March 1901, General Frederick Funston led a company of Macabebe scouts on a daring raid that captured Filipino leader

Emilio Aguinaldo. Resistance on many islands collapsed over the next few months. The *Annapolis* arrived in time to participate in the last stages of the war against the most committed of the Filipino insurgents.

The thousands of islands in the Philippines and numerous navigable rivers left the navy's warships stretched thin, even with the addition of thirteen former Spanish gunboats. The navy's gunboats played a vital role in the Philippine War. They patrolled Philippine waters to isolate the rebels on individual islands and prevented the flow of arms and supplies to them. They maintained communication with scattered army and marine garrisons and mobile columns and delivered their supplies, pay, and mail. They supported ground operations with their heavy weapons and Gatling guns, escorted troop transports, covered landings, and evacuated endangered garrisons. Without them, an American conquest of the Philippines would have proved impossible.[6]

The navy divided the gunboats among four cruising stations: (1) island of Luzon; (2) islands of Panay, Mindoro, Palawan, and Occidental Negros; (3) the Moro country of Sulu group and southern Mindanao; and (4) the Visayas group composed of Cebu, Samar, Leyte, Bohol, Oriental Negros, and northern Mindanao from the straits of Surigao to the Peninsula of Dapitan. This group included hundreds of smaller islands and was a favorite of many crews.[7]

The *Annapolis* first patrolled in the second of these sectors and served as the flagship of a varying number of old gunboats dubbed the "Mosquito Fleet." Her crew quickly fell into a routine, stopping and boarding passing ships to check their papers and cargo. They searched for arms smugglers while transporting messages and supplies to American garrisons. Rohrer worked to establish good relations with the villages in their area, and his crew traded rice captured from guerillas for all the fresh produce and meat they could eat. The patrols throughout May and June remained routine as American forces consolidated their gains before concentrating on the remaining centers of resistance. The closest the *Annapolis* came to combat was when a shark attacked members of the crew out for a swim. Despite being in a less than healthy part of the world, the *Annapolis* suffered little from contagious disease. Chambers, who had seen an epidemic sweep through his ship once, made certain the crew kept the *Annapolis* spotless.[8]

By July 1901, the United States' pacification program had proven largely successful. Only the province of Batangas and adjacent areas in southern

Luzon and the islands of the Visayan group, especially Cebu, Bohol, and Samar, continued armed resistance against American rule. On July 4, 1901, General MacArthur turned over control of the civil government of the islands to William Howard Taft and left Major General Adna Chaffee to crush remaining resistance.[9]

The *Annapolis* spent most of July anchored off Iloilo, Panay Island. Rohrer took her out for target practice on the 18th and 19th along with several smaller gunboats. Following an inspection by General Chaffee, the *Annapolis* led her squadron to Calahan, Mindoro, to support a renewed offensive. The gunboats escorted the army transports *Viscaya* and *Liscum* to Polak, Mindoro, and then helped ferry the soldiers upriver, towing the army's small boats with their steam launches. The mobility and firepower of the gunboats allowed the soldiers to outmaneuver and overwhelm the guerillas at every turn. Resistance collapsed in two weeks, and they returned to Cavite.[10]

After being scraped and repairing minor damage, the *Annapolis* sailed on September 14 to support army operations in Mindanao. While towing small boats, the inexperienced army crew of the transport *Buford,* a converted cattle carrier, managed to get the towing ropes wound around her propeller. The propeller jammed and the transport ran aground. Chambers organized a party of divers from the squadron and supervised their work underwater. It took a day to free the *Buford,* after which the gunboat towed her to Polloc for repairs. The *Annapolis* returned with supplies for another brief operation, and then sailed to Borneo to cut off arms sales to the Filipino guerillas. She spent a month sailing from port to port searching for arms smugglers, with limited success, though Chambers did rescue another grounded army transport. The *Annapolis* spent December trying to suppress the slave trade among the Moros in the Sulu Archipelago, southern Mindanao, and southern Palawan. They failed to capture any slavers, but captured some pirates.[11]

That same month, Brigadier General James Franklin Bell, commanding the newly created Third Separate Brigade, launched a major campaign against the Filipino fighters in southern Luzon. On December 7, he invoked General Order No. 100, calling for reprisals against civilians aiding the resistance. He closed all three of the region's ports and prohibited all trade by roads. Bell ordered most of the rural population into concentration camps to separate them from the guerillas. Numerous gunboats helped enforce Bell's blockade including the *Annapolis,* which spent January and February patrolling the area. Bell's campaign proved effective and General Miguel

Malvar surrendered to Bell on April 16, 1902, after the *Annapolis* had left for Mindanao.[12]

Chambers surveyed Polloc harbor and drew up new charts. He also supervised the expansion of the navy's machine shop there and oversaw the overhaul of several ships in dry dock.[13] Admiral Frederick Rodgers, in recognition of Chambers's role in several operations, transferred him to command the gunboat *Frolic* in March and placed the six smaller gunboats of the Samar Patrol Squadron under his command. After brief farewells, he caught a ride to his new command on board the transport *Zafiro*. Chambers would be the naval commander in the last major campaign against the Filipino resistance.

## The Samar Campaign

Vicente Lukban commanded the largest remaining Filipino guerilla group on Samar, the largest island of the Visaya group. Most of its 5,000 square miles were mountainous and covered by dense jungle, giving Lukban's soldiers excellent cover and numerous hiding places. Samar is separated from Leyte by a narrow, easily crossed strait through which supplies flowed at night to Lukban's army. Samar's principle crop was hemp, and its inhabitants needed to import food through its principle ports of Calbayog and Catbalogan, making the island vulnerable to blockade.

The U.S. Army's initial operations on Samar had gone well. Resistance seemed to collapse, and many garrisons became complacent over time. Filipino soldiers shattered this perception on September 27, 1901, when, helped by the local populace, they infiltrated the town of Balingiga and surprised its eighty-eight-man garrison of Company C, 9th Infantry. They killed fifty-nine of these soldiers and wounded twenty-three of the twenty-nine who escaped. Americans throughout the Philippines screamed for revenge.

General Chaffee sent Brigadier General Jacob H. Smith's 6th Separate Brigade to repacify the island along with a battalion of three hundred marines under Major Littleton W. T. Waller. It was Smith who issued the infamous order to turn the island into a "howling wilderness," to "kill and burn," taking no prisoners and killing "anyone capable of bearing arms." Smith's campaign met with initial success, but failed to cleanse the island of guerillas. Waller and his men ignored Smith's harsher orders, and Smith returned to a more benevolent vision of pacification in January and February.

Navy gunboats escorted army and marine units throughout the islands. The *Frolic* and *Villalobos* carried Major Edwin F. Glenn's soldiers on a series of raids in Samar and Leyte that destroyed several guerilla storehouses and yielded important intelligence. American soldiers captured Lukban in February, but the guerillas persevered under their new leader, General Claro Guivaras.[14]

Chambers arrived in March, and in April his gunboats supported General Frederick D. Grant's new campaign against the guerillas. Grant pressed deep into the island's interior by river in navy gunboats and small boats, while the navy tightened the blockade around the guerilla stronghold. In three weeks, Grant and Chambers harried the guerillas across the island and overran their main camp on the Gandara River. On April 26, General Guivaras and his staff boarded the *Frolic* as prisoners. With the prisoners apportioned among the various army transports and navy gunboats, the little fleet sailed to Catbalogan for an official surrender ceremony. On the 29th, Chambers hosted a reception on board the *Frolic* for the senior army and navy officers, while the enlisted ranks celebrated on shore. Chambers and Grant had crushed the last center of resistance, and reported that they had captured every gun on the island but two. On June 16 they turned over control of Samar to civilian authorities, ending "the longest and most brutal pacification in the Philippine War." Admirals Crowninshield and Frederick Rodgers both credited the navy's close blockade of Samar for the victory and singled out Chambers and his gunboats for praise.[15]

Chambers turned over command of the *Frolic* to Lieutenant Commander William R. A. Rooney in August, and returned to the United States with his career well in hand. Despite his lack of prestigious assignments, senior officers admired his work and abilities, and he had once again received excellent ratings from all his superiors. He possessed a wide range of experience having served on some of the largest and smallest ships of the navy, and commanded his own ship as well as a small squadron.

# 11 / Torpedoes, *Dreadnoughts,* and the General Board

Chambers reported to the Torpedo Station on October 11, 1902, but despite his long familiarity with torpedoes, his destiny lay elsewhere. His appreciation of technological change and technical expertise made him a valuable officer as the navy continued to modernize and expand. As the pre–Civil War generation of officers retired, more aggressive reformers rose to positions of influence. Rear Admiral Henry C. Taylor became Chief of the Bureau of Navigation at the end of 1902, and did his best to assign Chambers and other "young Turks" to prominent positions. He brought the best officers of the navy together on the General Board and its associated staff, ensuring that reformers would be in positions of influence—especially if, as Taylor hoped, the General Board evolved into a full-fledged naval general staff.

## Back to the Torpedo Station

The Torpedo Station had grown considerably during Chambers's absence. Its staff had modernized and expanded the production facilities to supply the navy's growing number of torpedo-armed warships. They had also added new docks for the growing number of torpedo boats and the navy's first submarines, then under construction. Shortly after Chambers arrived, they installed a new wireless mast and finished beautifying the grounds with dozens of new trees. Chambers's friend, Commander Frank F. Fletcher, commanded the station and assigned Chambers as his assistant with the title of Senior Assistant Inspector of Ordnance. Despite its expansion, the station's staff remained small. Lieutenants Archibald H. Davis and Leonard R. Sargent were the only other line officers stationed there. A surgeon, a paymaster, and six gunners completed the station's naval staff, though it also employed several dozen civilians.[1]

Chambers supervised the construction of torpedoes and mines at the station. His friend, Lieutenant Lloyd Chandler, had made several minor improvements to his torpedo guidance system, and Chambers picked up where Chandler left off, further refining and improving his guidance system.[2] Increasingly though, innovations in torpedoes came from the private sector.

Private industry in the United States became interested in torpedoes following the Spanish-American War as the navy ordered more and more torpedoes for the fleet. In 1900, Frank McDowell Leavitt began experimenting with torpedoes and tested several designs. The following year his company, E. W. Bliss, purchased a license to manufacture Whitehead torpedoes in the United States. Leavitt continued his own experiments, and in 1902 offered the navy an improved version of the Whitehead torpedo powered by a turbine engine. Chambers supervised the tests of this torpedo in September 1903, and the navy ordered three hundred of them on his recommendation. The following April, he supervised more tests of an improved Bliss-Leavitt design and recommended a number of improvements. In September, Chambers, Lieutenant Mark L. Bristol, and Lieutenant Commander Walter J. Sears judged a competition between the standard navy gyro (the modified Chambers design) and a Leavitt gyro. Both performed well, and the navy settled on a torpedo that remained true to Chambers's original design but incorporated features of the Leavitt gyro.[3]

Chambers hoped to reverse the trend toward larger and larger torpedo boats. Along with his other duties, he presented a series of lectures on torpedoes and torpedo boats to visiting officers, and he used these to push for smaller, faster, and cheaper craft. It was a point he would return to repeatedly over the next few years as many officers argued that bigger was necessarily better when it came to warships. Commander Bradley Fiske, for example, called for the construction of large, armored torpedo cruisers in 1905. Chambers's published response, apart from highlighting Fiske's ignorance of both torpedoes and torpedo boat tactics, emphasized that for the foreseeable future, guns would considerably outrange torpedoes. Torpedoes would be "a secondary weapon" rarely used by large warships. Torpedo boats needed to be fast and small to have any chance of closing with their targets to deliver their weapons. At the station, Chambers pushed the navy to replace torpedo boats' steam engines with oil and later gasoline engines and organized several tests that proved his points. At the last of these, all the judges recommended switching to oil or gasoline engines.[4]

An experimental submarine began trials just before Chambers had concluded his previous tour at the Torpedo Station. John Philip Holland began experimenting with submarines in the late 1870s, but the U.S. Navy did not place an order with Holland until 1895. That submarine, the *Plunger,* completed trials after the Spanish-American War. Few officers showed interest in the *Plunger,* but Admiral George Dewey did. After the war, he championed this new technology and argued that he would have been unable to hold Manila Bay had Spain possessed a single submarine.[5]

A navy trial board rejected the *Plunger* and recommended numerous changes. The most important was switching from a steam engine to a gasoline-powered internal combustion engine. The *Plunger's* two triple expansion steam engines had quickly brought temperatures within the cramped hull to unendurable levels. Holland designed a more modest submarine, and the navy ordered four of these in 1900 and three more the following year. Constant changes and frequent redesigns delayed their construction, but all neared completion when Chambers arrived at the Torpedo Station.[6]

Along with Bristol and Sears, Chambers supervised the trials of several of these new submarines in 1903. On June 1, 1904, he attended a much-publicized submarine sail-off competition, but only Holland showed up to compete. His rivals were far behind him in most areas of technology, although one of them, Simon Lake, impressed Chambers and other officers with his design. While Lake's submarine, the *Protector,* was slower than Holland's, it had greater endurance. It also surfaced and rose level rather than at an angle and was considerably quieter. Holland had emphasized speed while Lake had produced a stealthy, coast defense submarine suited to laying mines. Chambers pointed out that stealth was more important in submarines than speed, and encouraged the navy to purchase submarines from both builders. This would keep the technological options open and allow the navy to benefit from the innovations of both designers. The navy bureaucracy, though, settled on Holland, in part due to the political influence of his backers. Simon Lake went on to make a fortune building submarines and employing them in salvage operations. Chambers continued to suggest that the purchase of major equipment be from at least two suppliers to stimulate innovation.[7]

Most naval officers had little faith in submarines. Bureau chiefs George Melville and Charles O'Neil believed they had yet to prove themselves. Even as they joined the fleet, the General Board and Secretary of the Navy Paul Morton denigrated their effectiveness. At best, critics admitted that submarines might be useful for defending the coast, but coast defense had ceased to be the navy's focus. Guided by a Mahanian vision of high seas confrontation, they focused on the battleship as the primary instrument of sea power. More optimistic, Chambers believed that submarines were essential for scouting, laying mines, and other missions requiring stealth, and that their deployment forced the complete redesign of battleships to increase armor below waterline.[8]

## The All-Big-Gun Battleship

Chambers's most important work in these years involved neither torpedoes nor submarines. As had often been the case during his career, Chambers found time at the Torpedo Station to pursue projects of his own, and he returned to designing warships. He had followed battleship developments closely since the design contest, and like a growing number of naval officers around the world, believed that current designs had reached a dead end. Increasing armor made battleships impervious to all but the largest of guns, but they mounted relatively few of these. Chambers believed that since only 11-inch or larger guns could penetrate battleship armor at reasonable combat ranges, designers needed to eliminate the battleship's intermediate battery of 6- or 8-inch guns to make room for more heavy guns. Battleships should be armed only with heavy guns to engage major warships and lighter, rapid-fire weapons to defend against torpedo boats and small craft. Chambers produced a conceptual design for a battleship that mounted twelve large caliber guns in dual turrets along the centerline rather than the usual four guns in two dual turrets. In June 1903, he sent his design to the Naval War College, and its president, Captain French Ensor Chadwick, arranged for students to test it in that summer's war games.[9]

Inspired by Chambers's work, other American naval officers also considered all-big-gun designs, but most missed his point. Commander Homer G.

Poundstone, for example, advocated larger battleships, on the assumption that bigger was necessarily better. While considered the forerunners of the United States' later all-big-gun designs, Poundstone's designs were simply larger versions of existing battleships and they retained their intermediate batteries. In 1905, Bradley Fiske similarly advocated a "compromiseless battleship," but still expected combat at short ranges within the reach of intermediate batteries. Chambers, like some European thinkers, anticipated combat at much longer ranges. His design marked a revolution, while those of Poundstone, Fiske, and other American officers were simply evolutionary.[10]

Poundstone and Chambers were not the only naval officers considering this problem. As Chambers later wrote: the idea was "permeating the ether in various parts of the world at about the same time." In 1902, Chief of the Bureau of Construction and Repair Admiral Francis T. Bowles had his staff sketch a plan for a battleship with no intermediate battery, but his successor, Admiral Washington L. Capps, dropped the idea. The 1903 edition of *Jane's Fighting Ships* contained an article by Italian navy engineer Vittorio Cuniberti titled, "An Ideal Battleship for the British Fleet." Cuniberti argued that a 12-inch gun was the minimum needed to penetrate modern battleships' thick armor. Navies should eliminate the intermediate batteries to maximize the number of these large-caliber guns. His proposed all-big-gun battleship influenced navies around the world. The Japanese modified the battleships *Aki* and *Satsuma* then under construction, increasing the caliber of their intermediate batteries from 8 to 10 inches, giving these battleships four 12-inch and twelve 10-inch guns. While not quite what Cuniberti or Chambers had in mind, this was a step in the direction they indicated.[11]

Chambers's design performed well in the Naval War College's 1903 war games and Captain Chadwick and Commander Nathaniel R. Usher commended his work. The college's new president, Captain Charles S. Sperry, was particularly impressed, and he and Chadwick presented Chambers's proposal to the General Board the following January. Equally impressed, Admiral Dewey and the board asked the Construction Board on January 24, 1904, to design a battleship mounting twelve heavy guns of at least 10-inch caliber (at least four of them of 12-inch caliber) with no intermediate battery and only 3-inch guns for defense against torpedo attack.[12]

On May 14, 1904, Admiral Taylor, the Chief of the Bureau of Navigation, assigned Chambers to the General Board's small staff. Exactly what Taylor had in mind for his protégé from his days at the Naval War College is uncertain, for Taylor died two months later on July 26, depriving the navy of one its greatest visionaries and reformers. It is likely that Chambers's pioneering work on designing an all-big-gun battleship played a role in Taylor's decision, since it had also impressed the admiral. When Chambers left the Torpedo Station with what Chief of the Bureau of Ordnance Admiral O'Neil called "the best torpedo guidance systems in the world," the U.S. Navy had finally embraced the weapon and planned to install torpedoes on all future armored warships as well as torpedo boats and destroyers.[13]

## The General Board

Pushed by admirals Dewey and Taylor, Secretary of the Navy John D. Long had reluctantly established the General Board in March 1900. It was the navy's first centralized planning institution, and Taylor and other reformers hoped it would overshadow the powerful bureaus, allowing the creation of a rational, coherent naval policy. They hoped it would evolve into a naval general staff. Long, though, had limited its powers to advising the Secretary of the Navy on strategic matters and helping "ensure the efficient preparation of the fleet in case of war and for the naval defense of the coast." It was to prepare war plans, recommend the types and armament of ships, and generally "act as clearing-house for all questions of naval policy." Dewey presided over the General Board for more than a decade. Its other members included the Chief of the Bureau of Navigation, the Chief Intelligence Officer and his assistant, the president of the Naval War College and his assistant, and three other officers. The average tour for an officer on the General Board or its staff was just over two years, and these two years made a remarkable difference in that officer's career. While the average Naval Academy graduate from the years 1865 to 1892 had a 13 percent chance of becoming an admiral, 79 percent of those attached to the General Board between 1900 and 1914 achieved flag rank. It was the place to be for an upwardly mobile officer.[14]

The General Board's request for an all-big-gun battleship inflamed its already tense relations with the Construction Board. While many line officers perceived the General Board as the preeminent policy-making institution in the navy, day-to-day control over affairs, and especially ship design, remained in the hands of the bureaus. Secretary of the Navy Benjamin Franklin Tracy had created the Construction Board in 1889 to facilitate ship design and encourage bureau coordination. It was composed of the Chief of Naval Intelligence and the heads of those bureaus involved in ship construction: Construction and Repair, Equipment, Ordnance, and Steam Engineering. The Chief of the Bureau of Construction and Repair (the Chief Constructor of the Navy) presided over the board and controlled its agenda. In 1903, Secretary of the Navy William H. Moody tried to subordinate the Construction Board to the General Board and turn the General Board into a navy general staff like that recently created for the army, but the plan died in Congress thanks to the Construction Bureau's lobbying.[15]

Line officers had long resented the control of ship design by staff officers, and they increased their efforts to wrest control of the process from the staff bureaus and Construction Board. While they were frequently correct in arguing that staff officers lacked tactical knowledge and strategic vision, the engineers were equally correct in pointing out that most line officers lacked the technical and engineering knowledge on which any ship design needed to be based. Chambers's projected all-big-gun battleship became the focus of the worst power struggle to wrack the navy's bureaucracy in more than a decade.

The Bureau of Construction and Repair dragged its feet on the matter. Admiral Washington L. Capps bounced the request around his bureau and later claimed his staff had lost the plans on which they were working. It finally produced plans on October 1, 1904, that differed little from the previous *Connecticut* class battleship. When asked about the all-big-gun design, Capps claimed that "the development of such a design would involve the uninterrupted attention of several officers and twenty or more skilled draughtsmen and computers for at least six months." The bureau did not have the staff to work on the project. This, as everyone on the General Board knew, was simply an excuse for the Construction Board to do nothing. The General Board issued a scathing critique of the bureau design and again asked for a concept sketch that eliminated the intermediate battery and increased the main armament.[16]

Several line officers looked to the Russo-Japanese War (February 1904–August 1905) to buttress their ideas. Analysts around the world followed its battles closely, especially the destruction of the Russian fleet at Tsushima. For a generation of officers schooled on Mahan, the Battle of Tsushima was exactly what they expected. The war, Chief of the Bureau of Navigation Admiral George A. Converse wrote: "proved the pre-eminence of the battleship."[17] For many, it also pointed to the superiority of the all-big-gun design. Admiral Heihachiro Togo's heavy guns had decided the Battle of Tsushima and several lesser encounters. The General Board repeated its request for an all-big-gun battleship design following news of the battle.

Relations between line and staff officers worsened over the course of the year, especially between their respective leaders on the Construction Board and General Board. Following the failure of Moody's campaign, several younger line officers launched their own assault on the bureaus and publicized a series of problems with American warships that they blamed on the inefficiency and general ignorance of the Construction Board. Commander William S. Sims, a protégé of Theodore Roosevelt then serving as the Inspector of Target Practice, led the attack. Sims overstated his case, but there were plenty of real problems to embarrass the Construction Board, including a series of battleship turret explosions caused by poor design. Sims argued that the Construction Board should be subordinated to the General Board to ensure that its designs reflected tactics and strategy developed by General Board planning and Naval War College war gaming. Bradley Fiske seconded Sims's arguments, condemning American ship design, tactics, and strategy. The origination of the all-big-gun battleship by line officers gave Sims more ammunition in this struggle.[18]

Sims and Fiske were both out of their depth in challenging the Bureau of Construction on technical points. As historian William McBride has argued, American designs were "the product of a conservative, well-founded appreciation of a complex technical problem." The Bureau of Construction defended its designs to the press, but line officers maintained their attack. The General Board made two suggestions to fix the situation that would have stripped the bureaus of much of their power. One was to strip the Construction Board of its duties and transfer them to a "Board on Designs" composed of two civilian naval architects and five naval officers. This board would examine all new designs and make recommendations directly to the secretary of the Navy. The second was to bring in private shipbuilders whose designs would compete with navy designs. The dispute received considerable attention in the press and Sims later presented his case to the Senate.[19]

While American officers argued, Great Britain pushed ahead. Sir Percy Scott, who had improved target practice and introduced continuous-aim firing to the Royal Navy, advocated all-big-gun battleships and attracted other officers to the cause. Influenced by Cuniberti's article, the Russo-Japanese War, and Scott, Admiral John Fisher presented an all-big-gun design to the Admiralty in October 1904. After some modification, this design would become the *Dreadnought,* an 18,000-ton battleship mounting ten 12-inch guns in dual turrets and powered by turbine engines that made her 2 knots faster than any battleship afloat. Fisher rushed the *Dreadnought* to completion in secret, well ahead of Britain's complacent rivals.[20]

In the United States, Chambers urged compromise between the General Board and Construction Board and offered suggestions to harmonize line-staff relations. Experienced with design and engineering problems, he knew his fellow line officers had overstated their case. The question, as he saw it, was: "to what extent the studies of the General Board and Naval War College" would "influence the chief characteristics and military details of our ships in the future?" He agreed that line officers needed a voice in ship design, but a voice and control were different issues. Chambers argued that the bureaus should be open to criticism from the General Board, and that the Construction Board should seriously consider all suggestions to improve the navy's ships, even those originating outside the navy. Unlike Sims and the vocal line advocates, Chambers argued for harmony and cooperation. He envisioned a system in which the General Board and the Construction Board functioned as equal partners. Dialogue rather than hierarchy would produce the best ships. The Construction Board would submit designs to the General Board and Naval War College for criticism. As Chambers argued: "just criticism strengthens and cannot weaken good work." His arrangement would clarify but preserve the balance of power between the line and staff. Warships would result from consensus between them.[21]

Slowly, a compromise evolved for the 1905 battleships. The Construction Board first proposed that the two 1905 ships carry a mixed battery of big guns: four 10-inch and four 12-inch, like Japan's *Aki.* The General Board rejected this, repeated its demand for an all-big-gun design, and sent the Construction Board another copy of Chambers's proposal. On July 8, 1905, the Construction Board replied with a new set of plans, which were closer, but still not an all-big-gun design. The exchange of memos and debate continued as the two bodies slowly settled on a compromise design that mounted eight 12-inch guns in dual turrets on the centerline, what eventually became the standard model for post-*Dreadnought* battleships. At 16,000 tons, it was still smaller than the General Board wanted, but the Board had won its main point. Congress approved the final plans for two battleships of this design later that year. On December 5, Great Britain laid down the *Dreadnought*—a ship much closer to what Chambers and the General Board wanted.[22]

The United States did not lay down its first *Dreadnought* type battleship, the *Delaware,* until 1907, the same year that Germany began work on a similar warship, the *Nassau.* Both nations were desperate to close the gap between them and Great Britain created by the *Dreadnought.* The *Delaware,* completed in 1910, was the first American battleship to feature both the new, centerline all-big-gun layout and turbine engines, but even this ship did not satisfy Sims and his coagitators. Dewey, who had often supported them in the past, ordered them to keep quiet, but the future of the service lay with the agitators, not Dewey.[23]

## Chambers's Work for the General Board

While the U.S. Navy competed to match the Royal Navy in technology, few officers saw Britain as a likely enemy. Sparked by German actions at Samoa and Manila, Dewey, Taylor, others became convinced of German hostility and territorial ambitions in America's sphere of influence. Increasing German operations in the Caribbean and Pacific confirmed this perception. In 1904, Dewey wrote Secretary of the Navy Moody that the United States should base its naval building and war planning on a war with Germany.[24]

Germany was building a fleet that included thirty battleships and would be second only to Great Britain's in size. The General Board, determined not to fall behind, began planning an even larger fleet and asked its staff and members for suggestions. Chambers recommended a fleet of forty-six battleships, twenty-four armored cruisers, forty-eight scout cruisers, seventy-five torpedo destroyers, thirty colliers, and assorted gunboats and auxiliaries. The General Board's recommendation closely matched his suggestions: forty-eight battleships with an armored cruiser, two smaller cruisers, and three destroyers for each battleship. Colliers, gunboats, and other smaller vessels and auxiliaries brought the proposed fleet to 370 ships. This became the basis of the General Board's recommendations for the next decade as it sought to keep pace with European naval building.[25]

Apart from the all-big-gun battleship debate, Chambers spent his time on the General Board's staff working on a variety of small projects. He served on a board that codified rules for ship construction and classification and another on the physical training of sailors. He returned to the Torpedo Station several times to oversee tests and continue his work on torpedoes, and made minor improvements to the navy's torpedoes and two navigational aids. He produced a concept sketch for a scout cruiser that elicited favorable comments and designed a floating dock for the Philippines. Due to his prior experience, Dewey put him in charge of a board to compile data on the endurance and maneuvering characteristics of the ships of the fleet—a problem that had worsened as more battleships joined the fleet and admirals attempted larger maneuvers. The navy needed a system to classify its ships based on their maneuvering characteristics to determine their division into squadrons. The Naval War College had attempted to gather and compile this data the previous year without success. Both the Bureau of Navigation and the Bureau of Construction and Repair had given its officers the runaround, demonstrating that bureau coordination was not merely a line versus staff issue.[26]

Aided by lieutenant commanders Phillip Andrews, Benjamin Bryan, and William White, Chambers produced a standardized methodology and sequence of maneuvers to calculate the speed, coal usage, steaming endurance, and turning radius of a warship. They perfected the system following trials on board the cruiser *Chattanooga* several months later, and their system went into use throughout the fleet by the end of 1906.[27]

At the board's request, Chambers studied the staffing and promotion policies of several foreign navies. Compared to its rivals, the U.S. Navy had a serious personnel problem. Foreign navies assigned their ships more officers and sailors, and their officers were generally younger for their rank than their American counterparts. The average age for a U.S. Navy captain was 58 compared to 48 in the Royal Navy, 46 in the German Navy, and only 44 in the Japanese Navy.[28] Chambers, promoted to commander shortly after his 49th birthday in 1905, hoped that the U.S. Navy would do something to speed up the slow process of promotion and also begin promoting officers based on merit rather than seniority.

Over the course of the previous two decades, Chambers's skills brought him to the attention of several of his immediate superiors who relied on his technical expertise. His pioneering work with torpedoes earned him the respect of a small number of technically sophisticated line officers including

Montgomery Sicard and his successors at the Bureau of Ordnance. His detailed intelligence-gathering skills brought him to the attention of the small staff at the Office of Naval Intelligence and Secretary of the Navy William Chandler. His all-big-gun battleship proposal did more for his career than any of his previous successes and brought him to the attention of the General Board and some of the highest ranking and most respected officers in the navy, including Admiral Dewey. It brought him into the inner, policy-making circle of the navy and set him on course to influential positions in the future, but as a voice of moderation, he angered several of the extremists among reform-minded line officers.

# 12 / The Caribbean and the Bureau of Ordnance

While Chambers served on the General Board, President Theodore Roosevelt inaugurated a more aggressive foreign policy in the American hemisphere. The navy established a permanent Caribbean squadron in the autumn of 1902, and Secretary of the Navy Moody ordered it to: "exert our influence towards maintaining order in those regions where disorder would imperil the lives and property of our citizens."[1] Later that year, Roosevelt dispatched a squadron of battleships to deter a combined British, German, and Italian fleet that blockaded Venezuela to force the payment of debts owed to European banks. In 1903, Roosevelt rushed warships and marines to support Panama's revolt from Colombia. The next year, he announced his corollary to the Monroe Doctrine and informed the world that the United States would police the Caribbean, where Chambers would soon sail in his new command.

## The Dominican Republic

Like Venezuela, the Dominican Republic faced a debt crisis, and the 1899 assassination of long-ruling dictator Ulises Heureaux plunged the nation into chaos as factions fought for power. Leaders in both the Dominican Republic and the United States feared European nations would send warships to collect on their debts.

Horacio Vasquez and Ramon Cáceres had launched the revolution against Heureaux. After Cáceres assassinated the dictator, Vasquez seized power and called for elections, throwing his support to Juan Isidro Jimenez, a merchant who had spent his fortune fighting Heureaux. In November 1899, Jimenez became president with Vasquez as his vice president, but they quarreled and Vasquez and Cáceres ousted Jimenez. Vasquez became president with Cáceres as his principle advisor. Their coup split the country into two factions: the "Jimenistas" who supported ousted President Jimenez and the "Horacistas" who supported Vasquez. A stream of defections and the emergence of splinter factions added to the nation's instability.[2]

As the debt situation worsened, a New York syndicate of banks formed the San Domingo Improvement Company and bought up much of the nation's debt. Vasquez gave it control of several customs houses whose revenues would pay off the debt, but collecting import duties in the midst of civil war proved impossible. Vasquez terminated the arrangement and searched for a more reliable source of funds. In February 1903, he met secretly with lieutenants Walter S. Crosely and William S. Smith, dispatched by the General Board to investigate rumors of German intrigues on the island. Vasquez promised the United States the excellent anchorage at Samana Bay in exchange for American support. The officers returned with an enthusiastic report, but President Roosevelt refused to act.[3]

Frustrated at every turn and losing support, Vasquez called for new elections and retired from politics. Before these could take place, Heureaux's old generals seized control of the capital in several weeks of bloody fighting, only to be overthrown by Jimenistas that autumn. The Jimenista leader, Carlos Morales, cemented an alliance with the Horacistas. They arranged his election to the presidency in 1904 with Cáceres as his running mate.

The fierce fighting of 1903 had caused considerable damage to foreign holdings. Jimenista soldiers burned sugar cane fields, harassed foreigners, and interfered with passenger and cargo vessels landing in the north. Captain Richard Wainwright brought most of the South Atlantic Squadron to the capital. When Jimenista rebels fired on his squadron, he returned fire and landed marines who drove them off. Germany, Italy, and the Netherlands also sent warships to protect their citizens, and word leaked to U.S. chargé d'affaires William F. Powell that Germany had opened negotiations with several rebel factions. Both the State and Navy departments saw this as further evidence of German ambition that might lead to another naval showdown.[4]

President Morales convinced the United States to blockade arms shipments to his nation, and the U.S. Navy began patrolling the island's coast. In January 1904, Commander Andrew C. Dillingham of the *Detroit* landed marines at Puerto Plata and Sosua to protect foreigners. Efforts to broker a truce failed, and American forces continued to intervene, separating government and rebel forces, usually to the advantage of the government. Morales offered the United States leases on Samana Bay and Manzanillo in exchange for guaranteeing the nation's foreign debt, reducing import duties, and managing his government's finances. Roosevelt sent admirals George Dewey and Henry C. Taylor and Secretary of State Francis B. Loomis to investigate the situation, and they reported favorably on Morales's deal. Roosevelt, worried about domestic support for another foreign adventure, decided to proceed slowly. The Department of State sent Morales an economic advisor and suggested that he renew his aid request after the 1904 U S. presidential election.[5]

While Roosevelt campaigned for his second term, Morales's support ebbed away, and pressure from European bankers increased. Fierce domestic opposition again prevented the transfer of customs houses to the San Domingo Improvement Company. Fearing European intervention, Roosevelt pressured Morales to pay off the debts and sent Thomas Dawson to negotiate peace with the rebels. Dawson and Commander Dillingham secured a tentative agreement in June 1904. In exchange for peace, Morales agreed to pay the revolutionaries' debts and leave the northern province of Monte Cristi under the control of the local Jimenista governor, Desiderio Arias.[6]

On January 21, 1905, the United States and the Dominican Republic concluded a treaty. The United States agreed to take control of all the Republic's customs houses, which provided 90 percent of the government's revenue. The United States would collect all customs duties, turning 45 percent of the money over to the government and using the rest to pay off the nation's debt. The U.S. Senate, wary of another foreign adventure, adjourned without ratifying it, but the State Department put the treaty's provisions into force anyway. This so-called modus vivendi went into effect on April 1. The Jimenistas, who like the government relied on customs house revenue, resented the customs receivership. Governor Arias vowed to resist a U.S. takeover of the Monte Cristi customs house, but relented after meeting with Commander Dillingham and Admiral Charles D. Sigsbee, who briefly commanded the American squadron.[7]

## Chambers in the Dominican Republic

On July 2, 1905, Chambers took command of the gunboat *Nashville,* then fitting out in Boston. Larger than his last command, the *Nashville* carried a crew of 170 and fifteen marines and was armed with eight 4-inch guns and a variety of smaller weapons. A radio had just been installed, but would prove of little value. Chambers supervised the outfitting of the ship and ordered regular small arms practice to prepare his crew for combat ashore. The *Nashville* sailed August 30 and arrived at Santo Domingo two weeks later. Chambers himself conned the ship into port, something he did routinely. Once moored he ordered gun drills and left to meet Admiral Royal B. Bradford, the patrol squadron's new commander.[8]

Bradford's command included seven gunboats, a collier, and his flagship, the cruiser *Olympia.* He had just received orders from President Roosevelt to prevent the importation of any arms, and "to stop any revolution." Roosevelt intended to maintain the status quo in the Dominican Republic until the Senate approved the customs treaty. Neither revolutionaries in the Republic nor "red tape" at home would upset the smooth functioning of the modus vivendi. Bradford warned Chambers to expect trouble "in the Monte Cristi area," and assigned him to patrol the northern coast between Monte Cristi and Puerto Plata.[9]

The *Nashville* joined the other warship assigned to the north, the auxiliary cruiser *Yankee,* under Commander William H. Southerland, who was senior to Chambers. The two ships patrolled the coast to prevent arms smuggling, under strict orders to land troops only if absolutely necessary. While the situation was calm, Chambers reported that the Jimenistas were mobilizing and resented the appearance of another American warship. The navy reinforced the South Atlantic Squadron and Bradford sent the gunboat *Scorpion* to assist Southerland and Chambers.[10]

Despite American help, and partly because of it, President Morales continued to lose public support. A rumored American landing in November provoked riots in Santo Domingo, and Vice President Cáceres narrowly dissuaded a mob from killing Morales. In response, new Secretary of State Elihu Root withdrew several American warships and ordered the navy not to land troops except to protect American lives and property. This was the last straw for Morales. Fearing a coup from his former Horacista supporters, he fled the capital in December, joined the Jimenistas, and launched a new revolt against the government. Ramón Cáceres assumed the presidency.[11]

After Morales arrived in the north, the Jimenistas resumed offensive operations. Chambers and Southerland sailed for Puerto Plata to protect the town from the depredations of both government and rebel forces. Chambers arranged a meeting between government and rebel forces to ensure the safety of the town, and transported the government commander, General Demetrio Rodriguez, to meet with Arias and the Jimenistas. Arias demanded the restoration of President Morales and the equal division of all government offices between the two parties, which Rodriguez refused. The meeting broke up without agreement, and skirmishing began later that day as government soldiers moved into the city. The Jimenistas repulsed the first government attacks but more government forces were on their way. On December 30, Southerland in the *Yankee* intercepted and turned back the Dominican gunboat *Independencia* to prevent the bombardment of the city.[12]

Puerto Plata was far from the only hot spot, and Southerland left the next day to confer with Bradford. Before leaving, he transferred the *Yankee*'s marines to the *Nashville,* and ordered Chambers not to land troops unless the fighting entered the city. If it did, he was to use his limited forces to protect foreign property and the civilian population as best he could. If the *Independencia* returned, he was to prevent her from bombarding anywhere within 3 miles of the city.[13]

A fierce battle followed as government soldiers forced the Jimenistas from their positions around Puerto Plata. Several times the fighting entered the outskirts of the city, but the American gunboat anchored in the harbor dissuaded both sides from entering the city in force, and Chambers resisted calls from the "panic-stricken population" to land men. As night fell, the remaining Jimenista soldiers withdrew. Chambers organized a medical unit led by the *Nashville*'s surgeon and sent it ashore. The party established a hospital, which treated the wounded of both sides as well as civilians. A landing force from the *Nashville* helped restore order. Chambers's humanitarian efforts cemented his good relations with the Dominicans and Southerland later commended him for his tact, and "cool headedness and judgment during a time of panic." Privately, Southerland, who was due for promotion, promised Chambers that "when he became an admiral," he would request Chambers "as his chief of staff."[14]

A week later, the *Nashville* sailed for Monte Cristi where Desidario Arias and the defeated Jimenistas had regrouped. They controlled the countryside and the city's government, though the port's customs agents continued to collect duties for the government in Santo Domingo. Chambers arrived in time to prevent the Jimenistas from seizing the customs house, and warned them that he would not permit them to interfere with any American ships. He assured U.S. Consul I. T. Petit that he would land men to support customs officials if it became necessary.[15]

Government forces followed close behind the retreating Jimenistas. On January 12, apparently sensing defeat, Arias asked for shelter on board the *Nashville,* which Chambers granted. Jimenista forces remained in the field and the town's civilian population began to flee in expectation of battle. Chambers again negotiated with local military leaders to keep the fighting out of the city. During these, he convinced Arias that his cause was lost. In exchange for sanctuary in Puerto Rico, Arias and several members of his staff agreed to capitulate and end their rebellion.[16]

Arias also agreed to help Chambers negotiate a peaceful settlement with the remaining rebel leaders. Chambers arranged for a dozen of the rebel generals to meet with Arias on board the *Nashville.* They arrived on the 18th, ragged from their recent defeats and "resembling Moros in general appearance." Instead of arranging a truce, they plotted to renew the rebellion. Learning of their deception and infuriated by this betrayal, Chambers stormed into the conference room and delivered a stern lecture. He reviewed "the turbulent history of Santo Domingo . . . particularly with reference to the honest collection of customs by the United States," complimented the island for its beauty and vast resources, and concluded by condemning "the evil effects of constant revolution." If only, he told them, they would adopt "American methods of settling their disputes," the Dominican Republic would enjoy peace and progress. Chambers's rhetoric convinced few of the generals. The majority returned to the shore to renew the struggle. The rest joined Arias in exile in Puerto Rican, for which the *Nashville* sailed the next day. Chambers gave his crew a few days leave, and returned to Puerto Plata on the 24th.[17]

Despite the generals' vows to fight on, the revolution was all but over. Cáceres proved more able than his predecessors. Keeping the Jimenistas confused and scattered, he crushed their generals one at a time. The *Nashville* spent the rest of February on patrol off Monte Christi, and Chambers sent the Secretary of the Navy a thirteen-page report on the collapse of the revolution.

After a brief stop for crude repairs at Guantánamo, Cuba, the *Nashville* continued her patrols in March and April. The ebbing of hostilities gave Chambers the opportunity to conduct reconnaissance for the General Board. He completed a new survey of Puerto Plata, explored several of the nearby islands, and the General Board detailed charts of the area as well as reports of German operations and landholdings in the area. The General Board incorporated his work into Plan Black, the plan for a war with Germany, which assumed a German fleet would seize a base in the Caribbean.[18]

The navy ordered the *Nashville* home in June. Before sailing, Chambers and his senior officers dined with President Cáceres. The customs receivership ran under the modus vivendi for the next two years when the Senate ratified a new treaty. By the end of 1906, the Dominican Republic's debt had fallen from $30 million to just over $17 million. Cáceres won reelection in 1908, and the situation remained calm.

## Intervention in Cuba

In August, Chambers, working for the Bureau of Ordnance, took command of the monitor *Florida* at the Naval Academy. The bureau planned to use the *Florida* to test modern, heavy ordnance and give the midshipmen experience with new ordnance. Chambers had just settled into his new command when the navy ordered him to take command of the cruiser *Newark.* Another emergency in the Caribbean required experienced captains with cool heads.

In Cuba, negotiations between rival factions broke down and observers expected a major revolt any day. While Secretary of War William Howard Taft tried to arrange a settlement in Havana, President Roosevelt ordered the navy and marines to assemble a landing force and prepare to intervene. The battleships *Louisiana, New Jersey,* and *Virginia* along with the cruisers *Denver* and *Des Moines* sailed first, and arrived in Havana with the first troops the night of September 21. Meanwhile, marines gathered from every ship in the North Atlantic Fleet and assembled into the 1st Provisional Brigade under Colonel Littleton W. T. Waller of Samar fame. The cruisers *Tacoma, Newark,* and *Minneapolis* each embarked 250 marines and sailed as they completed loading on the 16th, 17th, and 18th respectively and arrived in Cuba a week later. The last two marine battalions sailed on October 1.[19]

The marines secured the area around Havana, and the *Newark* and other cruisers spent the next several weeks transporting small detachments of marines to secure secondary targets. The worst storm to hit Cuba in fifty years forced the *Newark* out to sea on October 14, wrecked several ships in Havana harbor, and drove others aground including several American warships. Chambers and the *Newark* helped clean up the harbor when they arrived, pulling ships free and helping with quick repairs. The marines had the situation well in hand by the end of the month, and the navy ordered the *Newark* and other warships home.[20]

## The Bureau of Ordnance

Chambers then resumed command of the *Florida* and instructed the midshipmen in modern ordnance. On December 24, he sailed the *Florida* to the Norfolk Navy Yard where workers added two 12-inch guns over her existing turret for the ordnance tests. They needed to test the effects of blasts from heavy guns firing over adjoining turrets to determine the practicality of the centerline gun layout that Chambers and other reformers had fought for. No one knew what effect the guns of the upper turret would have on the lower turret when they fired. Chambers directed a series of test firings between March 6 and 15 and proved the safety of the turret arrangement to observers from the Bureau of Ordnance and the skeptical Bureau of Construction and Repair. Yard crews restored the *Florida* for normal operations and in time for Chambers's small crew to take some midshipmen on their summer cruise.[21]

The success of the ordnance tests led to Chambers's assignment to the Bureau of Ordnance as the Assistant Chief of the Bureau on November 11, 1907. The Chief of the Bureau was his longtime friend, Newton E. Mason. Chambers spent his first months inspecting the bureau's numerous facilities at each of the navy yards. Benefiting from his experience at the New York yard, he improved coordination, standardized procedures, and eliminated some functional duplications. That summer, he supervised another series of ordnance tests in Chesapeake Bay, commanding a small squadron of obsolete ships including the *Arkansas, Florida, Montgomery,* and *Morris.* This time the aging *Florida* was the target. The *Arkansas* fired several 12-inch rounds into her turret face to assess the strength of new armor and to test several new shells. Afterward, Chambers detonated a torpedo under the *Florida* to test a new layout for internal compartmentalization. After the detonation, a crew reboarded her and rushed her into dry dock for examination. The tests showed what Chambers had long argued: it would take several torpedoes to sink a well-designed battleship. His team also tested the damage resistance of cage masts, fire control devices, and other exposed systems planned for the navy's new battleships. As a result of these tests and those of the previous year, Chambers concluded that battleship design had reached a point of finality and agreement. While improvements would continue, the single-caliber main battery would mark all future warships. On December 17, 1908, the navy promoted him to captain.[22]

Most of Chambers's work at the Ordnance Bureau proved bureaucratic and routine. The continued construction of new, larger battleships kept the bureau constantly upgrading its facilities to produce larger and larger guns as well as ammunition hoists and other associated systems. Chambers replaced torpedoes throughout the fleet with a new Bliss-Leavitt model, built up stockpiles of ammunition, and supervised the expansion of the bureau's facilities, including the Indian Head Ordnance Factory.[23]

During these years, the attention of virtually everyone in the navy focused on the voyage around the world of President Roosevelt's "Great White Fleet." Officers desperately sought assignments with it, but Chambers again proved too valuable at home. The fleet sailed from Hampton Roads on December 16, 1907, and returned to the United States on February 22, 1909, having sailed 46,000 miles without a serious breakdown. It displayed in grand fashion the emergence of the United States as a naval power. At the Bureau of Ordnance, Chambers helped coordinate the logistics of the voyage whose success garnered support for battleship construction.

Despite his position within one of the technical bureaus, albeit the one with strong line affiliations, Chambers continued to argue against the domination of ship design by either line or staff. He suggested that the navy create a Board of Critics that would solicit suggestions from all officers and oversee ship design. "Those charged with the expensive matters of design," he contended, "should be able to stand the test of intelligent criticism." When the Bureau of Construction and Repair launched a campaign to absorb several smaller bureaus, Chambers spoke forcefully against it. He agreed that fewer bureaus would improve coordination and planning, but thought the gain marginal. This was clearly an effort by a handful of "power mongering, empire building officers who want to enlarge their own bureaus and authority at the expense of others." The Bureau of Construction was trying to take sole control of shipbuilding and design by absorbing its rivals. Chambers again sought a compromise and suggested that the bureaus divide their work on a rational and equal basis and appoint a line officer to coordinate their efforts. Strong opposition from Chambers and the Bureau of Ordnance helped derail the Construction Bureau's grab for power.[24]

Chambers used his time in Washington to cement his contacts throughout the navy's bureaucracy. His performance ratings remained excellent, and in May he received command of the battleship *Louisiana.* A promotion to admiral normally followed a two-year command of a battleship. At fifty-three, Chambers enjoyed excellent health and easily passed his physical exam. His brown hair had just begun to thin and he needed glasses to read. He looked forward to long service at flag rank, preferably on the General Board.[25]

# 13 / The Beginnings of Naval Aviation

Chambers eagerly took command of the battleship *Louisiana* on June 1, 1909. Typical of the last battleships built before the *Dreadnought,* the *Louisiana* displaced 16,000 tons and carried four 12-inch, eight 8-inch, twelve 7-inch, and twenty 3-inch guns with a crew of forty-two officers and 785 sailors and marines. Chambers and his crew spent June fitting out in the New York Navy Yard and then sailed to join the North Atlantic Fleet under Rear Admiral Seaton Schroeder. Throughout August and September, the fleet engaged in extensive maneuvers and battle practice that ranged from the Virginia Capes to Cape Cod. The *Louisiana* earned a commendation from Secretary of the Navy George von Lengerke Meyer for its target practice score. The fleet attended the Hudson-Fulton Celebration in New York that October during which Chambers became seriously ill and spent two weeks hospitalized with acute bronchitis.[1]

Admiral Schroeder rated Chambers excellent or very good in all categories other than "manner of performing duties," for which he deemed him only "good." While clearly a favorable assessment, it marked the first time he had received anything other than excellent ratings, and it must have disappointed him. His drop in ratings, though, is not surprising considering his illness, brief time in command, and the difference in size between the *Louisiana* and his prior commands.[2] No doubt he would have improved had he remained with the fleet, but the navy had other plans for him.

Secretary of the Navy Meyer introduced sweeping administrative reforms in 1909. The most important of these was his appointment of four aides to advise him on naval matters, each overseeing a different section of the navy. The senior of them, the Aide for Operations, oversaw war planning and coordinated the activities of the General Board, Office of Naval Intelligence, and the Naval War College. The Aide for Personnel oversaw the Bureau of Navigation and the Navy's educational institutions other than the Naval War College. The Aide for Inspections directed ship trials, and inspected the fleet and navy yards. The Aide for Material replaced the Construction Board and oversaw the four technical bureaus: Construction and Repair, Ordnance, Engineering, and Equipment. This was the most important step in creating a naval general staff since the establishment of the General Board. Meyer appointed Admiral William Potter to Personnel, Admiral William H. Swift to Material, Admiral Richard Wainwright to Operations, and Admiral Aaron Ward to Inspections.[3]

This plan was the recommendation of a committee chaired by Admiral Swift, who requested Chambers as his assistant. He knew Chambers would be reluctant to leave his new command but wrote that his services were of the "greatest importance" to the navy. "For the first time since I can remember there is an opportunity for the military side of the naval service to make itself felt definitely and powerfully in settling the tactical features of design and construction in our ships." Swift knew no one "better equipped for analyzing and judging these matters" than Chambers. It would put Chambers in a position to oversee ship design, coordinate the fractious bureaus, and possibly end their squabbling.[4]

Chambers demurred, pointing out that he needed more time in command at the grade of captain and rather enjoyed commanding a battleship. Could the navy wait for him to finish his tour at sea? Swift insisted that he needed him urgently. "No officer" was as "well equipped for that duty as you are." On December 7, 1909, Chambers accepted his assignment as the Assistant to the Aide for Material. He assumed he would soon return to sea in a battleship, almost a requisite for promotion to admiral.[5]

Chambers worked with Swift laying the foundation for the new organization and coordinating the construction of new warships. Captain Frank F. Fletcher, Chambers's commanding officer from his second tour at the Torpedo Station, soon succeeded Swift, and the two worked well together. Fletcher respected Chambers's judgment and the two made great strides in rationalizing the navy's administration and encouraging cooperation among the bureaus. Nine months after accepting this position, Secretary Meyer asked him to look into aviation in addition to his other duties.

## The State of Naval Aviation

Samuel P. Langley had successfully flown a small, steam-powered model of his ill-named aerodrome in 1896, fourteen years before the Secretary of the Navy dropped aviation in Chambers's lap. Director of the Geological Survey Charles D. Walcott approached then Assistant Secretary of the Navy Theodore Roosevelt to fund a full-sized version. Roosevelt pressured Secretary of the Navy John D. Long into creating a four-member board under Commander Charles H. Davis of the naval observatory to investigate aviation. While the Davis Board issued a favorable report, and suggested using flying machines for reconnaissance and possibly combat, the navy's technical bureaus remained dubious. The navy never funded Langley's research. The army gave Langley $50,000, but Langley twice failed to launch his full-scale aerodrome, both times nearly killing its pilot. On December 17, 1903, nine days after Langley's second attempt, Orville and Wilbur Wright successfully flew their Flyer at Kitty Hawk. Due to the ridicule Langley's disasters received in the press, few believed the Wrights had flown, and it took them several years to interest the army in their invention. More than having merely flown, the Wright Flyer could be controlled and maneuvered by its pilot. The Langley Aerodrome lacked sufficient controls, making its pilots almost helpless passengers.[6]

From September 3 to 17, 1908, the Wrights demonstrated their airplane to a number of Army Signal Corps officers at Fort Myer, Virginia. Two naval officers, Lieutenant George C. Sweet and Naval Constructor William McEntee, observed the flights. Despite the crash on the 17th that injured Orville and killed his passenger, Army Lieutenant Thomas Selfridge (the world's first airplane fatality), many officers left this exhibition with an optimistic view of aviation. Both Sweet and McEntee reported enthusiastically on what they had seen and recommended the navy purchase planes immediately. The army purchased its first airplane in 1909, but it took more than one exhibition to interest the navy.[7]

In 1910, Glenn Curtiss, flamboyant inventor, motorcycle racer, and aviator, flew one of his own planes nearly 150 miles down the Hudson River from

Albany to New York City to win a $10,000 prize offered by the *New York World.* Afterward, he told reporters that airplanes would soon take off from ships and that warships were already vulnerable to air attack. "The battles of the future," he proclaimed, would "be fought in the air." In July, Curtiss flew over a battleship-sized target on Keuka Lake in New York and dropped 8-inch lengths of lead pipe on it, striking it repeatedly.[8] As more aviators captured headlines, and more mail describing the marvels of aviation poured into his office, Secretary Meyer demanded that his aides assign someone to deal with it. In September, Fletcher added aviation correspondence to Chambers's duties.

## The Officer in Charge of Naval Aviation

Chambers had witnessed the flights of several lighter-than-air craft at the 1904 St. Louis World's Fair and watched Wilbur Wright's flights for the Hudson-Fulton Celebration from the bridge of the *Louisiana.* Aware of the recent strides in aviation, he had discussed them in general with Lieutenant Sweet, but had not followed its development closely until Fletcher assigned him the aviation mail. What he read turned him into an aviation enthusiast, and he read everything he could on the subject. He arranged for his friend, Captain Templin Potts, the navy's Chief Intelligence Officer, to send him copies of everything he received on aviation, and he convinced the navy's librarian to purchase everything available on the science of flight and aviation. Chambers soon received regular reports from the ONI's attachés on European military aviation as well as the latest books and articles from Europe, some of which he translated himself. The more he studied aviation, the more fascinated he became with it.[9]

There were few aviation advocates within the navy, despite the fact that the development of the all-big-gun battleship underlined the need for aerial artillery spotting. The *Michigan* and other new battleships could fire shells out to 21,000 yards, but observers on board could not see targets beyond 16,000 yards and had trouble directing fire beyond 10,000 yards. Once again, Admiral George Dewey stepped in to support new technology, advocating aviation as he had submarines. He repeatedly used his influence on the General Board to support Chambers's proposals and urged Meyer to investigate aviation "without delay."[10] While Meyer generally ignored Dewey, Assistant Secretary of the Navy Beekman Winthrop, who approved virtually all of the important decisions concerning naval aviation while Meyer was out of the office, did not.

Chambers's anomalous position in charge of aviation with neither staff nor title coupled with the lack of authority of his two key supporters did not bode well for naval aviation's future. Over the next two years, the General Board became more vocal in support of aviation, but its ability to influence policy waned as the Secretary of the Navy ignored it and his aides made decisions on their own.[11]

In October 1910, Dewey convinced the General Board to recommend deploying aircraft on board the new scout cruiser *Chester.* This sensible proposal gave the bureaus a new plum over which to fight. Chief of the Bureau of Construction and Repair Richard M. Watt sent a memo to Meyer asking him to place his bureau in charge of aviation. His counterpart at the Bureau of Engineering, Hutch I. Cone, sent a similar note. Fortunately, Winthrop was in the office when these missives arrived, and he ordered both bureaus to appoint officers to coordinate with Chambers. Naval Constructor William McEntee and Lieutenant Nathaniel Wright received the assignments.[12] This demarcation of responsibility, while not codified until two years later, remained in force throughout the early years of naval aviation. Chambers remained tenuously in charge of personnel, policy-making, and the general direction of the program. The Bureau of Construction and Repair had charge of the planes themselves, while the Engineering Bureau looked after their engines. Each would soon have a separate aviation budget, and both outranked Chambers thanks to the temporary rank of admiral that bureau chiefs received. They avoided him routinely, preferring to deal directly with Secretary Meyer.[13]

Later that month, Chambers took McEntee and Wright to observe the International Air Meet at Belmont Park, New York, the first international meet held in the United States. Aviators from around the world attended, as did the leading American airplane manufacturers: the Wright Brothers and Glenn Curtiss. Chambers examined airplanes and questioned the men who designed, built, and flew them. He spoke at length with the Wrights at Belmont and with Curtiss and his star pilot, Eugene Ely, at a meet in Halethorpe, Maryland. Chambers expressed special interest in their opinions of a recent report that French aviator Henri Fabre had taken off from the water using a pontoon-equipped plane. The implications for the navy were obvious. While the Wrights dismissed the idea, Curtiss embraced it. Chambers and Curtiss became close friends and developed an excellent working relationship.[14]

While Chambers left these meets convinced of the importance of aviation, the instability of the frail craft and the lack of scientific understanding of flight by both pilots and inventors troubled him. Even Curtiss and the Wrights, far ahead of their competitors, often operated more by trial and error than from a scientific understanding of aeronautics, which aviators and inventors were only beginning to discover. Chambers had participated in the introduction of scientific principles to ship design three decades before and he intended to introduce them into aviation as well. He requested the establishment of a national aeronautic lab to conduct research in all aspects of flight. This centralized research facility would support the efforts of both civilian and military inventors and aviators in advancing aviation and improving its safety. Safety and scientific research became Chambers's guiding principles, and he remained committed to them regardless of bureaucratic opposition to centralized research or the entreaties of his pilots to set records and participate in aviation competitions.[15]

Chambers also recommended that the navy establish a separate office of aeronautics to direct the aviation program, construct an airfield, begin training pilots, purchase planes for the *Chester*, and fund research to adapt aviation to the needs of the navy. Unlike many of his fellow aviation enthusiasts, he insisted that new technologies be adapted to serve current needs and doctrine. Despite simulated bombing runs at Belmont using sacks of flour, he believed it would be some years before planes could attack targets with any degree of success. For the time being, they were useful only for scouting and artillery spotting.[16]

To launch naval aviation, Chambers needed to demonstrate that planes could work with ships, landing on and taking off from them without difficulty. Curtiss was eager to help and Ely was willing to make the attempt. They needed a ship and funds to construct the landing and take-off platform. Chambers proposed the idea to Admiral Wainwright, the Aide for Operations, but he turned him down. Wainwright also opposed the General Board's request for a plane for the *Chester*, suggesting that kite balloons were preferable for spotting "considering the present state of aeroplanes." Captain Fletcher sympathized with Chambers's request, but could do nothing without authorization or funds. Determined to make the attempt, Curtiss and Ely cornered Secretary of the Navy Meyer in his office and presented their case. Meyer refused and dismissed the airplane as a "carnival toy."[17]

Undaunted, Chambers, Curtiss, and Ely looked elsewhere for a ship and funds. Millionaire publisher and aviation enthusiast John Barry Ryan had just offered a $1,000 reward for the first shipboard launch. Curtiss convinced him to use the money to fund the attempt instead. Ryan helped arrange for a flight off the *Pennsylvania,* a liner of the Hamburg-America Steamship Company. Everything was ready to go when an accident damaged Ely's plane, preventing takeoff since the liner had to sail before repairs could be made.

The liner's German registry gave Chambers the leverage he needed with the navy. He waited for Meyer to leave the office and then approached Winthrop, mentioning Germany's apparent interest in naval aviation. Winthrop quickly assigned the cruiser *Birmingham* to Chambers. On November 14, 1910, Eugene Ely flew his Curtiss plane off an 82-foot platform hastily constructed over the *Birmingham*'s deck. Ely's plane dropped toward the water, slowly gathering speed. His wheels touched the water and then his propeller, and repeated impacts with the water shattered its tips. Ely barely managed to gain altitude and landed five minutes later two and half miles away on Willoughby Spit, 10 miles short of his planned destination and convinced he had let Curtiss and Chambers down. Chambers rushed to Ely and proclaimed him a hero. He wrote Meyer that day, announcing their success and asked him to purchase planes for the navy.[18]

The next day, news of the flight made the front pages of papers around the country, but Meyer remained unconvinced. In his congratulatory letter to Curtiss he spelled out his requirements: "When you show me that it is feasible for an aeroplane to alight on the water alongside a battleship and be hoisted aboard without any false deck to receive it, I shall believe the airship of practical benefit to the Navy."[19] Essentially, he challenged Curtiss to build a seaplane, a project on which Chambers already had him working. Curtiss' aircraft was almost ready, but first Chambers arranged another demonstration for Meyer.

Two months later Chambers, Curtiss, and Ely were ready for the second half of their test—landing a plane on board a ship. Chambers arranged to use the armored cruiser *Pennsylvania,* commanded by Naval Academy friend Captain Charles F. Pond. Rear Admiral Edward B. Barry, the commander of the Pacific Fleet supported their preparations. Chambers ordered a 119-foot wooden platform built over the aft deck for Ely to land on. Needing some way to bring the plane to a halt, they settled on a series of twenty-two ropes stretched across the deck, each attached to two 50-pound sandbags. They attached three metal hooks to the bottom of Ely's plane to catch the ropes as he landed. On January 18, 1911, Ely took off from shore and landed on the *Pennsylvania* anchored in San Francisco harbor. Eight of the ropes caught, slowing the plane to a stop before it crashed into the canvas screen at the end of the platform. An hour later, Ely took off from the ship and returned to shore. Pond hailed the landing as a major triumph and placed himself "on record as positively assured of the importance of the aeroplane in future naval warfare." As Ely wrote to Chambers, "the value of the aeroplane for the Navy is unquestioned."[20]

Following the success of the *Birmingham* flights, Curtiss offered to train army and navy pilots at no cost. The Wrights made a similar offer, contingent on the purchase of planes, but few naval officers expressed an interest in becoming pilots. Those who did request aviation duty often found their orders delayed or even lost. Chambers selected Lieutenant Theodore G. Ellyson for pilot training, the first of the handful of naval officers who had applied for aviation duty. He reported to Curtiss's winter camp in San Diego in December 1910, where he learned to fly and repair planes. In March, Chambers sent his second aviator, Lieutenant John Rodgers, who had repeatedly ascended in kite balloons, to train with the Wrights. It took a major effort on the part of both Chambers and Ellyson to get more officers transferred to aviation. In July, after considerable delay, they managed to send Lieutenant John H. Towers to Curtiss, and Ensign Victor Herbster to the Wrights. Chambers repeatedly flew in planes as a passenger and handled the controls in a few flights with Curtiss, but he never found the time to qualify as an aviator. He later reasoned that his time was better spent as an administrator, but he clearly regretted failing to master flying.[21]

Chambers followed Ely's latest success by arranging for a naval escort for another Curtiss aviator, J. A. W. McCurdy, who attempted to fly from Key West to Cuba to claim the prize offered by the *Havana Post* for the first successful crossing. On January 30, 1911, McCurdy made it to within 12 miles of the Cuban coast when his oil pump failed and he had to land in the water. Commander Yates Stirling's destroyer squadron recovered pilot and plane, and Stirling joined Chambers's growing network of aviation supporters. Four days earlier, Curtiss successfully flew his seaplane near his San Diego base. Ellyson had helped him complete it and together they refined its design. On February 17, Curtiss flew it again and landed in the water near the *Pennsylvania.* Pond had it hoisted aboard, refueled, and returned to the water, and Curtiss took off again. The aviators had satisfied Meyer's terms.[22]

## The First Appropriation of Funds

Chambers's carefully guided progress in aviation slowly paid off, though the navy still regarded aviation as a "side show." He worked hard to publicize aviation and returned to writing. He published a summary of aviation progress in the Naval Institute's *Proceedings,* and worked closely with the aviation press, writing for a number of aviation magazines. With his growing number of supporters, he convinced Meyer to ask Congress for $25,000 to buy planes, a paltry sum considering the Royal Navy's $175,000 aviation budget. It was roughly equivalent to the cash prizes offered to pilots by a variety of newspapers and organizations for achieving important feats. Congress passed the appropriation on March 4, 1911, but Chambers could not spend any of the money until the beginning of the fiscal year in July.[23]

Meyer ignored most of Chambers's other recommendations, including the creation of an office of aeronautics, which would have given him a staff to help his work and the authority to oversee the bickering bureaus involved in aviation. The chiefs of the Construction and Engineering Bureaus both wanted to control aviation, opposed his efforts at coordination, and delayed work on aviation. Neither would spend any of his bureau's funds to buy planes. Nor could Chambers convince anyone to equip new ships with planes, and thus bypass the need for special aviation appropriations from Congress. In frustration, Chambers wrote F. H. Russell, the Wright Company's manager, that straightening out the aviation bureaucracy was his highest priority.[24]

Chambers finally convinced Meyer to clarify his duties and authority. The secretary ordered him to "keep informed" of the progress of aeronautics "with a view to advising the Department concerning the adaptability of such material for naval warfare, especially for the purposes of naval scouting." He was to guide the training of the navy's aviators and to consult with the navy's librarian in gathering aviation literature. He was also to consult with the bureaus that had "cognizance of the various branches" of his work, but the enforcement of his recommendations would "rest entirely with the bureaus having cognizance of the details."[25] It was an administrative arrangement guaranteed to magnify all the problems of bureau coordination that Meyer had sought to limit with the creation of the Aide system. Chambers continued to operate without a title, signing his correspondence as "the Officer in Charge of Aviation."

Chambers worked alone on aviation all these months, without even clerical support. On March 30, Dewey transferred him to the General Board where he could get staff support and have a stronger voice in influencing policy. Unfortunately, Congress placed the $25,000 aviation appropriation in the Bureau of Navigation's budget. Since only that bureau could spend the money, Chambers arranged for Fletcher to transfer him to the Bureau of Navigation. He left for his new home in the Bureau of Navigation on April 14; he had sat on the General Board for only two weeks.[26]

Chambers proved an oddity in the Bureau of Navigation. Next to its chief, Admiral Reginald F. Nicholson, he was its most senior officer, but almost everyone at the bureau ignored him. Despite numerous requests, he could not obtain the service of a single aide. Nicholson actually suggested that Chambers "work at home," but Chambers managed to secure a desk and filing cabinets in the corner of Room 67 in the dank basement of the War, State, Navy building. He described it as "a good place to catch a cold."[27]

Chambers often corresponded with civilian inventors during his career, but he never received the volume of mail he did as head of naval aviation. By February, he received a letter a day. Once newspapers announced his $25,000 appropriation, the floodgates opened and mail poured in from inventors around the country. Most of them had "not taken the trouble to inform themselves" on the progress of aviation. Many had probably never even seen a plane. Nonetheless, Chambers answered all of them, and during his first year, he was invariably polite, making an effort "to handle [them] with tact and with a humane effort to point out the errors." He encouraged those he thought had promise and politely discouraged the rest. The cranks were easy to spot because they were "loath to impart their secrets," but always promised to revolutionize aviation if only Chambers would send them money. He always refused. He would only purchase complete, well-tested products and challenged companies and inventors to back up their claims with proof. Blueprints were not enough. Chambers often gave detailed critiques of the better ideas. He suggested potential buyers, cited technical literature they should read, and even put people working on similar ideas in touch with one another so they could pool their efforts. In his replies, Chambers always emphasized his limited funds and frequently included a plug for whatever project he was then lobbying Congress, most often a national aeronautic lab to which he hoped to direct would-be inventors in the future. Over time, the strain of his workload began to show, and by 1913, he was far from tactful, telling several inventors that their ideas were simply "absurd." He tried to hand off the job to several of the aeronautical societies, but no one wanted such a thankless task.[28]

## The First Planes

Aviation work practically ceased in May when the navy assigned Chambers to sit on a naval retiring board.[29] These boards sorted through the lists of senior officers due for promotion and determined which of them would be "plucked" from the service (forcibly retired) to make room for the promotion of others. Progressive officers had long demanded a system of promotion by merit, but without effect. In theory, the plucking boards weeded out the inept and incompetent, but they had accomplished this in the previous decade. Increasingly, plucked officers had good records and promising careers.

On his return, Chambers decided to use his small budget to buy three planes: two from Curtiss and one from the Wrights. He hoped to establish a good relationship with both manufacturers and incorporate the best ideas of each into the navy's future planes. Over time, though, Chambers developed a closer and friendlier relationship with the outgoing and daring Curtiss than he did with the withdrawn and often taciturn Orville Wright. Curtiss also proved much more interested in developing seaplanes than the Wrights, who despite the repeated urgings of aviation pioneer Grover Loening, remained uninterested.[30]

Chambers specified a minimum speed of 45 miles per hour for the planes and room for a passenger. Later, he would insist on dual controls to make training easier. Each manufacturer agreed to train a pilot and mechanic for each plane purchased. The first of the Curtiss planes was to be a normal wheeled plane, the other was the famous "Triad" that Chambers had discussed with Curtiss—a seaplane with retractable landing gear so it could operate from land as well as water. Chambers requested a seaplane from the Wrights, but they ignored him and built it with the usual wheels. Curtiss delivered the wheeled plane, the A-1, on July 1, and the A-2 Triad on the 13th. The Wrights finished their plane, the B-1, a few days later, and Orville took Chambers for a ride in it.[31]

McEntee experimented with designs for seaplane pontoons at the Washington Navy Yard model tank for several months, and together with Naval Constructor Holden C. Richardson, designed pontoons for the Wright plane. The Bureau of Construction and Repair had transferred Richardson to aviation work following repeated entreaties by Chambers for technical assistance. Richardson learned to fly later that year and became Chambers's most important technical advisor.[32]

With a handful of pilots and planes in hand, Chambers's priority became establishing a base at which they could train, fly, and determine the potential of airplanes for the navy. He learned from friends that the navy had 60 acres of unused land across the Severn River from the Naval Academy. Chambers secured it for aviation and set up camp that summer. It was near College Park, Maryland, where the army aviators trained, and the two groups of pilots shared information and socialized together frequently. It was also near the Engineering Bureau's Experiment Station, which Chambers hoped would cooperate in research on aircraft engines. Unfortunately, the lack of "money and interest on the part of the Bureau of Engineering conspired to render this adjunct far from satisfactory."[33]

Always short of supplies, spare parts, fuel, and other essential materials, Chambers and his pilots often dug into their own pockets to buy what they needed. The navy proved slow to reimburse them for their travel and expenses. Along with their mechanics, the pilots often broke into the experiment station at night to borrow the parts and tools they needed. Chambers, miffed at the Bureau of Engineering, ignored their pilfering. He may even have suggested they write to companies requesting free samples of their products, which became an important source for extra gasoline and oil.[34]

## Aviation Safety

The desire of many of his pilots to set records and compete in civilian aviation meets presented a constant problem for Chambers. He worried about their safety and held paternal feelings toward many of them, since they were only a few years older than his son who had just entered the Naval Academy. Shortly after Ellyson completed his training, Chambers warned him against stunt flying and reminded him that he had chosen him because he was a "well balanced man who would be able to assist in building up a system of aviation training."[35] Eugene Ely's death while stunt flying in September reinforced Chambers's concerns over safety. He had repeatedly warned Ely to stop engaging in dangerous stunts. Over the next few years he repeatedly condemned the "spirit of sensationalism" that was "the cause of much imprudence, carelessness and consequent death to many of our best American aviators." His pilots were "fine officers," but "so zealous and eager to show what they can do that they are prone to make light of the deficiencies of their craft and to take risks that should be avoided." Ellyson and John Rodgers in particular worried him. He complained to Curtiss that Ellyson had "a bit of competition fever" and wanted to break records. Rodgers was even more zealous "to do something more startling than his rivals," and Chambers worried that it would get him killed. By October, he worried that Ellyson looked ill and was overworking.[36] Chambers, too, worked long hours, but it took some time for the toll to catch up with him.

By 1912, four army aviators had died in mishaps, but not a single navy aviator had perished, though Ellyson suffered severe injuries in a crash on March 14, 1912. It took more than a month for him to return to flying, and his neck injury troubled him for the rest of his life. While Ellyson recovered, Towers took charge of the camp at Annapolis and supervised most of the flight instruction. He blossomed as an administrator, slowly displacing Ellyson as Chambers's right-hand man. Ellyson, plagued by pain, remained nervous and irritable.[37]

In the wake of Ellyson's crash, Chambers launched a major safety campaign, addressing the issue in a series of speeches before aeronautical clubs, publishing several articles, and emphasizing it in interviews with the press. He banned his flyers from exhibition flying, which had cost the lives of numerous pilots and some spectators. The army did the same two years later. Privately, he pressed both Curtiss and the Wrights to make their planes safer. He wrote Russell that "the burning issue in aviation" was reducing the danger of flying. "There are devices which can produce it and they doubtless can be improved. Why is it that manufacturers don't want to touch the question without being forced?" He warned Orville Wright that Congress was "hysterical over the number of accidents" and reluctant to increase aviation funding. All of his reports to Meyer and the General Board emphasized the need for improving safety. Aviation's death toll was too high, and unless these issues were addressed, aviation would "not merit a role of the first order."[38]

The lack of a standardized control system for planes exacerbated Chambers's concerns. The Wrights and Curtiss employed completely different control systems, forcing pilots to specialize in one or the other. Curtiss used a shoulder yoke to control the ailerons and a wheel that controlled the elevators by pushing and pulling and the rudder by turning. In their new "C" model, the Wrights used two control levers, one on each side of the twin seats, forcing specialization as either right-side or left-side pilots. The center lever included a bent-wrist control that turned the rudder. Chambers insisted that his pilots learn both Wright and Curtiss controls so that they could settle on a standard, but they did so reluctantly. He pressed Curtiss and the Wrights to work on the problem, but their continuing court battles made any standardization impossible. Besides, there was little agreement as to what the best system would be. Each pilot remained partial to the system he first learned. Ellyson strongly favored the Curtiss system, though Towers kept an open mind. He observed the European, Deperdussin control system at an aviation show in 1912 and recommended it, but it took another year for Chambers to agree that foot pedals were the best system. He continued to hope that American manufacturers would settle on a standard of their own.[39]

Chambers hoped that his pilots would form a bond like "Nelson's band of brothers," but considerable tension existed among them. He discussed the situation with Curtiss, worrying that they were becoming jealous of one another over their accomplishments and competing for his attention.[40] It was no secret to many of the pilots that Chambers was grooming Ellyson to succeed him, and this offended John Rodgers in particular. Chambers's growing reliance on Towers offended other pilots. The patent dispute and court battles between Curtiss and the Wrights worsened matters as the Wrights refused to have anything to do with Curtiss-trained pilots, encouraging the division of pilots and the growing number of civilian aeronautic clubs into rival camps until 1917 when the government helped broker a settlement. While Chambers would have preferred to develop good relations with both companies, the difficulties he encountered working with the Wrights and in getting them to accept new ideas, build seaplanes, and modify their designs to suit the navy's needs contrasted sharply with his growing friendship with Curtiss and Curtiss's eagerness to work with the navy to develop seaplanes. So, while the army strengthened its relationship with the Wrights and continued to purchase mostly Wright airplanes, the navy embraced Curtiss.[41]

## Progress by the End of 1911

Toward the end of 1911, the navy planned to use the obsolete battleship *Texas* (renamed the *San Marcos*) as a target for ordnance experiments. The Bureau of Construction and Repair suggested that Chambers send one of his planes to participate in the tests and drop bombs on the ship—a seriously premature suggestion, since none of the navy's three planes had been designed to drop bombs, nor did properly fused aerial ordnance exist.[42]

What motivated the suggestion mystified Chambers, but participation in the tests would only make the navy's infant aviation program look bad. Besides, he reasoned, what would dropping bombs on a defenseless target prove? Real ships would fire in their defense and maneuver fast enough to make them difficult targets for his slow planes. At best, Chambers figured he could get one of his planes in the air with 200 pounds of ordnance by leaving the second seat empty, and having the pilot drop the bombs—a rather difficult task considering the state of control systems. A 200-pound bomb, though, would not significantly damage the *San Marcos.* That would require at least a 500-pound bomb. Of course, the pilot could not drop even a 200-pound bomb. He would have to use bombs small enough to toss over the side of the plane. Chambers argued that if the issue was accuracy, they should just sketch out a ship on land and bomb it, so they could easily and precisely measure accuracy. If the issue was the damage resistance of battleships, he suggested they try dropping the bombs from kites. Dropping bombs from planes would have to wait for larger aircraft with more powerful engines.[43]

Despite being repeatedly called away during the year to the Naval Examining Board and other temporary assignments, Chambers managed to make real progress in building the aviation program. The training of new pilots continued without him, while Ellyson handled a growing amount of the administrative burden. The year ended with significant experimental progress, achieved against consistent bureaucratic opposition. Chambers had pilots, planes, and a base. He hoped the next year would be even more productive.[44]

# 14 / Building Naval Aviation

During 1912, Chambers built on the previous year's successes and emphasized the integration of aviation with the fleet. He needed to find a way to launch aircraft directly from the navy's existing ships without extensive modifications to them. The only option at the time was lowering them into the water by crane—a slow process that required the ship to stop. In September, Theodore Ellyson and Glenn Curtiss had tried launching an airplane by sliding it down greased guide wires, but this proved awkward and practical only in calm seas. Chambers set to work on a solution.[1]

Inspired by his work with torpedoes, Chambers decided to use compressed air. He knew that any ship equipped with torpedoes (and most cruisers and battleships were) would have the equipment to supply compressed air. Utilizing his contacts at the Bureau of Ordnance, especially Lieutenant Commander G. L Smith, who directed the drafting room at the Naval Gun Factory, he designed a compressed air catapult using the parts from an old ammunition hoist. It was a simple design. An air-driven piston propelled the plane on a launching shuttle down a track and into the air. Chambers's team installed the catapult on the *Santee*'s dock at the Naval Academy for tests that summer. On July 31, their attempt to launch Ellyson in the Triad failed when the airplane lifted off the shuttle prematurely and a crosswind tossed it into the water. Chambers rebuilt the shuttle mountings with Richardson's help and they tried again on October 12. This time it propelled Ellyson into a perfect takeoff. Several friends suggested that Chambers patent his catapult, but he told them he no longer cared "to have anything to do with patents." He turned the catapult over to Richardson who continued to refine it.[2]

Despite Chambers's professed motto to "work quietly until you get results and then let these speak for themselves," he announced in a newspaper interview that summer that airplanes had proven themselves. He confidently predicted that each of the fleet's battleships would carry a seaplane by the end of 1913. Chambers hoped to use the press to goad the navy's bureaucracy to actively support aviation. Everyone who worked on the catapult assumed the navy would begin installing it on warships within a year or two.[3]

Chambers turned to other inventive work shortly afterward, working on wing designs and aircraft engines. Safety and navigation equipment soon became his focus, especially an aerial compass and a drift indicator at which he worked intermittently. One of aviation's most pressing safety needs was a stabilizer that would help pilots keep their planes level and make flying less physically exhausting. Inventor Elmer Sperry, son of gyroscope-pioneer Lawrence Sperry, had begun work on a gyroscopic stabilizer, and Chambers actively encouraged his research. He assigned pilots to work with him and shared his own knowledge of gyroscopes. Along with Curtiss, Chambers helped Sperry test his prototypes, but he never had the money to buy one for the navy. Sperry would eventually sell his invention overseas after winning a $10,000 prize in France.[4]

The funding battle resumed anew in 1912. Chambers asked for $50,000 for each of the three bureaus involved in aviation, but the bill introduced in Congress provided only $10,000 for the Bureau of Construction and Repair to buy planes and $20,000 for the Bureau of Engineering for engines and research. The $10,000 would barely purchase two planes, leaving no money to maintain those already in operation. Chambers still hoped that the navy would begin purchasing planes as ship equipment, as it did small boats, but he still needed money for training, experiments, and replacement parts, and additional planes for pilot training. He launched a new lobbying effort and asked all his friends and aviation contacts to write their members of Congress and explain how little funding aviation received in the United States compared to Europe. He managed to get the appropriation increased slightly, but not back to the original sums. Several months later, he discovered that the bureaus had asked Congress for a lower appropriation, believing the smaller amounts adequate.[5] Once again, the bureaus had set back progress in aviation. The final appropriation included $10,000 for the Bureau of Navigation, $20,000 for the Bureau of Engineering, and $35,000 for the Bureau of Construction and Repair. Chambers condemned the paltry appropriations in his report that year and again argued that planes should be paid for out of the large appropriations for shipbuilding. The General Board seconded Chambers's proposal, but was also ignored.[6]

Despite the disappointing funding, Chambers managed to add three planes to his small force that year. The navy bought another Curtiss seaplane (the A-3), and Chambers's team assembled another Wright (the B-2) from spare parts. The third plane was a new Curtiss design, the flying boat (the C-1). It again owed much to his collaboration with Chambers. Instead of simply attaching pontoons to a land plane, the flying boat was designed from the beginning to be a seaplane with a carefully designed boatlike fuselage that made it much more seaworthy. Ellyson tested the new plane on November 30, 1912, and was greatly impressed with it. Along with new planes, Chambers also added new pilots that year, including marine First Lieutenant Alfred A. Cunningham, who arrived that summer, and lieutenants Patrick N. L. Bellinger, William D. Billingsley, and Godfrey DeCourcelles Chevalier who came on board a few months later. Cunningham was unique in that he had learned to fly on his own from the local Aero Club while stationed in Philadelphia, against his wife's urgent pleadings.

The Marine Corps, then seeking to clarify its mission and develop its capabilities for amphibious operations, became interested in aviation, and Chambers worked hard to encourage this interest. The Marine Corps had begun making plans for an Advance Base Force whose mission would be to establish and defend naval bases to support naval operations. The Commandant of the Marine Corps requested planes in 1912. Chambers supported his request and offered to train marine pilots, though he could only handle two at a time. Secretary of the Navy George Meyer responded that there were no funds for the marines to have their own planes, but he did approve training marine pilots. First Lieutenant Bernard L. Smith and Second Lieutenant William M. McIlvain arrived for instruction at the end of the year. This, as Chambers emphasized, was more important. Planes could be purchased later. Chambers clearly also hoped that these marine aviators would disseminate the importance of aviation to the Marine Corps.[7]

Chambers became interested in the problems of the Advance Base Force and believed aircraft would play a critical role in its operations. He returned to work on the Triad design, hoping to develop a plane that could operate from both water and land, a plane that would travel with the fleet but then be able to operate from the land base established by the marines. This design developed into the E-1 OWL (over water and land). Slow and unstable, it never performed up to his expectations. Most pilots hated it, but Bernard L. Smith also considered it important for the Marine Corps and worked with Chambers to improve it.[8]

Chambers had proved that planes could operate off the navy's ships, but he needed to prove their utility to a fleet at sea. In June, the General Board asked Chambers to assign several planes to accompany the fleet in maneuvers that winter. Chambers eagerly agreed and confidently announced to the press that he expected these maneuvers would finally prove the value of aviation to the navy.[9]

The officers of the General Board, led by Admiral George Dewey, became even more aggressive in promoting aviation that summer, and solicited the advice of Chambers and his aviators on its future, asking detailed questions about the capabilities of airplanes. In August, the General Board declared that a "complete and trained air fleet is a necessary adjunct to the Navy" and called "for the immediate organization of an efficient naval air service." In December, it issued a full report on aviation that echoed the points Chambers had been making for more than a year. Planes were essential for naval reconnaissance. While they had "no great offensive power" at that time, this would soon change. Planes would be used to bomb critical shore targets such as fuel depots, powder plants, arms factories, and possibly the locks of the Panama Canal. They suggested using planes to defend against aerial attack, arming them with machine guns and small bombs to drop on enemy aircraft.[10]

Chambers's aviators spent the summer and fall testing and experimenting with their planes to be certain they would be ready to sail with the fleet. Their most pressing need was a way to communicate with ships from the air. The Bureau of Engineering again proved unhelpful, but John Towers knew Ensign Charles Maddox from their time together on board the battleship *Michigan.* Maddox was rapidly becoming the navy's premier expert on radio, and Towers convinced him to work on a transmitter small enough to fit in an airplane. Maddox spent the summer at Annapolis and designed a set that weighed only 40 pounds. They mounted it in a plane and on July 27 sent a simple Morse code message to a receiver on the ground. The transmitter had only a 12-mile range and its long, trailing antenna kept snapping off, but they had proved it could be done. Planes would be able to communicate directly with ships, making it possible for them to direct their fire.[11]

Earlier that year, the French had successfully used planes to spot submarines in tests off Cherbourg. Chambers had long predicted this would be possible, but he had met with little cooperation in arranging a test. In October, he spoke with Lieutenant Chester W. Nimitz, the commander of the Atlantic submarine flotilla, and arranged a test. The submarines submerged in Chesapeake Bay while Towers and Victor Herbster flew overhead trying to spot them. They each carried a submarine officer who helped them spot periscopes, air bubbles, and other signs of submarines. They successfully spotted submarines close to the surface, but the muddy waters of the Chesapeake prevented seeing anything at depth. Just before these tests, Towers set an endurance record when he remained aloft in the A-2 for six hours and ten minutes, proving that planes could stay in the air long enough for a prolonged search.[12] The aviation unit stood ready to prove itself to the fleet.

## Chambers's Thoughts on Aviation

As airplanes developed, questions naturally arose as to their role in combat. Early on, Ellyson and Chambers suggested the navy use planes to attack targets on land, and they became more optimistic over time. In his 1912 report on aviation, Chambers still emphasized scouting as the primary role of aircraft. They would be the "eyes of the fleet," locating enemy forces, directing fire, scouting for expeditionary forces, supporting blockade operations, and allowing rapid communication with detached squadrons or forces on shore. They would also locate and destroy submarines, mines, and dirigibles, and attack land bases including docks, ships under repair, magazines, and fuel depots.[13]

Chambers was always cautious in making predictions. He saw progress as "a step by step process," that would not be "found in radical changes all at once." While many civilian writers argued that airplanes made battleships obsolete, Chambers knew that time had not come. More importantly, as he warned the editor of the *Aero Club Bulletin:* "there will be an angry reaction in the Navy if the 'aeroplane phobia' gets far enough along in its efforts to discredit the battleship." Chambers needed to support aviation without threatening the status of the battleship and repeatedly emphasized in his correspondence and reports that command of the air would never have the "vital significance" of control of the sea.[14] Whether he actually believed this is uncertain, but it certainly held true for his time.

To deflect criticism from aviation, Chambers repeatedly insisted that "no airship or collection of airships" would "ever take the place of a battleship in the maintenance of sea power," and argued that a battleship would "be able to destroy a fleet of airships." Yet, Chambers had a very different battleship in mind from what aviation advocates would later deride as "the gun club." Chambers understood that warships evolved and changed over time, having participated in the process throughout his career. While technology would change, large warships would remain the backbone of any fleet that sought to control the seas. Planes would add to the capabilities of surface ships, but would not supplant them. Chambers believed that future battleships would carry airplanes. Airplanes would intercept and fight other airplanes and those "not overburdened with missiles intended for dropping will have the advantage." He dismissed dirigibles as particularly vulnerable to airplanes, and believed they would never "be a serious menace to any American city" or ships at sea.[15]

Chambers repeatedly emphasized to his civilian correspondents that offense and defense in war had always acted to balance each other. "For every new method of attack there is always some very effective means of defense." Improved defensive firepower and early warning would offset the larger, more accurate bombs carried by more advanced aircraft. Planes would not scour the seas of naval vessels. For the foreseeable future, "such bombs as an aeroplane might drop would be mere flea bites to a battleship." It was a position shared by all the world's navies at the time. The German navy believed that a hit achieved from a plane flying above the range of a ships' guns would "be a complete accident." Torpedoes proved a more serious threat to battleships, but Chambers argued that air-launched torpedoes would no more displace the battleship than those launched by torpedo boats or submarines. Battleships would protect themselves with their own aircraft and defensive armament. Smaller warships, submarines, and troopships, though, would be particularly vulnerable to airplanes. This, though, was for the future. As Chambers wrote to one aspiring inventor, "we are not so much interested in bomb dropping devices now as we are in getting satisfactory aeroplanes from which to drop them."[16]

The Royal Navy had considered building an aircraft carrier in 1913, but decided it needed more experience operating planes first. Chambers also considered specialized aircraft-carrying warships to be premature. Rumors in the press circulated repeatedly that the United States was going to construct some type of "hanger ship," but none of them were true, and Chambers always acted quickly to denounce them. He knew Congress would never fund such a vessel even if he managed to convince the navy to ask for one. The navy could not get Congress to fund auxiliary vessels in adequate numbers and remained short of colliers and other important auxiliaries. More importantly, a hanger ship would concentrate aviation officers at one spot, limiting their influence on the navy as a whole. This was one of Chambers's great fears, that aviation would find itself isolated and ignored as the Torpedo Station had been for most of its history. He wanted aviation to spread thorough the fleet, so that it would become part of every officer's normal experience—even those who would never fly. Every cruiser and battleship should be equipped with planes. Specialized aircraft carriers, he argued, would come later.[17]

## A National Aeronautic Lab: The Woodward Commission

Aviation enthusiasts and manufacturers had sought government support for several years. F. H. Russell, for instance, wrote Chambers that "the success of aviation in this country . . . depends vitally upon the support which the government gives to the few concerned who are organized on a solid basis for experimental and manufacturing work."[18] A 1911 effort by the Aeronautic Society to get President Taft to create a national aeronautic research laboratory was derailed by Admiral Richard M. Watt and the squabbling among several government agencies over its control.

In 1912, Chambers, assisted by Dr. Albert F. Zahm, launched a vigorous campaign to create a national lab. Zahm, a professor of mechanics at Catholic University and the governor of the Aero Club of America, had built the first wind tunnel in the United States in 1901. Like Chambers, he believed unwaveringly in the future of aviation and that a national research lab was vital to advance aviation. Together, Chambers and Zahm rallied the nation's numerous aeronautic clubs behind the cause and built support for it within the government and academia. Zahm used the *Aero Club Bulletin* to spread the word, blaming the "halting, haphazard, and fortuitous" progress of aviation in the United States on its lack of a centralized, aeronautic research facility. Chambers, too, published a series of articles on the need for the lab and devoted most of his September report on aviation to explaining its need and presenting an organizational model for it. He argued that it was time for the "methods of scientific engineers" to replace those of crude inventors, and recommended that the president appoint a commission to study the matter. In "fifteen tightly worded pages," Chambers presented the "rationale and the blueprint for the National Advisory Committee for Aeronautics," which would be created in 1916.[19]

On December 12, 1912, President Taft finally formed a nineteen-member commission to consider creating an aeronautic lab. The seven government appointees included a representative from the Weather Bureau, the Smithsonian, and the National Bureau of Standards as well as two army and two navy officers. Chambers and Captain David D. Taylor from the Bureau of Construction represented the navy. Robert S. Woodward, the president of the Carnegie Institute of Washington chaired the committee, which quickly ran into problems. Since it had no congressional authorization or appropriation, Chambers arranged for a friend to introduce a bill to fund it. The bill passed in the Senate, but failed in the House. Unfunded and with questionable authority, the commission met anyway.[20]

All of the commission's members agreed on the importance of a national lab, but arguments erupted almost immediately over where it would be located and under whose authority it would operate. Richard Maclaurin, the president of the Massachusetts Institute of Technology, wanted it located near his university, which had a growing aeronautics program. Samuel Stratton, the director of the National Bureau of Standards, wanted it under his agency. Chambers, along with Woodward, Zahm, and Charles Walcott (the president of the Smithsonian) argued adamantly in favor of a research lab under the Smithsonian. Chambers believed the Smithsonian was not only in the best position to run the lab but also just as important to raise public awareness in order to further the development of aviation. He wanted the lab to do independent research, as well as verify the research of others and serve as a source of information for all inventors. A military-sponsored lab, by its very nature, could not be open about its work. Chambers also argued that a Smithsonian lab could draw on private as well as government support.[21]

Chambers's main opponent in these debates was Taylor. Taylor's chief, Admiral Watt, had consistently opposed the creation of any government-sponsored aviation research facility. Taylor, who had been the driving force in establishing the model basin and putting naval research on a truly scientific basis, took the same position. The model basin had just finished installing a wind tunnel and was finally pursuing aviation research with real dedication. He argued that any funding for another establishment would be a needless duplication and waste of money.[22]

This was hardly a convincing argument, and in the end, the commission voted thirteen to three with three abstentions in favor of establishing a lab at the Smithsonian and issued a report to Congress advocating its establishment. Taylor and its other opponents, though, proved effective lobbyists, and a bill establishing the lab failed to pass the 62nd Congress before its term expired in March. Reintroduced in the 63rd Congress, the bill died in committee.[23]

## Problems at the End of the Year

The failure to get the lab established inaugurated Chambers's most trying months in charge of aviation. While he could boast in 1911 that the United States was ahead of European nations in exploring the potentials of naval aviation, the situation had changed by the end of 1912. The British matched Ely's pioneering flights that year and were working on a torpedo plane. The French converted a collier into seaplane tender. Each of the European powers spent at least ten times what the United States did on military aviation, some of them considerably more. In 1912, France spent $6.4 million, Russia $5 million, Britain $2.1 million, Italy $2 million, and Germany $1.5 million. "Our statesmen," as Curtiss complained to Chambers, "do not seem to be taking a serious interest in aviation." Underfunded and haphazardly supported, U.S. naval aviation was losing its lead.[24]

Chambers also had problems with his older pilots. Their sense of optimism from the previous year was clearly waning. Isolated from the rest of the navy, some of them feared for their careers. Tempers began to run short and they clashed with Chambers over a host of issues ranging from aircraft design to pay and expense reimbursement. Few realized Chambers's delicate political position and resented his inability to do more for them. John Rodgers, following the fatal crash of his stunt pilot cousin, Calbraith Perry Rodgers, announced he was seeking a position at sea. Shortly afterward, Ellyson announced his interest in returning to the fleet. Chambers's decision to give command of the aviation detachment for the winter maneuvers to Towers, while Ellyson remained in the United States to continue work on Curtiss's flying boat, may have been the last straw for Ellyson.[25] Regardless, Chambers lost his two most senior aviators early in 1913.

Chambers had also been eying a return to the sea, but he wanted the aviation program solidly established and in competent hands before he would leave. In October 1912, he had learned that the navy planned to give him command of the new battleship *Florida.* Chambers thought it was too soon for him to leave aviation. He wrote to his friend Philip Andrews, the new Chief of the Bureau of Navigation, to get his orders to sea withheld until the spring, by which time he hoped "that an officer may be detailed to assist me with a view to carrying on the work without embarrassment after I am relieved." In delaying his orders to go to sea, Chambers knew he was hurting his career. In his fitness report earlier that year he had felt the need to point out that he "had never sought duty in aviation, and had only become interested in it after receiving the assignment." He concluded his letter to Andrews reminding him that his request for a delay "should not be construed as a request to escape orders to sea." Chambers was ready to go to sea "regardless of the absorbing interest that my present duties inspire in me to be in the van of progress with Naval Aviation."[26]

Andrews wrote Meyer in support of Chambers, arguing that his departure "would seriously affect the progress of naval aviation." Work on aviation would "practically stop" if Chambers went to sea. No one could take up his work "without extensive preparation." Unfortunately, with misplaced honesty, Andrews added that he did not believe that Chambers wanted to go to sea "but plainly he cannot put himself in the position of asking not to go." The latter was certainly true. A deliberate effort to avoid sea duty would doom his career. Chambers had already damaged his reputation with his commitment to aviation. Admiral Charles Vreeland, the Aide for Operations, had "put Chambers down for continuous shore duty, in the belief that he is not fit for divisional or fleet command"—a statement that would have astounded Admiral Dewey and any of Chambers's commanders. Meyer approved the change in Chambers's orders, and everything seemed set for him to go to sea in the spring.[27]

## 1913 and a New Administration

In January, virtually the entire aviation unit sailed with the North Atlantic Fleet to Cuba for its winter maneuvers, including Bellinger, Billingsley, Chevalier, Cunningham, Herbster, G. L. Smith, and Towers. It was the first use of airplanes in conjunction with fleet operations and the aviators worked hard to demonstrate what their planes could do and to sell aviation to higher officers. After setting up camp in Guantánamo, they spent the next six weeks scouting, photographing, and even making a few bombing runs. They managed to spot submarines as deep as 60 feet below the surface and to locate mines from the air. While they continued to have problems with the radio, which failed repeatedly, they proved the value of aerial spotting to the fleet. They also took more than two hundred officers for practice flights, among them Lieutenant Commander Henry C. Mustin, who soon joined the aviation program and learned to fly.[28]

Back in the United States, a change in administration compounded the uncertainty of aviation's future. New President Woodrow Wilson had promised to eliminate corruption and run the government in strict accordance to regulations and the law. Josephus Daniels, the new Secretary of the Navy, knew nothing about the navy's bureaucracy and did not trust it. He was particularly suspicious of Meyer's aide system, which he increasingly bypassed, choosing to work directly with the bureau chiefs, especially Admiral Victor Blue, an old friend and fellow North Carolinian, whom he appointed Chief of the Bureau of Navigation.[29]

Along with the new administration came a new Aide for Operations, Rear Admiral Bradley Fiske. Meyer appointed him on February 11, 1913, to replace Rear Admiral Charles Vreeland who had taken ill. It was one of Meyer's last official actions, and one that would have grave consequences for the navy and for Chambers. Fiske had excellent credentials as a reformer and a number of inventions to his credit. He was also one of the most outspoken officers in the navy and among the loudest proponents of a naval general staff.

With Fiske's record of invention, it would be logical to expect him to embrace aviation, but his record of supporting it was questionable. While on the General Board in 1911, Fiske had advocated deploying torpedo-armed airplanes to defend the Philippines. Richard Wainwright ridiculed his idea as a "wildcat scheme," pointing out that the General Board had to base its plans on what was possible in the present rather than the future.[30] Fiske left for a command at sea shortly thereafter and did not return to Washington until January 6, 1913, when Meyer appointed him Aide for Inspections. Apart from getting a patent for his sketch of a crude apparatus for dropping a torpedo from a plane, there is no indication that he paid any attention to aviation developments while at sea.

As Aide for Operations, Fiske had a few conversations with Chambers, but paid little attention to naval aviation during his first year in office. Instead, he focused on matters more important to him, especially creating a naval general staff, which he wanted to lead. He used his position as Aide for Operations to isolate the General Board and other officers from the Secretary of the Navy and to enlarge his own power base. Aviation, as well as everything else, took a back seat to Fiske's personal ambitions. Had Fiske, as Chambers later wrote "subordinated his personal schemes to the best interests of the government, he could have succeeded in establishing many necessary reforms."[31] If Chambers had expected support from Fiske, he must have been sorely disappointed.

As one of his first actions on taking office, Daniels ruled that he would not promote officers who did not have the sea duty required for their rank. This immediately posed serious problems for the navy as Meyer had violated this policy routinely to ensure that the best officers staffed his new administrative arrangement. Now these officers found their prospects for promotion in danger. The first victim of this abrupt change in policy was Chambers's longtime friend Templin Potts. Meyer had removed him from command of the battleship *Georgia* to become the Chief Intelligence Officer. Potts, who had since become the Aide for Personnel, was due for promotion to flag rank. Daniels denied his promotion due to lack of sea service. Dewey, and to a lesser extent Fiske, intervened on Potts's behalf, arguing his case to Daniels, but the secretary remained adamant and sent Potts back to sea unpromoted. Shortly afterward, the retirement board (or "plucking board") followed Daniels's policy, declared Potts short of sea service, and placed him on the retired list. The career of an excellent officer and noted reformer was over.[32]

Daniels's treatment of Potts triggered an exodus from Washington as senior officers on shore rushed to find appointments at sea to save their careers. Over the next few months, the navy's Washington bureaucracy underwent one its greatest changes in personnel in its history. Chambers's network of friends and supporters on shore evaporated. Among those who left was

Philip Andrews, who gave up his position as Chief of the Bureau of Navigation and reverted to his regular rank of commander. So did Hutch I. Cone, who resigned as the Chief of the Bureau of Engineering and returned to sea as a lieutenant commander.[33]

Chambers knew his days in aviation were numbered. Daniels would not approve an extension of his time on shore as Meyer had. He needed to ensure the aviation program's position in the navy and he needed to do it quickly. Towers, following his return from Guantánamo, became Chambers's primary assistant. He did his best to help with Chambers's "legislative engineering," as well as supervising the pilot training program and day-to-day operations at Annapolis.[34]

Chambers had testified before Congress that January, but could not convince its members to increase aviation funding. The budget for 1913 remained the same as the previous year: $10,000 for the Bureau of Navigation, $20,000 for the Engineering Bureau, and $35,000 for the Bureau of Construction and Repair. Following this defeat, Chambers wrote to Daniels and several friendly members in Congress asking them to switch unused funds for "transportation navigation" to naval aviation, but without success. Chambers also tried to get Congress and the navy to sponsor prizes for aviation record setting and invention, hoping they would spur aviation developments in the United States as they had in Europe—especially if the navy purchased planes and instruments from the winners. Congress would not appropriate the funds. On April 24, the National Aeronautical Society presented him with a gold medal for his efforts to advance aviation, and Chambers used the opportunity to again make his case for aviation funding and a national research lab. He followed his speech with another long letter that Daniels again ignored.[35]

Walcott also continued to fight for the lab, and convinced the Regents of the Smithsonian Institution to reopen the Langley Laboratory and resume aeronautical research, which President Wilson later approved. Walcott appointed an eleven-member board that included Chambers and Holden Richardson to oversee its operation. The lab's mission and organization were virtually identical to what Chambers had outlined in his 1912 report. Over the next two years, Walcott, Chambers, and their supporters lobbied Congress to fund the lab. Assistant Secretary of the Navy Franklin Roosevelt weighed in on their side in the final legislative battle, and helped get funding for it tacked on to the 1915 naval appropriations bill. The lab became an integral part of the National Advisory Committee for Aeronautics created the following year.[36] Chambers finally had his lab, but by then his career was all but over.

## The Billingsley Crash

On June 20, 1913, Chambers found himself confronted by what he had most dreaded. Towers had accompanied Ensign William D. Billingsley on a flight. As the Wright B-2 skirted a storm, a sudden updraft threw both men into the controls. Neither had worn the plane's crude and uncomfortable safety straps. The plane plunged into a steep dive, tossing Billingsley to his death. Clinging to the rigging, Towers fell 1,600 feet with the plane into the water. He survived, severely injured, and would spend most of the next four months in the hospital.[37]

The crash "cast a pall over naval aviation." Chambers ordered the Wright planes, which had developed a particularly deadly reputation (having killed five Army aviators and now Billingsley), grounded. Cunningham, at the behest of his fiancée, left aviation. Chambers lost virtually his entire first generation of pilots. His remaining senior aviator, Victor Herbster, while a good pilot, proved a terrible administrator and repeatedly clashed with most of the other pilots. Chambers had no choice but to put Lieutenant (j.g.) James Murray in charge of the Annapolis base. While the most experienced pilot available, he had flown solo for only ten hours.[38]

It must have seemed to Chambers that naval aviation's situation could hardly get worse, but it did. On June 23, 1913, Daniels issued General Order 41, which codified Meyer's division of aviation responsibilities into law with the Bureau of Construction and Repair in charge of airframes, the Engineering Bureau in charge of engines, and the Bureau of Navigation in charge of instruments, clothing, and personnel. This division would remain in force until 1921, complicating the efforts of Chambers and his successors to rationalize the administration of naval aviation. An even worse blow befell Chambers one week later.

## Plucked

Chambers was to be assigned to command the new battleship *Utah* in March as he had arranged with Andrews, but the change in administration stalled the bureaucracy. The navy failed to assign anyone to relieve him. Chambers tried to get Mustin as his replacement, but he could not arrange the transfer. Chambers knew he was in a tenuous position, but he decided to pass on the proffered command.[39]

Chambers's friend Theodorus Mason had been in charge of the plucking board the previous year and had protected Chambers. He had written to both Chambers and Meyer asking if Chambers's "failure to secure the command of a first-class ship has been due to the requirements of the public interests." Meyer affirmed that he indeed required Chambers on shore. Chambers apparently assumed that this arrangement would cover him for another year. He also incorrectly believed that he still had several years to make up his deficiency in time at sea.[40]

Meyer's support and well-placed friends were all Chambers had needed in 1912 to safeguard his career, but the situation had changed. Henry Mayo and other friends phoned and wrote Chambers warning him to apply for sea duty. Chambers did not take them seriously, believing that if the navy could drag him from sea to shore, it could send him back just as well. Oblivious to the urgency of the situation and bogged down by work, Chambers did not apply for sea duty until May 1913.[41] In typical fashion, Chambers indicated his "readiness for sea duty," summarized his accomplishments, complained about his lack of support and funding, and repeated his request for a qualified relief to continue his aviation work. He foolishly concluded his letter: "I am perfectly willing to risk the chances of promotion if the Department should find it expedient to delay my orders. Nevertheless, I wish to record the fact that I am not working assiduously in the development of aviation for the purpose of avoiding sea duty and that I am ready for such duty at any time."[42]

Victor Blue approved Chambers's assignment to sea, writing to Daniels that while Chambers had "done valuable work in directing the progress of aviation along scientific lines," the Bureau of Navigation would not stand in his way of going to sea. When a few days later Daniels replied that, "no action will be taken towards ordering Captain Chambers to sea at this time," Chambers still thought everything was in order. He was only fifth on the list of captains, so five admirals would have to retire before the navy could promote him. He saw no reason for urgency.[43]

The plucking board did not agree. Possibly pressured by Daniels to clear out higher ranks, it met later that month. It plucked five captains, the maximum allowed by law, among them Chambers. The ostensible reason for most of these pluckings was lack of sea service in the grade of captain. The deliberations of the plucking boards were kept completely secret, so there was no way for Chambers or anyone else to find out why or how they had made their decision. Blue phoned Chambers on June 30 and notified him of his forced retirement. The news stunned Chambers, but when Blue asked him to remain on active duty and continue to direct naval aviation, he agreed.[44]

Blue confirmed this arrangement in writing the next day. Chambers agreed to continue his work for a short time, though he pointed out that he would "not care to continue this duty, at the pay of a Lieutenant, any longer than necessary" to complete his most important work. (Federal law mandated that retired officers returned to active duty could not be paid more than an active duty lieutenant, a few dollars more than the retired pay of a captain.) Chambers, crushed by his plucking, plaintively asked "whether the Department appreciates not only the difficulties surrounding the problems involved and the importance of aerial navigation to the future of naval warfare, but the peculiar difficulties, the discomforts of my position, the sacrifices I have made in my zeal for this work." Daniels accepted his willingness to continue on active duty and replied that he "hoped that an officer can be assigned to duty with you with a view to becoming your relief."[45] Chambers would remain in charge of aviation for the next seven months, and it would be in this awkward position that he presided over his final achievement.

Several years later Chambers discovered the circumstances that led to his plucking, though he probably never learned all the details. At first, he thought that Daniels wanted to purge the navy's upper ranks to further the career of his friend Blue, a commander whose promotion was accelerated by plucking Potts, Chambers, and the other captains. Later, he correctly focused on Fiske, who could have prevented his "sacrifice by a wink of his eye." Fiske had intervened with Daniels and arranged for Chambers to stay on shore. Fiske had witnessed the destruction of Potts's career and arranged the same fate for Chambers. The question, of course, is why. In his autobiography, Fiske simply stated that aviation needed "new blood" because the "captain in charge of aviation [Chambers] . . . was more occupied with making certain inventions connected with aeroplanes than with the subject of developing an aeronautical service."[46]

Fiske's biographer supports this, and argues that Fiske incorrectly believed Chambers "was more interested in solving the theoretical problems of flight than in quickly developing a naval air service."[47] This complaint, coming from Fiske, is simply absurd. Fiske had spent the better part of his career tinkering with a variety of inventions and had complained repeatedly about the lack of support inventors received from the navy. Even as Aide for Operations, he still found time to experiment and test his inventions. If the issue were new blood, sending Chambers to sea would have cleared the way for Fiske to appoint a new officer to command aviation. Fiske's destruction of Chambers's career was deliberate, personal, and vindictive. His use of the plucking board was masterful. Chambers's carefully cultivated network of friends and supporters could do nothing to save him.

Chambers later came to believe Fiske turned against him because he failed to support Fiske's torpedo plane idea. He apparently dismissed Fiske's premature advocacy of armed aircraft as he had that of so many other inventors, stating that it needed to wait until larger planes capable of lifting torpedoes (which weighed 2,000 pounds) had been developed. Fiske envisioned waves of torpedo planes sweeping obsolete warships from the sea. The pragmatic Chambers repeatedly told Fiske and other visionaries that it would be many years before anyone built planes capable of the feats they envisioned. Scientists and inventors first had to solve the very real (and very many) problems of aviation.

It is also likely that Fiske was annoyed that Chambers was not interested in creating an independent aeronautics bureau that would have equal standing with the other bureaus. Much as he had in the debate over ship design, Chambers took a middle position between line officer extremists like Fiske and the staff bureaus. He sought ways to harmonize interbureau cooperation and tried to work with the system as it was rather than fighting to change it. He was not motivated by any love for the bureau system. Rather, he preferred to focus his efforts on practical, achievable goals. Congress would never have approved the creation of a new bureau in the navy even had Daniels been convinced to support it. The battle over the creation of an aviation bureau would have antagonized the technical bureaus that Chambers relied upon to purchase aircraft. Fiske remembered which side Chambers had been on in the debates over ship design, and may also have been offended by his criticism of his ideas on ship design and torpedoes at that time.[48] Whatever his motivations, Fiske brought Chambers's career to a premature end.

In just under three years, Chambers had built up the navy's aviation program from nothing to a small but respectable force that included a dozen aviators and eight aircraft. His aviators set several world records and managed to lead the world in achievement if not in numbers. He had managed to carve a niche for aviation within the fleet and convince numerous, doubting senior officers of its importance. Operating under serious budgetary constraints and with virtually no support within the navy's bureaucracy, his achievements testified to his technical and organizational skills and his tenacity. Caught between his pilots and aviation enthusiasts who always wanted more than he could possibly give them and a navy bureaucracy that was at best indifferent, Chambers persevered. Key officers in the bureaucracy, such as Fiske and many of the bureau chiefs, often evinced more interest in their own empire building than the future of naval aviation and supported it only when it suited their own ends.

During these years, aviation became Chambers's entire life, and despite being plucked, he would continue to work in the aviation program for six more years. Long into his retirement, Chambers remained most proud of the safety record of naval aviation under his command. By the end of 1913, the slightly larger army aviation program had lost fourteen aviators in crashes while the navy had lost only Billingsley. The army made little effort to improve pilot safety and did not even ban its aviators from exhibition flying until 1914, two years after Chambers had made that unpopular decision for his pilots.[49]

Chambers's forced retirement stands in stark contrast to his record for these years. Dewey, Reginald Nicholson, and Andrews had rated him excellent in every category in evaluation after evaluation. Nicholson surprisingly wrote that he "would be glad to serve under him," and that he considered Chambers's work on aviation "excellent." Dewey remarked that he had a "special aptitude" for the General Board. Andrews cited his remarkable "success with development of aviation," and considered him "calm, even tempered, forceful, industrious," and fit for promotion.[50] Had he not been plucked, Chambers would have left an even more dramatic mark on the navy. Despite his retirement, Chambers would leave the navy one final legacy.

# 15 / Retired

Chambers's plucking exacerbated his already weak position within the navy's bureaucracy as the battle for the control and funding of naval aviation continued. Chief of the Bureau of Construction and Repair Richard Watt disagreed with Chambers on virtually every issue of aviation policy, and opposed many of his initiatives. Chambers's support for the Langley Lab particularly angered him, as did his efforts to create a recognized office of aeronautics within the navy. Josephus Daniels seemed completely oblivious to aviation's desperate need for funding. Chambers needed a replacement with official standing in the navy to fight for the aviation program. He tried to get John Towers to fight for the position, but Towers knew it required a higher-ranking officer to deal with the bureau chiefs. Chambers suggested Henry Mustin and several other officers to replace him, but Bradley Fiske ignored him. Fiske alone would choose Chambers's replacement, and it would take him some time. Officers were understandably reluctant to accept the position after what had happened to Chambers.[1]

While Fiske looked for Chambers's replacement, he also tried to hijack the aviation policy from him. On July 16, 1913, Fiske asked Daniels to obtain the General Board's opinion on the utility of aviation for the fleet, hoping to use its recommendation to support his effort to create an Aeronautics Bureau. The General Board sent Daniels to Chambers, despite the fact that

Fiske and Daniels had destroyed his career just two weeks earlier.[2] Chambers would have one last chance to influence the future of naval aviation.

## The Chambers Board

Daniels and Assistant Secretary of the Navy Franklin Roosevelt had visited the Annapolis aviation camp that summer, and Towers and Victor Herbster had taken them for plane rides. Roosevelt, at least, returned to Washington convinced of the importance of aviation. Like many of his predecessors, Roosevelt would wait until Daniels was out of the office and then act forcefully to support projects he believed in. Often he would phone friends to see if he could do anything for them.[3] On October 7, 1913, probably at Dewey's suggestion, Roosevelt put Chambers in charge of a special Aeronautic Board (usually referred to as the Chambers Board) to make recommendations for aviation policy. Chambers appointed Towers to the board, the Marine Corps sent Alfred Cunningham, and the bureaus each sent a representative: Commander Carlo B. Brittain from Navigation, Holden C. Richardson from Construction and Repair, Commander Samuel S. Robison from Engineering, and Lieutenant Manly H. Simons from Ordnance. Chambers, Towers, and Richardson dominated the board's discussions and carved out a plan for the future that closely followed Chambers's previous recommendations.

Before the board met, Chambers sent Towers on a six-week fact-finding mission to gather information on the progress of aviation in the United States. The two of them discussed aviation policy in detail before the board met and reached agreement on most issues. The one contentious issue between them was aircraft design. Chambers had an engineering background and had worked hard to learn everything he could about aeronautics. He had repeatedly involved himself in the aircraft design process, but lacked experience as an aviator. Towers wanted all aircraft designs passed by a board of pilots. He had suffered too many bad experiences with designs from nonflyers. He was particularly opposed to Chambers's OWL design. Nonetheless, they worked out most of their differences and presented a united front during the board's deliberations.[4]

The Chambers Board met in mid-November. At the first meeting, Chambers gave each member the data Towers had gathered and his own proposal for the expansion of naval aviation. He then adjourned the meeting so the members could read everything. When the board reconvened, most of the discussions focused on Chambers's proposal. The board issued its unanimous report on November 25 after deliberating for twelve days. Its recommendations differed hardly at all from Chambers's initial proposal.[5]

The Chambers Board recommended expanding the pilot training program, establishing a larger and more permanent base on shore, and assigning a ship to aviation to serve as a mobile base. Most important, they recommended the immediate purchase of fifty airplanes and three dirigibles, and the future purchase of even more aircraft. It was a modest proposal considering that by the end of the year the militaries of Germany, France, and Russia each fielded about five hundred aircraft. Even Belgium had twenty-seven planes, more than the U.S. Army and Navy combined. Administratively, the board supported Chambers's repeated recommendation to create an office of naval aeronautics, but not the separate aviation bureau that Fiske wanted. A navy captain would direct the office with an assistant and representatives from the Marine Corps and the four bureaus involved in aviation. To sidestep potential opposition, they recommended funding research at both the navy's model basin and the Smithsonian. They requested $1,297,700 to fund their recommendations.[6]

This blueprint for the future of naval aviation contained most of Chambers's proposals of the past three years. Had Chambers not been plucked, it would have been a fitting legacy to cap his time as director of naval aviation before returning to sea. Chambers, though, had nowhere to go and simply continued to work on aviation with ever-diminishing authority and influence.

The Chambers Board's report offended Fiske because it accepted the current bureau division of responsibilities. Fiske tried to bury it. He refused to present its recommendations to Daniels or the General Board, and prevented Chambers from meeting with Daniels. Chambers passed his board's report on to the General Board and from there it reached Daniels. Unfortunately, despite his statements to the press, Daniels was not willing to fight hard for aviation, especially since the Wilson administration was worried about a budget deficit. The "word had been quietly passed along to squeeze expenditures." Chambers lost the stenographer he had managed to get for the Aeronautical Board, and once again worked alone. When Daniels presented the navy's proposed budget to Congress, he asked for only $350,000 for aviation and he did not fight for it. Congress appropriated only the same low amount it had the previous two years—a total of $65,000 split between the bureaus of Navigation, Construction, and Engineering.[7] It was another setback for aviation.

## Mark Bristol

On December 17, 1913, Fiske arranged the assignment of recently promoted Captain Mark L. Bristol to work on aviation under him in the Division of Operations. He intended Bristol to replace Chambers, but it would be several weeks before Fiske announced his plans to anyone else. Chambers learned from newspapers on January 5 that he would be subordinated to Bristol. On January 8, Fiske had Chambers detached from the Bureau of Navigation and ordered to his Operations Division. Fiske then systematically stripped Chambers of all his authority over aviation. Fiske had to approve all expenditures of funds and all correspondence. He reduced Chambers's duties to work on the OWL flying boat and liaison to the Langley Lab, though the latter could not "be openly recognized."[8]

Chambers protested to Daniels that he had not consented to remain on active duty "to perform the drudgery of this work under the direction of an officer who is junior to me." If he and Fiske wanted him to stay, they would have to give him interesting work to do. Chambers also sent a long memo to Fiske that pointedly demonstrated just how little Fiske knew about aviation in general or the day-to-day business of naval aviation. In apparent retaliation, Fiske took the OWL project away from Chambers, but acknowledged the importance of the Langley Lab and placed Chambers in charge of aeronautical research. Fiske placed Bristol in charge of day-to-day operations and establishing the new Naval Air Station at the abandoned Pensacola Navy Yard. Bristol would eventually relieve Chambers, but Fiske set no date for this. A few weeks after this bitter exchange of memos, the strain and overwork finally caught up with Chambers—his health collapsed and he entered the hospital with pneumonia.[9]

Fiske's choice of Bristol, however, proved a good one. While Bristol was not particularly interested in aviation (he had hoped to be appointed Chief Intelligence Officer), he proved a good administrator, quickly installing Mustin and Towers at Pensacola and securing the obsolete battleship *Mississippi* for aviation training, and later the armored cruiser *North Carolina* when the United States sold the *Mississippi* to Greece. Bristol and Chambers worked well together as they had on board the *Texas* and at the Torpedo Station. Chambers brought Bristol up to speed on aviation over the next year. There is no indication that Chambers vented any of his frustration over his situation at Bristol. He repeatedly emphasized his great respect for Bristol and supported him in bureaucratic battles.[10]

## Reinstatement

When he recovered from his bout with pneumonia, Chambers focused on undoing his plucking and getting reinstated into the navy. Following his plucking, mail had poured into Chambers's office from a host of well-wishers. Charles Gove and other classmates wrote to express their surprise and anger about both Chambers's and Potts's forced retirement. Chambers's sister proclaimed him a "martyr to his sense of duty." Robert Peary wrote that "aviation is the loser by your retirement," a sentiment shared by many in the aviation community. The navy's aviators were also quite upset by Chambers's plucking. They did not have to like Chambers to know what his fate meant for the aviation program as a whole and those officers too closely associated with it. So many letters arrived that Chambers soon had to respond with form letters. He vowed to fight on and continue working on aviation, though he likened it to "trying to swim in a turbulent stream with a stone tied to his feet."[11]

Friends in the aeronautical societies pressured members of Congress to reinstate Chambers. Their efforts worried Chambers because he thought they would offend the navy's bureaucracy. He asked his friends to coordinate their efforts through him and launched his own effort at reinstatement. He began building support within the navy's bureaucracy in September and wrote to Dewey for advice. He put his campaign on hold while he chaired the Aeronautics Board, and did not resume work on saving his career until February. As it had for the past three years, aviation took precedence over everything else.[12]

In February, Chambers received Daniels's permission to petition Congress for reinstatement "in strict conformity with Navy regulations." Potts and several other officers also worked for reinstatement, but without success. The Bureau of Navigation opposed all their petitions, fearing a flood of plucked officers demanding reinstatement.[13]

In his petition, Chambers summarized his accomplishments and explained that when plucked he had still had time to make up his deficiency in sea duty. He also pointed out that as part of the amalgamation of the line and staff, the navy promoted five former engineers to the rank of admiral despite their serious deficiencies in time at sea. Since Chambers's duties in charge of aviation had involved engineering, he argued that the navy should make an exception for him as well. The Aeronautical Society unanimously backed his petition, and its president wrote that Chambers was "principally responsible for the present progressive policy of the Navy" in aviation. Other aeronautic organizations also chimed in to support Chambers. Philip Andrews confirmed that the navy pulled Chambers from the *Louisiana* because of his "well known technical knowledge," and his importance to the "Meyer organization."[14] On March 9, 1914, Senator James A. Reed introduced Senate Bill 4623 "to Restore to the Active Duty List of the Navy for Special Duty Captain W. I. Chambers, USN Retired." It died in committee.

## Aviation in 1914

The following month, naval aviation received its first taste of combat. The Wilson administration, concerned about the civil war in Mexico, had concentrated a growing number of warships off Mexico's coast under the command of Chambers's friend Rear Admiral Henry T. Mayo. In April, Mayo demanded an apology and a twenty-one-gun salute from Mexico following the detention of several American sailors in Tampico. The local governor agreed to the apology but not the salute. The arrival at Veracruz of the German steamer *Ypiranga* loaded with arms and ammunition brought the crisis to a head. President Wilson ordered the navy to occupy the Veracruz customs house and seize the arms shipment. The navy ordered Towers and Patrick Bellinger, commanding the 1st and 2nd Aeroplane Squadrons of two planes each, to support the landing. The aviators flew reconnaissance patrols over the area, observed troop movements, and helped direct artillery fire in the confused street battle that followed the landing of 4,000 sailors and marines. Admiral Frank Fletcher commended their work.[15]

On July 1, 1914, Fiske succeeded in establishing the Office of Naval Aeronautics under his Division of Operations and placed Bristol in charge of it. Like Chambers, Bristol found himself bogged down with paperwork, but he did get one clerk to assist him. Fiske ignored Chambers's recommendations for more administrative officers, especially for the Pensacola Naval Air Station. The senior aviator there continued to handle all administrative details in addition to training new pilots and other aviation work. Chambers briefly commanded naval aviation again in October while Bristol observed the army's aviators on the West Coast. On his return in November, Bristol officially assumed the title of Director of Naval Aviation.[16]

The success of the aviators at Veracruz along with the outbreak of war in Europe encouraged Bristol to push Daniels and Congress to fund the Chambers Board's proposals. Supported by Fiske, Bristol requested two planes for each of the navy's sixteen battleships. After careful lobbying, he managed to get $1 million added to the naval appropriation for 1915. He also secured congressional support for the aeronautical advisory committee that would become the NACA the following year. The first shipboard launch from Chambers's catapult that November underlined aviation's readiness for fleet deployment. Chambers's dreams for aviation were finally coming true.

Fiske, meanwhile, continued his campaign to create the office of Chief of Naval Operations. He convinced Daniels of its importance and helped draft the legislation that created it, but was infuriated when Daniels chose relatively obscure Captain William S. Benson as the first Chief of Naval Operations on May 11, 1915. Daniels, tired of his constant quarrels with Fiske, appointed him president of the Naval War College in July to get him out of Washington. Fiske retired from the navy the following year.[17]

Bristol's Office of Naval Aeronautics, along with Chambers, moved from the now defunct Operations Divisions to the office of the Chief of Naval Operations. This should have strengthened the position of aviation, but Benson systematically stripped Bristol of his authority. While hostile to Chambers and bent on personal aggrandizement, Fiske had at least believed in and fought for naval aviation. Benson virtually ignored it. Bristol, who had no time at sea at the rank of captain, left aviation in March 1916 to command the *North Carolina* and its attached aircraft. He had no desire to share in Chambers's fate. Benson placed Lieutenant (j.g.) Clarence K. Bronson in charge of aviation until Towers returned from Britain that October and took charge. Benson remained apathetic in support of aviation until the United States entered World War I and even then failed to understand its importance.[18]

## Dwindling into Obscurity

In 1915, Chambers, Potts, and ten other plucked officers combined forces and again petitioned Congress for reinstatement into the navy with their seniority intact and the rank of admiral, which they would have attained had they not been plucked. They also pressed Congress to change the navy's promotion system. In an article that appeared in *The Navy,* Chambers condemned the plucking system and "the selfish scramble for promotion."[19] Congress, faced with numerous plucked officers with good records seeking reinstatement, voted to change the navy's promotion policy from seniority and plucking to selection on merit and authorized President Wilson to reinstate recently plucked officers. The navy, though, opposed reinstating any officers. Removing Congress from the promotion process had long been a goal of reform-minded officers. Having achieved it, they opposed any exceptions that would set a precedent for renewed congressional influence in officer promotion. Wilson, unwilling to involve himself in what he considered a navy matter, avoided the issue entirely.

Chambers redoubled his efforts at the next session of Congress, getting Fletcher (who had served on the plucking board) to support him. Fletcher wrote to Congress that "some very able officers were caught short of sea service." He argued that if "any officers are to be restored to the active list there is no one more entitled than Captain Chambers." Friends introduced another bill to reinstate Chambers in May, but Congress was determined to leave matters to the president. It again authorized Wilson to reinstate Chambers and the other petitioners, and Wilson again chose not to act. Chambers petitioned again on February 12, 1917, and yet again on April 7, 1917, expecting that Wilson would recall the plucked officers since the United States had declared war on Germany, but Wilson never reinstated any of them.[20]

By 1916, the navy had removed Chambers from the day-to-day operations of naval aviation. For a time, he had coordinated intelligence work on the British and French war effort. Then, given broad discretion to keep track of aeronautic research, he traveled the country visiting inventors and manufacturers, particularly Glenn Curtiss, and working on a number of his own projects. He spent a considerable amount of time investigating the orphans of American aeronautic research: dirigibles and helicopters. Chambers never had much confidence in the combat capabilities of dirigibles, believing that the "high speed of the aeroplane would seem to annul the useful employment of dirigibles." Their ability to hover and observe, though, would be particularly useful to the navy. The solution seemed to be the helicopter, or ornithopter as several inventors called it. Helicopters had other advantages as well. They could be easily based on board ship, requiring neither runways nor catapults. Unfortunately, as Chambers repeatedly complained, no one seemed able to make them work.[21]

Chambers spent several months in 1916 with ornithopter designer John O'Leary and his financial backers in Cohoes, New York. O'Leary's *Dragon Flyer* was one of the most ambitious designs of the time—a tilt-rotor vertical take-off airplane. Chambers had corresponded with O'Leary on and off through the years, making several suggestions to improve his design, but always remained dubious about his chances for success. As he wrote in his first letter to O'Leary, "the ill-success that has attended the many efforts in this direction hitherto, justify caution and a certain skepticism as to your immediate success." The navy had even less confidence in helicopters in these years and recalled Chambers from Cohoes to work in Washington. The project collapsed two years later following O'Leary's death. Chambers tried to help O'Leary's daughter salvage something from the project, but the *Dragon Flyer* had never been practical.[22]

Chambers continued to work on a variety of projects over the next two years, virtually ignored by the navy. In 1917, Admiral Benson complained that while Chambers had indicated he was "engaged in research and investigation of the science of naval aeronautics," he had "received from him no data upon which a judgment of his efforts in this line may be made." Chambers later complained that Benson had repeatedly promised to secure for him a solid place in the navy's bureaucracy with a recognized job title, but never made any effort to do so. Benson had no interest in aviation.[23]

Naval aviation expanded dramatically during World War I, from fifty-four planes to over two thousand, but Chambers's duties remained relegated to research. During the war, he developed a new motor, an improved hydraulic crane, and helped make several minor improvements to the navy's new seaplanes. He also resumed work on the aerial compass he had designed in 1912 and a drift indicator. Unfortunately, the standardization required for rapid production left little opportunity for the kinds of incremental improvements at which Chambers excelled. He bitterly complained to friends that the navy had made a serious mistake "in abandoning research entirely for standardization." By the end of the war, Chambers felt completely isolated. He avoided the officers club and the other haunts of his "so called brother officers," and pursued alone whatever project interested him. The navy finally relieved him of active duty on October 31, 1919.[24]

## Retirement

During his retirement, Chambers kept up with naval aviation. Admiral William A. Moffett consulted with Chambers before assuming command of naval aviation and corresponded with Chambers periodically. Bellinger and some of the other aviators from the early years visited Chambers at home, bringing him news of their successes but also of the constant battle for funding.[25]

Chambers was the guest of honor at numerous aviation meetings in the early 1920s, but the aviation community lost interest in him after he lost his influence on policy. For a time, he threw himself into writing music and poetry so as not to think about his "disgrace and avoid having it gnaw away at him." He managed to publish a few pieces, and also sent his work to friends as Christmas presents. Many of them expressed surprise at this, such as family friend F. Law Olmstead, who had never realized his "great gift in the direction of music and song." Chambers donated the proceeds of his poem "Belgium, Brave Belgium" to the Belgian relief effort in which he was active. He tried to market several of his inventions to manufacturers, most notably his aerial compass, but the collapse of the aviation market after the war made that impossible. He never managed to sell his compass despite the help of Richard Byrd and other friends in the aviation community.[26]

Over time, Chambers became increasingly bitter about both his plucking and Fiske's efforts to portray himself as an aeronautic visionary. When Fiske overstepped himself in enforcing his torpedo plane patent, he took his opportunity for a bit of revenge. In 1912, Fiske, working with retired naval officer and *Scientific American* editor Park Benjamin, filed for a patent on a device for dropping a torpedo from a plane. It was simply a release lever with a switch to arm the torpedo. They never built or tested the device, but on July 16, 1912, the Patent Office improperly awarded them a patent based on their sketches.[27] The navy ignored the device, and Fiske soon had bigger things on his mind. Other nations were also working on torpedo planes, and on July 28, 1914, the Royal Navy tested the first air-dropped torpedo. By the end of World War I, many nations had deployed torpedo planes.

During his retirement, Fiske worked to portray himself as a visionary martyred by Daniels and the Wilson administration, a prophet who had predicted the future of aviation and aerial warfare. As proof of this, he pointed to his 1911 proposal to the General Board to defend the Philippines with airplanes and his torpedo plane patent. On February 10, 1922, Fiske decided to exercise his patent. He demanded that the Bureau of Aeronautics pay him a $500 royalty for each torpedo plane the navy deployed.[28]

Aside from the obvious problems with the patent itself and Fiske's very broad claim to royalties, it was also questionable as to whether Fiske had the rights to it. He had developed it while on duty. Fiske spent the rest of the decade in and out of court fighting to collect his royalties. Harry C. Workman, the patent secretary of the Justice Department, investigated Fiske's claim and wrote to Chambers for information. Chambers responded that he did not recall Fiske "spending much time on aviation." He was always more concerned with his "schemes for advancement" and his patents than his duties as a naval officer. Chambers also pointed out, quite correctly, that dropping a torpedo from a plane was easy given an airplane powerful enough to carry it. Building a torpedo that would survive impact with the water and then proceed to its target was the hard part. Fiske had not solved any pressing technical problem.[29] In 1931, the Court of Appeals of the District of Columbia ruled against Fiske. He could not patent an idea, only a real, executed invention. The Supreme Court refused to hear the case and brought the long legal battle to a close.

By 1930, Chambers's health was failing and he decided to launch one last effort for promotion to admiral, this time on the retired list. The promotion of Richard E. Byrd to admiral on the retired list had established a precedent and Chambers hoped Congress would similarly reward him, expunging the stain of his plucking and finally recognizing him for his pioneering work in naval aviation. Chambers rallied a number of politicians and naval officers to his cause, including Senator Robert Wagner who introduced a bill to have him promoted. Admiral Moffett testified in support of Chambers's promotion, but Moffett's enemies in the navy opposed it on principle. The navy's senior leaders again opposed the bill, citing both the cost (an extra $1,500 a year for Chambers's pension) and the precedent it would set. What would prevent other officers from demanding promotions after their retirement? This bill, too, died in committee.[30]

Chambers regrouped from this defeat and tried one last time in 1932.

Wagner introduced a new bill, this time giving Chambers the promotion without the pay increase. Moffett again supported Chambers, as did Mark Bristol and Rear Admiral T. T. Craven, who had directed naval aviation at the close of World War I. Most importantly, Chief of the Bureau of Navigation Frank B. Upham, a former commander of the Pensacola Naval Air Station, reversed his position and supported the bill since it would not cost the navy any money. Unfortunately, the remainder of the navy's bureaucracy remained adamantly opposed to the promotion. Admiral William V. Pratt, the Chief of Naval Operations, believed it would set a bad precedent and testified to Congress that there was no evidence of inequity in Chambers's plucking. It "must be presumed that their [the plucking board's] action was just and equitable." In the midst of the hearings, Chambers's health failed. His wife continued the fight for him, but without success. The Committee of Naval Affairs rejected the bill.[31] Chambers's health deteriorated over the next year. He died on September 23, 1934, near Chillicothe, Ohio, while en route to Washington DC, for medical care. He was buried in Arlington National Cemetery four days later.

# Conclusion

Many officers worked to improve and modernize the U.S. Navy between the Civil War and World War I. Some focused on institutional reform, envisioning and creating the navy's new institutions and bureaucratic infrastructure. Other officers focused on improving the technology of the new fleet, investigating, testing, and reporting on a host of new weapons systems, technologies, and warship designs. Chambers did both. The new, modern navy required the work of both groups, and both groups of officers supported and benefited from the modernization and expansion of the fleet.

The interests of both institutional reformers and technological innovators often coincided, and their projects were frequently complementary. Technological innovators benefited from the data gathered and published by the Naval Institute, the Office of Naval Intelligence, and the other new institutions that supported the navy. Institutional reformers capitalized on the successes of the new navy and the rapid pace of technological change to push for more reform and for greater autonomy from civilian authority. The fastest progress came in projects that achieved broad support across both groups of officers. The best example of this was the all-big-gun battleship—a warship that merged the latest weapons systems and shipbuilding technologies with Mahanian strategic concepts. The all-big-gun battleship quickly achieved virtually unanimous support among line officers, and its opponents in the Construction Bureau gave way. A similar case can be made for the Panama Canal. It had long fascinated engineers with its scale and complexity, but it also offered great commercial and strategic possibilities. Virtually all naval officers agreed on its importance long before its construction.

In general, individual reformers tended to specialize in either new technology or institutional reform. Stephen B. Luce, Alfred Thayer Mahan, and Henry C. Taylor led the way in creating a new strategy and new strategic planning institutions for the navy, but they were often in the dark when it came to technology. Officers with a technological bent tended to enter the navy's engineering corps and focus their attentions there. The navy produced great engineers in these years including Francis Bowles, Holden C. Richardson, and David Taylor, but these officers rarely participated in strategic discussions.

Relatively few naval officers made important contributions as both technological innovators and institutional reformers. These included Bradley Fiske, William Sims, and Chambers. In particular, Chambers worked to ensure the compatibility of new strategic concepts with technological advances. It was a consistent pattern throughout his career demonstrated by his work at the Office of Naval Intelligence, his 1884 Prize Essay, his lectures and planning at the Naval War College, his numerous efforts to create compromise during internal navy debates on bureaucratic organization, and finally his guidance of the navy's infant aviation program. His interest in new technology, though, was paramount and colored his work as a reformer. Like many reformers in the Progressive Era, he took efficiency as his guiding principle. He hoped to rationalize technological, strategic, or administrative planning in the navy and clarify its organizational structure.

Chambers would be called an early adopter today—a person fascinated with new technology and eager to examine the latest products of scientists and inventors. He read widely and kept up with scientific developments. He also enjoyed the experimental process. He developed a number of inventions of his own and improved on those of others. Discerning and analytical, he excelled at assessing and refining the inventions of others. During his career, he made a host of minor improvements to numerous devices and made important contributions to torpedoes, ship design, and aviation.

Chambers took a pragmatic approach to technology, insisting that new technologies work. He refused to support incomplete inventions, and recommended only those he had thoroughly examined and tested. His friends commented that Chambers had "a longer vision of the future than most people," but it was a carefully considered vision.[1] He believed progress was the result of carefully taken and measured steps rather than sudden, revolutionary change. While individual inventors spurred this process from time to time with remarkable new devices, only careful, scientific research produced long-term results. Technological progress resulted from incremental evolution rather than radical revolution.

In his own inventive work, and especially in guiding aviation, Chambers insisted that new technologies be adapted to support existing doctrine. He avoided what historian Clark Reynolds has labeled "one of the great evils of modern machine warfare"—the "weapon dictating doctrine, rather than the reverse"—a common pitfall "to which advocates of new weapons have always been particularly susceptible."[2] While Chambers worked to perfect aviation technologically and determine its utility for combat and other missions, he kept it focused on scouting and artillery spotting, where it fit within existing doctrine. He expected doctrine to change as the navy integrated aircraft into the fleet and officers learned their capabilities. Chambers believed that educating his fellow officers about the benefits and potential of airplanes was critical to its success, and did everything he could to popularize aviation and demonstrate its capabilities.

Chambers became an active participant in the new educational institutions of the new, professional navy, including the Office of Naval Intelligence (1883–88), the Newport Torpedo Station (1898–99 and 1902–4), and the Naval War College (1892–93). He worked to educate not only himself, but his fellow officers as well. He studied history, strategy, and the other subjects valued by the founders of the Naval War College, as well as science and engineering. He joined the U.S. Naval Institute and several of the emerging professional engineering organizations. He came to see himself as both an engineer and a naval officer, and some of his fellow line officers came to regard him with the same suspicion they did the navy's engineering and construction officers.

Many of the navy's best technical minds left to pursue the greater opportunities offered by the private sector, but Chambers remained in the navy despite frequent frustrations. Even his forced retirement in 1913 did not drive him away. He voluntarily remained at work for six more years at little more than his retired pay. Chambers continued to hope for reinstatement during these years, but he also desperately wanted to ensure the place of aviation in the fleet. He remained convinced that the navy's future lay with the airplane, and he was willing to sacrifice his career to integrate aviation into the fleet. The strength of his commitment to aviation puzzled his friends, offended conservative officers, and frustrated those who sought to control aviation for their own ends. In his enduring commitment to the navy despite all the difficulties he encountered, Chambers epitomized the new professional officer the young Turks and their mentors had worked to create.

Chambers's conception of naval officership was at times quite romantic. As a young officer, he wanted a glorious career. It was in search of glory that he joined the Greely Relief Expedition and later fought for a shipboard assignment in the Spanish-American War. Over time, he seemed to find the glory he sought in bureaucratic battles. He challenged senior officers over ship design and navy yard administration. He fought for a number of causes including torpedoes, expanding the fleet, the Naval War College, and eventually aviation. Once committed to a cause, he fought for it without regard to the consequences to his career. At times, he seemed to actively pursue martyrdom. This could be tolerated in a young officer, but he still needed the protection of senior officers such as Mahan and Henry Taylor when he went too far.

The fight over the Naval War College dulled Chambers's taste for bureaucratic infighting, but he returned to his old habits when he took charge of naval aviation. He aggressively lobbied for change, regularly writing members of Congress and influential people to press his case and rally their support. He was willing to work around Admiral Wainwright and Secretary of the Navy Meyer to arrange Eugene Ely's flights and to get the support he needed to expand and improve naval aviation. Eventually, he even became willing to antagonize the Bureau of Construction and Repair on which he depended for airplane purchases.

Like most innovators and reformers, Chambers encountered resistance to his ideas throughout his career. When Chambers's technological vision coincided with that of the navy, his career went well. High-ranking officers supported his efforts and rewarded him with choice assignments. When he tried to push the navy too fast or into places it did not want to go, such as aviation, he encountered opposition. Many of his proposals and inventions, especially early in his career, were simply filed away and ignored. The navy isolated torpedoes and later submarines at the Newport Torpedo Station and ignored them. Torpedo tactics and practice never received the attention that gun target practice did. Other officers denigrated what Chambers sought to create and at times actively interfered with his work. Chambers's perseverance and technical expertise nullified the hostility of some of these officers. Francis Bunce and Francis Ramsay, for example, continued to rely on his knowledge of engineering and ship design even after the fight over the Naval War College. Sheer ability, though, could not win over all his enemies. In the end, his personal enemies united with those suspicious of aviation to use his lack of sea duty to terminate his career.

Aside from the pervasive conservatism of the officer corps, the navy's bureaus were often the greatest obstacles to innovation. Without their support innovation moved forward slowly, or not at all. The Bureau of Construction and Repair's opposition delayed the adoption of the all-big-gun battleship by several years. Even an already accepted idea or technology could be derailed by a power struggle over its placement within the navy's bureaucracy. Naval aviation faced these problems. Critics derided its military potential and effectiveness while its proponents fought over its control and placement within the navy's bureaucracy.

Over the course of his career, Chambers witnessed efforts at innovation both succeed and fail. He learned what worked both from his own mistakes and from his mentors. Successful innovators worked slowly, carefully building support for their ideas. All-out battles over policy, such as those instigated by Sims and Fiske, generally failed. Successful innovators and reformers popularized new technologies and methodologies while placating the defenders of the status quo. They presented new ideas or technologies in as nonthreatening a manner as possible, as Taylor presented first the Naval War College and then the General Board. Innovation in the navy was the result of long preparation and carefully arrived at consensus. It was a process of incremental evolution rather than radical revolution, a process that matched Chambers's conception of the steady, incremental advance of science and technology.

Successful innovators often emphasized the improvement of current capabilities rather than the development of completely new ones. Sims's introduction of continuous-aim firing succeeded not just because of the support of Theodore Roosevelt and its adoption by the Royal Navy, but also because of the relative ease with which the fleet could adopt it and its coherence with existing doctrine that emphasized battle-line gun duels. Submarines, in contrast, suffered because of their unique characteristics, which required a new style of warfare and a new doctrine for their effective employment. Aviation suffered from many of the same problems as submarines. They differed markedly from surface warships and were prone to fatal accidents. Most officers had great difficulty integrating these technological wonders into their conception of naval combat.

The introduction of aviation to the fleet proved the greatest challenge of Chambers's career. He may well have based his campaign to popularize aviation on Taylor's careful, decade-long campaign to create the General Board. He started small and built on his successes, using each success to lobby for just a little more support. He sought to mollify the navy's technophobes by repeatedly explaining that aircraft would not displace the navy's warships. Rather, airplanes would enhance their capabilities, making them more effective at their current role. Chambers carefully built up a network of supporters within Congress and courted people in positions of influence. He was particularly effective in rallying the aviation societies to support his initiatives, though the aviation community never influenced government to the extent that he hoped.

Chambers also worked to build support for aviation in the press, which avidly followed the adventures of early aviators. He had seen the press mobilized to support naval expansion during his time at the Office of Naval Intelligence, following the Greely Relief Expedition, and both for and against the Naval War College. Unlike many reformers of his generation, Chambers consistently portrayed the navy in a positive light when speaking to the press. He assumed that good publicity would lead to increased funding. Fiske and Sims took the opposite approach, believing that muckraking exposure would force the navy or the government to institute reforms. Even when U.S. naval aviation had fallen well behind the European powers, Chambers continued to emphasize the achievements of his small aviation group. Certainly, he asked for increased funding, but he never exposed the inner workings of the navy's bureaucracy to public scandal no matter how much it interfered with his efforts to expand naval aviation. Even after he was plucked, Chambers continued to report favorably on the progress of naval aviation.[3]

Chambers proved less effective in gaining support for aviation within the fleet. He was opposed both by those with little confidence in the technology, such as Wainwright and Meyer, and by those who sought to control it or add it to their personal empires, such as Watt and Fiske. Still, he managed to form a network of aviation supporters within the navy. Templin Potts, Frank

Fletcher, and a number of his old friends supported his work on aviation from his earliest days in command. Like Chambers, they were innovators and reformers who had finally risen to positions of influence. Chambers slowly managed to convince other officers of the importance of aviation, especially after the 1912 fleet maneuvers, but these tended to be younger officers. Among the older officers of the navy, especially those in positions of influence, Dewey was almost unique in believing in the future of aviation. He was also confident of Chambers's ability to successfully guide the navy's aviation program.

The Bureau of Construction and Repair and the Bureau of Engineering were already maneuvering for control of aviation when Meyer handed Chambers the aviation mail. Chambers had railed against the navy's convoluted bureau system early in his career and worked to rationalize its division of responsibilities while stationed at the New York Navy Yard. Over time, though, he found it easier to work with the bureaus than against them. This was particularly true after the battle to control ship design in 1903–5. Chambers argued for cooperation and for the creation of institutions that would coordinate the bureaus and ensure line officer input. He challenged the bureaus only if he saw no other option.

During Chambers's three years in charge of naval aviation, the bureaus constantly frustrated his efforts. Their refusal to support him in appropriations battles kept the aviation program small and starved of planes, personnel, and spare parts. Chambers tried to goad them into action and often worked around them to get what he needed. At first, he avoided direct confrontations with them. If the General Board backed by the Secretary of the Navy could not defeat the technical bureaus, what chance did a lone captain with virtually no authority have?

Chambers reversed this policy when he became convinced of the need for a national aeronautic research lab. He lobbied for it aggressively against the wishes of the Bureau of Construction and Repair, and refused to back down. Chambers needed to advance aviation to the point where its usefulness to the fleet was so obvious that no one could sensibly oppose it. Better planes were more important for this goal than more planes. He became increasingly critical of the bureaus during his last year in charge of aviation and condemned their inaction in his January 1913 testimony to Congress. Still, he kept his protests within narrow bounds, focused on appropriations and research. He never asked for the establishment of a separate aviation bureau. To do so would have launched an all-out war with the technical bureaus rather than the narrow, issue-focused battles he preferred and that he thought he could win. Instead, Chambers campaigned for the authority to coordinate bureau work on aviation and for the creation of a recognized and staffed office of naval aviation.

Reform is an ongoing process and successful reformers generally attract younger officers to carry on their work. The older generation of reformers that included Mahan and Taylor clearly selected Chambers to carry on their work, and like them, Chambers sought out young officers who would continue his aviation work. The question of his successor was one of his earliest concerns at aviation and it guided his selection of the navy's first pilots. His initial choices proved excellent. Theodore Ellyson, John Rodgers, and especially John Towers would all continue to make important contributions to aviation during their careers, though fatal crashes cut short the careers of Ellyson and Rodgers. Despite the termination of his own career, Chambers had ensured that others would carry on his work, though it would be some years until they achieved sufficient rank to influence policy.

Faced with growing opposition even from officers whose support he had expected, Chambers refused to back down. His successes in earlier bureaucratic battles may well have given him a false sense of confidence in fighting for aviation. He may also have expected more support from Dewey and the General Board than they could give. Chambers believed unwaveringly in the importance of aviation to the navy. Convinced that he was the best officer to lead the program through its early years, he was willing to risk promotion, and possibly his career, to see it through. In the end, he remained true to the advice that Mahan had given him twenty years before. He went down with his colors flying.

# Notes

## Introduction

1. Holden C. Richardson, "History of Naval Aviation," unpublished manuscript, 1923, 85–87, quoted in Paolo Coletta, *Patrick N. L. Bellinger and U.S. Naval Aviation* (Lanham, MD: University Press of America, 1987), 73.

2. Peter Karsten, "Armed Progressives," in *The Military in America from the Colonial Era to the Present,* ed. Karsten (New York: Free Press, 1980), 236.

## Chapter 1

1. Park Benjamin, *The United States Naval Academy: Being the Yarn of the American Midshipman* (New York: G. P. Putnam's, 1900), 254; W. D. Puleston, *Annapolis: Gangway to the Quarterdeck* (New York: D. Appleton-Century, 1942); James Russell Soley, *Historical Sketches of the United States Naval Academy* (Washington, DC: GPO, 1876); Jack Sweetman, *The U.S. Naval Academy: An Illustrated History* (Annapolis, MD: Naval Institute Press, 1979); and "Departments," U.S. Naval Institute's *Proceedings* (hereafter USNIP) 61 (October 1935): 1414–40.

2. The designation for Naval Academy students changed repeatedly in these years. For simplicity, I have used the term midshipmen to describe all students regardless of the date.

3. Frederick Sawyer, *Sons of Gunboats* (Annapolis, MD: U.S. Naval Institute, 1946), 17.

4. Chambers Journal, 1876–79, Chambers papers, Box 42; Benjamin, *Naval Academy,* 300.

5. Naval Academy, Register of Cadets; Peter Karsten, *The Naval Aristocracy: The*

*Golden Age of Annapolis and the Emergence of Modern American Navalism* (New York: Free Press, 1972), 7–16.

6. William F. Fullam, "The System of Naval Training and Discipline Required to Promote Efficiency and Attract Americans," USNIP 16 (1890): 481.

7. Chambers Journal, 1876–79; Menu, 1871, Chambers papers, Box 42; Benjamin, *Naval Academy,* 294.

8. Soley, *Historical Sketches of the United States Naval Academy,* 112–13.

9. Conduct Roles for 1871–72 and 1873–74, Naval Academy Archives; Benjamin, *Naval Academy,* 294; *Army and Navy Journal,* January 1, 1876.

10. Chambers Notebook, March 14, 1874, Chambers papers, Box 42; Tom [no last name] to Chambers, February 17, 1875, and Gymnastics Exhibition Announcements, both in Chambers papers, Box 5; Naval Academy Register, 1871–72 and 1872–73.

11. Albert Caldwell to father, quoted in Karsten, *Naval Aristocracy,* 37.

12. Naval Academy Annual Register, 1871–72 through 1875–76 (Washington, DC: GPO, 1872–76).

13. Journal of the Officer of the Day, January 10, 1873; Chambers Journal, 1873–76, Chambers papers, Box 41; Tom [no last name] to Chambers, February 17, 1875, Chambers papers, Box 5; Conduct Roles, 1873–76, Naval Academy Archives.

14. Sweetman, *U.S. Naval Academy,* 104; Karsten, *Naval Aristocracy,* 39; Robert Seager II, *Alfred Thayer Mahan: The Man and His Letters* (Annapolis, MD: Naval Institute Press, 1977), 119.

15. Chambers's classmate Albert B. Crittenden drew a knife and attacked another midshipman, Journal of the Officer of the Day, U.S. Naval Academy, February 13–15, 1872; William Green to Hunt Priddy, October 1, 1873, quoted in Karsten, *Naval Aristocracy,* 40.

16. *New York Times,* November 8, 1875; Worden to Board of Investigation, October 28, 1874, Hazing File, Naval Academy Archives; and R. L. Field, "The Black Midshipman at the U.S. Naval Academy," USNIP 100 (April 1978): 28–30.

17. Worden to E. J. Horton, Hazing File, Naval Academy Archives; Benjamin, *Naval Academy,* 287–90.

18. Naval Academy Conduct Role, 1872–73.

19. The other eighteen were: W. G. Cutler, G. D. Donnelly, H. W. Ford, G. C. Foulk, H. C. Gearing, E. C. Goss, A. L. Hall, Nicholas J. L. T. Halpine, W. G. Hammon, Richard Henderson, C. W. Horton, S. B. Mallory, R. T. Milligan, C. F. Pond, T. M. Potts, A. W. Rollins, F. H. Sherman, and W. L. Varnum.

20. Report of Board on Order of March 31, 1874, Hazing File, Naval Academy Archives.

21. Conduct Role, 1874; Journal of the Officer of the Day, April 1, 1874, and Report of Board on Order of March 31, 1874, Hazing File, Naval Academy Archives.

22. Benjamin, *Naval Academy,* 301; *Army and Navy Journal,* October 2, 1875; and Robert E. Coontz, *From the Mississippi to the Sea* (Philadelphia: Dorrance, 1930), 65.

23. Coontz, *From the Mississippi to the Sea,* 63 and 74; Paolo E. Coletta, *Admiral*

*Bradley A. Fiske and the American Navy* (Lawrence: Regents Press of Kansas, 1979), 5; Chambers Practice Logbooks, 1872 and 1873, Chambers papers, Box 41.

24. Chambers Notebook, 1876, and Practice Logbook, 1874, Chambers papers, Boxes 41 and 42.

25. Chambers Practice Logbooks, 1872 and 1873, Chambers papers, Box 41.

26. *New York Times,* October 3, 1884.

27. Coontz, *From the Mississippi to the Sea,* 73; Hop Announcements, Chambers papers, Box 5; Chambers Notebook, 1875–76, Chambers papers, Box 42. The other members of the hop committee were D. R. Case, A. E. Jardine, Walter McLean, R. T. Mulligan, J. T. Newton, R. C. Ray, C. G. Rodgers, and B. S. Tappan.

28. Stephen Howarth, *To Shining Sea: A History of the United States Navy, 1775–1994* (New York: Random House, 1991), 216; Sean Dennis Cashman, *America in the Gilded Age* (New York: New York University Press, 1984), 10–11; Journal of the Officer of the Day, U.S. Naval Academy, June 6, 1876.

## Chapter 2

1. Bureau of Navigation to Chambers, October 20, 1876, Chambers papers, Box 1; Chambers Journal, 1876–79, Chambers papers, Box 42.

2. Chambers Journal, 1876–79, Chambers papers, Box 42.

3. Ibid.

4. Chambers to parents, November 25, 1876, Chambers papers, Box 5; and Chambers Journal, 1876–79, Chambers papers, Box 42. Some pages are torn from Chambers's journal, so it is impossible to say more about this relationship.

5. Chambers to parents, January 13, 1877, Chambers papers, Box 5.

6. Chambers to parents, December 26, 1876, Chambers papers, Box 5; Logbook *Pensacola,* National Archives, Record Group (hereafter cited as NARG) 24.

7. Chambers to parents, January 13, 1877, Chambers papers, Box 5.

8. Chambers to parents, November 25 and December 26, 1876, Chambers papers, Box 5.

9. George Foulk to Chambers, December 28, 1883, Chambers papers, Box 5.

10. Chambers Journal, *Pensacola,* Chambers papers, Box 42; Logbook *Pensacola,* NARG 24.

11. Chambers to parents, December 26, 1876 and April 12, 1877, Chambers papers, Box 5.

12. Chambers to parents, December 26, 1876, Chambers papers, Box 5.

13. Chambers to Irwin, February 19, 1877, Chambers papers, Box 1.

14. Chambers to parents, April 12 and May 8, 1877, Chambers papers, Box 5.

15. Ibid.

16. Chambers Journal, 1877, Chambers papers, Box 42; Irwin to Secretary of the Navy Thompson, October 8, 1877, Chambers papers, Box 1.

17. Chambers to Ammen, September 1, 1877; Ammen to Chambers, September 15,

1878; and Bureau of Navigation to Chambers, September 20, 1877, Chambers papers, Box 1.

18. Caspar Goodrich, *Rope Yarns from the Old Navy* (New York: Naval History Society, 1931), 84.

19. Farquhar to Thompson, March 6, 1878, Chambers papers, Box 1; Logbook *Portsmouth,* NARG 24.

20. *New York Times,* March 12, 1878, 4.

21. *London Times,* August 22, 1878; *New York Times,* July 7 and 12, September 2 and 9, and October 22, 1878; Chambers Journal, 1876–79, Chambers papers, Box 42; Jeffery Dorwart, *The Office of Naval Intelligence* (Annapolis, MD: Naval Institute Press, 1979), 15–20.

22. Chambers to parents, February 13, 1878, Chambers papers, Box 5; Logbook *Portsmouth,* NARG 24.

23. McNair to Thompson, August 21, 1878, and Crowninshield to Thompson, December 21, 1878, Chambers papers, Box 1.

24. Hugh Rodman, *Yarns of a Kentucky Admiral* (Indianapolis: Bobbs-Merrill, 1928), 44; and Peter Karsten, "No Room for Young Turks?" USNIP 99 (March 1973): 37–50.

25. *Congressional Record,* 48th Cong., 2d sess., February 23, 1885, 2044.

26. J. W. King, *The War-Ships and Navies of the World* (Washington, DC: GPO, 1880; reprint, Annapolis, MD: Naval Institute Press, 1982), 394; Donald L. Canney, *The Old Steam Navy: Frigates, Sloops, and Gunboats* (Annapolis, MD: Naval Institute Press, 1990).

27. Bunce to Whitney, December 12, 1885, Chambers papers, Box 1.

28. Goodrich, *Rope Yarns,* 65–66; Chambers Journal, 1876–1879, Chambers papers, Box 42; Chambers to Bureau of Ordnance, June 10, 1879 and June 24, 1879, Chambers papers, Box 1.

29. Chambers, Notes on the *Hiawatha,* Chambers papers, Box 34.

30. Sicard to Chambers, November 9, 1881, and Chambers to Sicard, September 4, 1881 and June 27, 1882, Chambers papers, Box 1; Chambers, "A Modified Monitor, with a New Method for Mounting and Working the Guns," USNIP 7 (1881): 437–46.

31. Bunce to Whitney, December 12, 1885, Chambers papers, Box 1.

32. Chambers, "Rescue of the *Trinity*'s Crew," USNIP 9 (1883): 121; and Logbook *Marion,* NARG 24.

33. Chambers to Walker, August 4, 1882, Walker to Chambers, October 16, 1882, and Terry to the Secretary of the Navy, December 11, 1885, Chambers papers, Box 1; Robert G. Angevine, "The Rise and Fall of the Office of Naval Intelligence," *Journal of Military History* 62 (April 1998): 291–312; Dorwart, *Office of Naval Intelligence,* 17.

34. Oliver to Chambers, May 5, 1882, Chambers papers, Box 1.

35. Chambers, "Reconstruction and Increase of the Navy," USNIP 11 (1885): 41–42; Buckingham to Chambers, February 2, 1883 and April 1, 1883, Chambers papers, Box 5; Sicard to Chambers, January 10, 1883, and Mason to Chambers, December 9, 1882 and February 9, 1883, Chambers papers, Box 1.

## Chapter 3

1. Buckingham to Chambers, April 1, 1883 and September 1, 1883, Chambers papers, Box 5; Mason to Chambers, January 9, 1883, Chambers papers, Box 1.

2. For more on the *Jeannette* Expedition see Edward Ellsburg, *Hell on Ice: The Saga of the "Jeannette"* (New York: Dodd, Mead, 1938); George Melville, *In the Lena Delta* (Boston: Houghton Mifflin, 1892); Raymond Lee Newcomb, ed., *Our Lost Explorers: The Narratives of the "Jeannette" Arctic Expedition as Related by the Survivors and Last Journals of Lieutenant De Long* (Hartford and San Francisco: American Publishing and A. L. Bancroft, 1884).

3. John E. Caswell, *Arctic Frontiers: United States Explorations in the Far North* (Norman: University of Oklahoma Press, 1956), 96–98.

4. Winfield Scott Schley and J. R. Soley, *The Rescue of Greely* (New York: Scribner's, 1885), 23.

5. Caswell, *Arctic Frontiers,* 106–8; David G. Colwell, "The Navy and Greely: The Rescue of the 1881–1884 Arctic Expedition," USNIP 84 (January 1958): 71–79; Winfield Scott Schley, *Forty-Five Years under the Flag* (New York: Appleton, 1904), 144–45.

6. William H. Goetzmann, *New Lands, New Men: America and the Second Great Age of Discovery* (New York: Viking, 1986), 433; David Wragg, *Wings over the Sea* (New York: Arco, 1979), 9; James M. Merrill, "The Greely Relief Expedition, 1884," USNIP 77 (September 1951): 971; Schley, *Forty-Five Years,* 148; and *New York Herald,* August 5, 1884, 5.

7. Schley and Soley, *Rescue of Greely,* 155; *New York Times,* March 18, 1884 and March 19, 1884.

8. Schley to Chambers, April 25, 1884, Chambers papers, Box 1; William A. Kirkland to Bureau of Navigation, April 14, 1884, NARG 181; and Schley and Soley, *Rescue of Greely,* 155.

9. Chambers Journal, 1884–85, Chambers papers, Box 42.

10. Ibid.; Schley and Soley, *Rescue of Greely,* 153–54; Winfield Scott Schley, *Report of Winfield S. Schley: Commanding Greely Relief Expedition of 1884* (Washington, DC: GPO, 1887), 27–28.

11. Logbook *Thetis,* NARG 24.

12. *New York Herald,* July 27, 1885, 8; and Logbook *Thetis,* NARG 24.

13. Schley, *Forty-Five Years,* 150–51.

14. Schley and Soley, *Rescue of Greely,* 165–66; and Schley, *Forty-Five Years,* 150–59.

15. Logbook *Thetis,* NARG 24.

16. Chambers Journal, 1884, Chambers papers, Box 42; Schley, *Report of the Greely Relief Expedition,* 72.

17. Albert Gleaves, *The Life of an American Sailor: Rear Admiral William Hemsley Emory* (New York: George H. Doran, 1923), 66.

18. Chambers, "Reconstruction and Increase of the Navy," Discussion, 74.

19. *New York Herald,* July 27, 1885, 8.

20. Unknown newspaper clippings, Chambers papers, Box 42.

21. Richard S. West, *Admirals of American Empire* (Indianapolis: Bobbs-Merrill, 1948), 113.

22. Mark Russell Shulman, *Navalism and the Emergence of American Sea Power* (Annapolis, MD: Naval Institute Press, 1995), 32, 52–54; *New York Times,* December 19 and 20, 1884, and April 18 and 20, 1885.

23. William A. McGinley, *Reception of Lt. A. W. Greely, U.S.A., and His Comrades, and of the Arctic Relief Expedition, at Portsmouth, N.H.* (Washington, DC: GPO, 1884), 45.

24. Schley, *Report of the Greely Relief Expedition,* 73; Schley to Whitney, December 19, 1885, Chambers papers, Box 1.

25. Clarence G. Lasby, "Science and the Military," in *Science and Society in the United States,* ed. David D. Van Tassel and Michael G. Hall, 256–58 (Homewood, IL: Dorsey Press, 1966).

26. Goetzmann, *New Lands, New Men,* 445.

## Chapter 4

1. Frederick C. Drake, *The Empire of the Seas: A Biography of Rear Admiral Robert Wilson Shufeldt, USN* (Honolulu: University of Hawai'i Press, 1984), 147–55; Jackson Crowell, "The United States and a Central American Canal, 1869–1877," *Hispanic American Historical Review* 49 (1969): 27–52.

2. Daniel Ammen, "Inter-Oceanic Ship-Canal across the American Isthmus," *American Geographical Society Bulletin No. 3* (1878): 142–62, and *The American Inter-Oceanic Ship Canal Question* (Philadelphia: Hamersly, 1880).

3. Drake, *Empire of the Seas,* 35, 135–41, 151–52, 396–97; Thomas O. Selfridge, *What Finer Tradition: The Memoirs of Thomas O. Selfridge, Jr., Rear Admiral, USN* (Columbia: University of South Carolina Press, 1987), 255; *Survey of the Darien Canal Routes,* House Miscellaneous Document 113, 42nd Cong., 3d sess.; Gerstle Mack, *The Land Divided: A History of the Panama Canal and Other Isthmian Canal Projects* (New York: Alfred A. Knopf, 1944), 210–11; and Senate Executive Document 15, 46th Cong., 1st sess., 1–2. Lull's final report is *The Nicaragua Canal,* Senate Executive Document 57, 43rd Cong., 1st sess.

4. J. Fred Rippy, "Justo Rufino Barrios and the Nicaraguan Canal," *Hispanic American Historical Review* 13 (1930): 190–97.

5. Representative Finerty, March 1, 1884, *Congressional Record,* 48th Cong., 1st sess., 1534; Shufeldt to the editor of the *Nautical Gazette,* 1874, quoted in Drake, *Empire of the Seas,* 152; and Dexter Perkins, *The History of the Monroe Doctrine* (Boston: Little, Brown, 1963), 163.

6. Aniceto G. Menocal, "Discussion upon Inter-Oceanic Canal Projects," *American Society of Civil Engineers Transactions* 9 (November 1880): 429–46.

7. Mack, *Land Divided,* 214.

8. James D. Richardson, *Compilation of the Messages and Papers of the Presidents, 1789–1897* (Washington, DC: GPO, 1899), 8:257–58.

9. William H. Hobbs, *Peary* (New York: Macmillan, 1936).

10. Chambers to Chandler, January 9, 1885, Chandler papers; Chambers Journal, 1884–85, Chambers papers, Box 42.

11. Kenneth Hagan, *American Gunboat Diplomacy and the Old Navy, 1877–1889* (Westport, CT: Greenwood Press, 1973), 156–57; Chambers to Chandler, October 15, 1884, and Chandler to Chambers, December 15, 1884, Chandler papers, Box 72; and "Reports of Naval Officers on Panama Canal," Senate Executive Document 123, 48th Cong., 1st sess.

12. Chambers Journal, 1885, Chambers papers, Box 42.

13. *Report of the U.S. Nicaragua Surveying Party, 1885,* Senate Executive Document 99, 49th Cong., 1st sess., 20.

14. *Report of the U.S. Nicaragua Surveying Party,* 1–14.

15. Chambers, "Notes on the Nicaragua Ship Canal, as Relocated and Revised by the U.S. Surveying Expedition of 1855," USNIP 11 (1885): 807–8; Menocal to Chambers, February 28 and April 13, 1885, Chambers papers, Box 1; John Edward Weems, *Peary the Explorer and the Man* (Boston: Houghton Mifflin, 1967), 50–55; Chambers Journal, February 11, 1885, Chambers papers, Box 42.

16. Chambers Journal, February 6–24, 1885, Chambers papers, Box 42.

17. *Report of the U.S. Nicaragua Surveying Party, 1885,* Senate Executive Document 99, 49th Cong., 1st sess., 12, 14–21; Chambers Journal, March 29, 1885, Chambers papers, Box 42.

18. Chambers, "Notes on the Nicaragua Ship Canal," 809–14; *Report of the U.S. Nicaragua Surveying Party,* 40; R. P. Rodgers to Menocal, October 2, 1885, Chambers papers, Box 1.

19. *Report of the U.S. Nicaragua Surveying Party,* 40–41.

20. *Papers Relating to the Foreign Relations of the United States, 1885* (Washington, DC: GPO, 1931), v–vi.

21. House Report 3035, 51st Cong., 1st sess.

22. Thomas B. Atkins, *The Interoceanic Canal across Nicaragua and the Attitude toward It of the Government of the United States* (New York: New York Printing Co., 1890); The Nicaragua Canal Construction Company, *Annual Report,* 1890 and 1891; and Chambers, "National Importance of a Canal," Chambers papers, Box 30.

23. Chambers, "National Importance of a Canal"; Josiah Strong, *Our Country: Its Possible Future and Its Present Crisis* (New York: American Home Missionary Society, 1885), 29; Walter LaFeber, *The New Empire* (Ithaca, NY: Cornell University Press, 1963), 70–79.

24. Henry C. Taylor, "The Control of the Pacific," *Forum* 3 (June 1887): 416; and C. H. Stockton, "The Inter-Oceanic Canal," USNIP 25 (December 1899): 753–97.

## Chapter 5

1. Thomas Hunt, *The Life of William Henry Hunt* (Brattleboro, VT: E. L. Hildreth, 1922); Secretary of the Navy Annual Report (hereafter cited as SONAR), 1881, 5.

2. Angevine, "The Rise and Fall of the Office of Naval Intelligence," 297.

3. SONAR, 1882, 107–8.

4. Dorwart, *Office of Naval Intelligence,* 16; C. C. Rogers, "Naval Intelligence," USNIP 9 (1883): 659–92.

5. Wyman H. Packard, *A Century of Naval Intelligence* (Washington, DC: ONI and NHC, 1996), 3.

6. James Robert Green, "The First Sixty Years of the Office of Naval Intelligence" (master's thesis, American University, 1963), 13; Dorwart, *Office of Naval Intelligence,* 15; Packard, *Century of Naval Intelligence,* 158.

7. Angevine, "The Rise and Fall of the Office of Naval Intelligence," 299; Index to Register of the Office of Naval Intelligence, July 1882–December 31, 1885, NARG 38; Packard, *Century of Naval Intelligence,* 40; and F. T. Bowles, "Our New Cruisers," USNIP 9 (1883): 627–31.

8. Albert P. Niblack, *History and Aims of the Office of Naval Intelligence* (Washington, DC: GPO, 1920); Green, "The First Sixty Years of the Office of Naval Intelligence," 17–18; Packard, *Century of Naval Intelligence,* 5.

9. Register of Personnel of the ONI, NARG 38.

10. Dorwart, *Office of Naval Intelligence,* 22.

11. Foulk to Chambers, March 13, 1886, Chambers papers, Box 5; Tyler Dennett, "Early American Policy in Korea, 1883–1887: The Services of Lieutenant George T. Foulk," *Political Science Quarterly* 37 (1923): 82–103; Angevine, "Rise and Fall of the Office of Naval Intelligence," 305; Dorwart, *Office of Naval Intelligence,* 32–34.

12. Sicard to Chambers, July 3, 1883, Chambers papers, Box 1; Chambers to the West Point Foundry Association, October 5, 1883, Chambers papers, Box 5.

13. Chambers to the West Point Foundry Association, October 5, 1883, and West Point Foundry Association to Chambers, October 10, 1883, Chambers papers, Box 5; Chambers to Chandler, February 8, 1884, Chambers papers, Box 1; Chambers to Billy [no last name], March 19 and March 22, 1884, Chambers to Commissioner of Patents, February 29, 1884, and Commissioner of Patents to Chambers, March 3, 1884, all in Chambers papers, Box 5.

14. James Howden to Chambers, February 12, 1884, Chambers papers, Box 5.

15. See Charles Belknap, "The Naval Policy of the United States" [1880 Prize Essay], USNIP 6 (1880): 375–91; Edward W. Very, "The Type of (I) Armored Vessel, (II) Cruiser, Best Suited to the Present Needs of the United States" [1881 Prize Essay], USNIP 7 (1881): 43–83; and J. D. J. Kelley, "Our Merchant Marine: The Causes of Its Decline, and the Means to Be Taken for Its Revival" [1882 Prize Essay], USNIP 8 (1882): 3–47.

16. Chambers, "Reconstruction and Increase of the Navy," 58.

17. Ibid., 12.

18. Robert Seager II, "Ten Years before Mahan," *Mississippi Valley Historical Review* 40 (December 1953): 491–512.

19. Chambers, "Reconstruction and Increase of the Navy," 35–36; United States Senate, *Report of the Select Committee on Ordnance and War Ships* (Washington, DC: GPO, 1886); SONAR, 1881, 31.

20. Chambers, "Reconstruction and Increase of the Navy," 40–41.

21. Ibid., 52.

22. Caspar Goodrich, "Discussion of Reconstruction and Increase of the Navy," USNIP 11 (1885): 68; Foulk to Chambers, September 11, 1884 and March 13, 1886, Chambers papers, Box 5.

23. Dorwart, *Office of Naval Intelligence,* 21; Register of Personnel of the Office of Naval Intelligence, NARG 38; and General Information Series Numbers V, VI, and VII (Washington, DC: GPO, 1885–88).

24. Packard, *Century of Naval Intelligence,* 4–5, 40, 317.

25. Very to Chambers, February 11 and June 23, 1885, and William A. Fredenburgh to Chambers, September 7, 1886, Chambers papers, Box 5.

26. Munson & Phillips to Chambers, April 1, June 27, and July 25, 1885, and Weeks to Chambers, August 3 and August 11, 1885, Chambers papers, Box 5; and U.S. Patent 328919.

27. Rodgers to Chambers, May 2, 1888, Chambers papers, Box 1; Chambers to Hotchkiss, March 24, 1888, Chambers papers, Box 5.

28. Bowles to Chambers, September 13, 1886, and Charles Henige to Chambers, September 15, 1886, Chambers papers, Box 5.

29. Draft plans of the *Iowa* and *Ohio,* Chambers papers, Boxes 33 and 34.

30. Naval Advisory Board to Chambers, August 12, 1887, and Chambers to Whitney, June 18, 1887, Chambers papers, Box 1.

31. William E. Stillings to Chambers, February 8, 1887 and March 2, 1887; Howden to Chambers, September 6, 1887; J. D. J. Kelley to Chambers June 29, 1887, all in Chambers papers, Box 5.

32. Chambers to the editor of the *Army and Navy Journal,* undated, 1887, Chambers papers, Box 5.

33. Chambers to Whitney, June 18, July 13, and September 30, 1887, and Whitney to Chambers, July 12 and October 15, 1887, Chambers papers, Box 1.

34. Gherardi to Chambers, April 26, 1888, Henige to Chambers, April 26, 1888, and Patterson to Chambers, June 13, 1886, Chambers papers, Boxes 1 and 5.

35. R. P. Rodgers to Chambers, April 25, 1888, Chambers papers, Box 1.

## Chapter 6

1. SONAR, 1892, 49; Mark D. Hirsch, *William C. Whitney, Modern Warwick* (New York: Dodd, Mead, 1948), 264.

2. Leonard D. White, *The Republican Era* (New York: Macmillan, 1958), 162; SONAR, 1883, 117; and Leon Burr Richardson, *William E. Chandler, Republican* (New York: Dodd, Mead, 1940), 309.

3. Captain S. Norton to the Board on Navy Yard Organization, July 2, 1891, NARG 40, item 186.

4. Charles Oscar Paullin, *Paullin's History of Naval Administration, 1775–1911* (Annapolis, MD: U.S. Naval Institute, 1968), 180; and Porter to Luce, quoted in Walter R.

Herrick, *The American Naval Revolution* (Baton Rouge: Louisiana State University Press), 46.

5. Henige to Chambers, May 1, May 16, and July 4, 1888, Chambers papers, Boxes 1 and 5.

6. Rodgers to Chambers, January 26, 1889; Coudert Brothers to Chambers, March 9 and October 24, 1889, and Coudert Brothers to Tracy, September 3, 1889; Chambers to the editor, *New York Herald,* June 14, 1891; John F. Stickly to Chambers, July 14, 1890 and October 23, 1891; James Gordon Bennett to Chambers, June 16, 1891, all in Chambers papers, Boxes 1 and 5.

7. Chambers, "Responsibilities of Commandant in Building the *Maine,*" undated 1888, Chambers papers, Box 30; and "Report of the Investigating Board," undated 1888, NARG 181.

8. For the conflicting versions of this story see Leonard Swann, *John Roach, Maritime Entrepreneur* (Annapolis, MD: Naval Institute Press, 1965), 185–208; Richardson, *William E. Chandler, Republican,* 290–95; and Hirsch, *William C. Whitney, Modern Warwick,* 274–88.

9. Chadwick to Ramsay, April 2, 1889 and June 17, 1889, NARG 181.

10. Chief of the Bureau of Ordnance (Sicard) to Gherardi, December 29, 1888, NARG 181. Bradley Fiske, then overseeing the installation of ordnance on the *Atlanta,* approved their work. Coletta, *Admiral Bradley A. Fiske,* 19–22.

11. Chambers, "Responsibilities of Commandant in Building the Maine," undated 1888, Chambers papers, Box 30.

12. Monte Calvert, *The Mechanical Engineer in America, 1830–1910* (Baltimore, MD: Johns Hopkins Press, 1967); and Henige to Chambers, February 2, November 16, and November 25, 1888, Chambers papers, Box 5. Chambers and Henige frequently used people's initials when discussing them in their letters.

13. Pook to Gherardi, June 7, 1888, NARG 181; Henige to Chambers, May 11, 1888, Chambers papers, Box 1.

14. Henige to Chambers, November 25, 1888, Chambers papers, Box 5; *New York Times,* December 18, 1888, 2.

15. Henige to Chambers, February 2 and November 25, 1888, Chambers papers, Box 5.

16. Ramsay to Chief of Construction Bureau, January 21, 1889, NARG 181; *New York Times,* June 17, 1889, 4.

17. Tracy to Ramsay, April 20, 22, and 23, May 13, and July 26, 1889, NARG 181; Ramsay to Head of the Department of Steam Engineering, March 12, 1889, NARG 181; Tracy's efforts to please both reformers and the spoilsmen are described in Benjamin Franklin Cooling, *Benjamin Franklin Tracy: Father of the Modern American Fighting Navy* (Hamden, CT: Archon Books, 1973).

18. *New York Times,* June 24, 1889, 4; Ramsay, "Memo to All Yard Officers," undated, NARG 181.

19. Ramsay to Chambers, April 20, 1889 and April 24, 1889, NARG 181.

20. Ramsay to Jos. W. Kay, Chairman of Veteran Rights Union, June 4, 1889; Ram-

say to John Buchanan April 25, 1889; Ramsay to unknown job applicant, April 17, 1889; and Tracy to Sicard, October 12, 1889, all in NARG 181.

21. Orders to Board Relating to Navy Yard Organization and Examinations at Various Navy Yards, NARG 80; SONAR 1892, 51.

22. NARG 80, item 184; Charles Bandle to Tracy, September 5, 1889, quoted in Herrick, *American Naval Revolution,* 46–47; SONAR 1892, 52–3.

23. Ramsay to Department Heads, March 2, April 15, and May 6, 1889, NARG 181.

24. Ramsay to Thomas Reynolds, April 20, 1889, NARG 181.

25. Ramsay to Commandant of Boston Navy Yard, August 5, 1889, NARG 181.

26. Chambers to Ramsay, May 10, 1889, Chambers papers, Box 1; Chambers to Mason, undated draft, 1888–89, Chambers papers, Box 5.

27. Chambers, "Progressive Improvement at the Navy Yard," Chambers papers, Box 30; Chambers, "Reconstruction and Increase of the Navy," 57.

28. Tracy to Ramsay, May 28, 1889; "Inventory and Appraisement of Property," March 1, 1889; Chief Engineer H. Smith Craven to Ramsay, September 13, 1889, all in NARG 181.

29. Henige to Chambers, November 25, 1888, Chambers papers, Box 5; and Tracy to Ramsay, June 20, 1889, and Ramsay to Chambers, June 22, 1889, Chambers papers, Box 1.

30. Chambers to Ramsay, February 20, May 31, and August 7, 1889, and Ramsay to Chambers, May 31, 1889, Chambers papers, Box 1; Chambers, "Report on Navy Yard Improvements," May 10, 1889, Chambers papers, Box 30.

31. Gherardi to the Secretary of the Navy, June 3, 1891, NARG 24; Ramsay to the Secretary of the Navy, June 9, 1891, NARG 24; Ramsay to Chambers, December 10, 1889, Chambers papers, Box 1.

32. Paullin, *History of Naval Administration,* 396; Chambers, "General Notes on Consolidation of Navy Yards," undated circa 1900, Chambers papers, Box 30.

## Chapter 7

1. Daniel H. Wicks, "The First Cruise of the Squadron of Evolution," *Military Affairs* 44 (1980): 64–68.

2. *New York Times,* May 26, 1890, 5; Wicks, "The First Cruise of the Squadron of Evolution," 67.

3. Frank M. Bennett, *The Steam Navy of the United States* (Pittsburgh: Warren, 1896), 789; *New York Times,* November 10, 1890; John D. Alden, *The American Steel Navy* (Annapolis, MD: Naval Institute Press, 1972), 39–42.

4. Logbook *Petrel,* NARG 24.

5. Ibid.

6. Ibid.; *New York Times,* November 10, 1890, 2.

7. John M. Ellicott, "Three Navy Cranks and What They Turned," USNIP 51 (October 1924): 1617–18; *New York Times,* June 13, 1890, 8.

8. Logbook *Petrel,* NARG 24, *New York Times,* May 25, 1891, 2.

9. Brownson to Bureau of Navigation, June 4, 1891, Chambers papers, Box 1.

10. *New York Times,* October 14 and 16, 1891.

11. Ibid., October 16 and 17, 1891.

12. Logbook *Atlanta,* NARG 24.

13. Chambers, 1892 memorandum, Chambers papers, Box 1; Chambers Fitness Reports, NARG 24; J. D. J. Kelley to Chambers, October 31, 1892, Chambers papers, Box 1; James Gordon Bennett to Chambers, June 16, 1891 and October 23, 1891, Chambers to the editor of the *New York Herald,* June 14, 1891, and Robert Bridges to Chambers, November 14, 1891, all in Chambers papers, Box 5.

14. Walker to Chambers, April 26, 1892, and Higginson to Chambers, September 11, 1892, Chambers papers, Box 1; *Atlanta* and *Chicago* Logbooks, NARG 24

15. Mahan to Chambers, July 27, 1892, in Robert Seager II and Doris D. Maguire, eds., *The Letters and Papers of Alfred Thayer Mahan* (Annapolis, MD: Naval Institute Press, 1975), hereafter LPATM; Higginson to Chambers, October 4, 1893, Chambers papers, Box 1; and Chambers Fitness Report, 1892, NARG 24.

## Chapter 8

1. SONAR, 1885, 114; Ronald Spector, *Professors of War: The Naval War College and the Development of the Naval Profession* (Newport, RI: Naval War College Press, 1977), 21.

2. Ramsay to Taylor, September 13, 1893, quoted in Spector, *Professors of War,* 66; Seager, *Mahan,* 221–22.

3. SONAR, 1889, 4.

4. Seager, *Mahan,* 193.

5. Mahan to Chambers, July 27, 1892, LPATM.

6. Ibid.

7. Aside from Chambers and Mayo, the students that year were commanders C. H. Davis, and M. L. Johnson; lieutenant commanders R. E. Impey, and L. C. Logan; lieutenants J. H. Bull, G. A. Calhoun, W. P. Day, L. C. Heilner, J. C. Irvine, J. L. Purcell, J. A. Rodgers, E. H. Tillman, F. H. Tyler, B. T. Walling, W. P. White, and J. C. Wilson; and ensigns Philip Andrews, C. B. Brittain, W. H. G. Bullard, H. K. Hines, and N. A. McCully.

8. Opening Address, 1892, Naval War College Archives; Seager, *Mahan,* 243.

9. Mahan to Soley, October 29, 1892, LPATM; Austin M. Knight and William D. Puleston, *History of the Naval War College* (Newport, RI: unpublished typescript, 1916); Seager, *Mahan,* 244; *New York Times,* December 17, 1892, 4.

10. Chambers, Naval War College Notes, Chambers papers, Box 29; Spector, *Professors of War,* 42.

11. Unknown newspaper clipping, 1892, Naval War College Archives; William McCarty Little, "The Strategic Naval War Game or Chart Maneuver," USNIP 38 (1912): 1212–33.

12. Higginson to Chambers, November 28, 1892; and Francis Isabella Chambers to W. I. Chambers, May 19, 1893, Chambers papers, Box 5. Virtually all personal materials were removed from Chambers's papers, making it impossible to say much about his relationship with Isabella.

13. Chambers to Very, November 18, 1893, Chambers papers, Box 1; and Alfred Thayer Mahan, *The Influence of Sea Power upon the French Revolution and Empire, 1793–1812* (Boston: Little, Brown, 1892), 111–14.

14. Chambers, "Notebook on Tactics, Strategy, and Torpedo Warfare," and Chambers, "Introductory Lecture on Torpedoes," Chambers papers, Boxes 32 and 33.

15. Mahan to Sampson, February 13, 1893, Chambers papers, Box 1; and Spector, *Professors of War,* 148.

16. Spector, *Professors of War,* 49, 86; Chambers, "Scheme for Departments at the War College," undated 1893 paper, and Chambers's War College Notebook, Chambers papers, Box 29.

17. Chambers, Notebook on Tactics, Strategy, and Torpedo Warfare, Chambers papers, Box 43.

18. "Scheme for Departments at the Naval War College," Chambers papers, Box 29.

19. Spector, *Professors of War,* 68–70; Seager, *Mahan,* 274–75.

20. *New York Times,* May 29, 1893, and July 9, 1893, 2; *Congressional Record,* 49th Cong., 2d sess., February 25, 1887; Spector, *Professors of War,* 53–54, 64; Seager, *Mahan,* 274.

21. Ramsay to Chambers, January 17, 1893, June 1 1893, and July 7, 1893, Chambers papers, Box 1.

22. Mahan to Chambers, June 1, 1893, LPATM.

23. Herbert to Mahan, October 4, 1893, LPATM; *New York Times,* October 17, 1893, 2.

24. Bureau of Navigation to Chambers, November 3, 1893, and Chambers to the Chief of the Bureau of Navigation and the Secretary of the Navy, November 6, 1893, Chambers papers, Box 1.

25. Handwritten note on bottom of Chambers to the Chief of the Bureau of Navigation and the Secretary of the Navy, November 6, 1893, Chambers papers, Box 1.

26. Sears to Chambers, December 15, 1893, Chambers papers, Box 5.

27. Taylor to Luce, December 28, 1893 and January 22, 1894, Luce papers; Spector, *Professors of War,* 70.

28. Spector, *Professors of War,* 66; C. H. Stockton to Chambers, December 5, 1893, Chambers papers, Box 1.

29. Mahan to Ellen Evans Mahan, December 18, 1893, January 5, 1894, and February 9, 1894, LPATM.

30. Seager, *Mahan,* 276.

31. Henige to Chambers, November 11, 1893, and Taylor to Chambers, May 24, 1895, Chambers papers, Box 5.

32. Naval War College, *Abstract of Course, 1894,* 12, 14, 20, 24.

## Chapter 9

1. Ernest Andrade, "The Great Samoan Hurricane of 1889," *Naval War College Review* 34 (1981): 73–81; LaFeber, *New Empire,* 130–36, 210–18, 243–82; Kenneth J. Hagan, *This People's Navy* (New York: Free Press, 1991), 198–205.

2. Benjamin Franklin Cooling, *Gray Steel and Blue Water Navy* (Hamden, CT: Archon Books, 1979), 121. This price was actually below Bethlehem's cost of production. A later contract raised the price to $524, but the damage to Bethlehem's reputation had been done.

3. Chambers, "Petition to Congress," 5, Chambers papers, Box 4.

4. *New York Times,* July 1, 1894, 9.

5. Ibid., July 4, 1894, 9, and December 26, 1894, 9.

6. Ellery Ingham (U.S. District Attorney for eastern Pennsylvania) to Chambers, December 24, 1894, Chambers papers, Box 5; Chambers, travel receipts, Chambers papers, Box 2.

7. Commander C. J. Sperry to Chambers, May 17, 1895, Chambers Correspondence, NARG 24; and Sperry to Chambers, May 20, 1895, Chambers papers, Box 2.

8. Alden, *American Steel Navy,* 56.

9. Chambers, "*Minneapolis* Notebook on Seamanship and Fleet Drill," 1895–96, Chambers papers, Box 43; Logbook *Minneapolis,* NARG 24.

10. *New York Times,* October 22, 1895, 1; and William N. Still Jr., *American Sea Power in the Old World* (Westport, CT: Greenwood Press, 1980), 113–14.

11. Logbook *Minneapolis,* NARG 24; *New York Times,* November 21, 1895, 5.

12. Chambers to C.O. *Minneapolis,* April 18, 1896, Chambers papers, Box 2; Chambers, "Notebook: *Minneapolis* Seamanship and Fleet Drill," 1895–96, Chambers papers, Box 43.

13. Selfridge, *What Finer Tradition,* 252–77; Still, *American Sea Power,* 124–25; Selfridge to Chambers, July 10, 1896, Chambers papers, Box 2; Chambers, "Notes on Target Practice," Chambers papers, Box 43.

14. Selfridge to C.O. *Minneapolis,* January 1, 1897, Chambers papers, Box 2; Selfridge, *What Finer Tradition,* 278–80; *New York Times,* October 23, 1894, 1.

15. Chambers, Notebook: Fleet Maneuvers 1897, Chambers papers, Box 43; *New York Times,* March 16, 1897, 4; Logbook *Minneapolis,* NARG 24; Alden, *American Steel Navy,* 240. The navy recommissioned both cruisers for the Spanish-American War the following year.

16. *New York Times,* July 3, 1897, 4.

17. Ibid., December 5, 1896, 1, and January 3, 1897, 17.

18. Ibid., April 8, 1897, 3, April 9, 1897, 3, April 11, 1897, 4, and July 30, 1897, 5.

19. Cooling, *Gray Steel and Blue Water Navy,* 141.

20. Chambers, "A Characteristic Action of Mr. Roosevelt While Secretary of the Navy," undated, Chambers papers, Box 24; Cooling, *Gray Steel and Blue Water Navy,* 142.

21. *New York Times,* December 2, 1897, 3; House Document 95, 55th Cong., 2d sess., 20–21.

22. LaFeber, *New Empire,* 348–49; Cooling, *Gray Steel and Blue Water Navy,* 145.

23. T. C. McLean to Chambers, January 1, 1898, and Crowninshield to Chambers, January 11, 1898 and January 29, 1898, Chambers papers, Box 2; Chambers to Bureau of Navigation, January 10, 1898, NARG 24.

24. Charles M. Arnhault, "The Employment of Torpedoes in Steam Launches against Men of War," USNIP 6 (1880); Edwyn Gray, *The Devil's Device* (London: Seely, Service, 1975).

25. Bruce McCandless, "The Howell Automobile Torpedo," USNIP 92 (October 1966): 174–76; and Gray, *Devil's Device,* 122–31.

26. Gray, *Devil's Device,* 155–58; Seaton Schroeder, "The Development of Modern Torpedoes," *General Information Series No. VI* (Washington, DC: ONI, 1887), 1–44, 333–36.

27. Larry R. Smart, "Evolution of the Torpedo Boat," *Military Affairs* 23 (Summer 1958): 99–101; *New York Times,* March 26, 1898, 1.

28. McLean to Chambers, January 22, 1898, Chambers papers, Box 2; Chambers, "Petition to Congress," 4–6.

29. H. C. Poundstone to Chambers, November 29, 1898, Chambers papers, Box 2; Chambers, "Petition to Congress," 4–6; and SONAR, 1899, 486 and 504.

30. McLean to Chambers, March 20, 1899, Chambers papers, Box 2.

31. Dorwart, *Office of Naval Intelligence,* 68; Chandler to Chambers, October 25, 1899, Chambers papers, Box 6.

## Chapter 10

1. *New York Times,* January 1 and January 4, 1896, and September 30, 1897, 12; Bennett, *Steam Navy,* 794.

2. Charles O'Neil to Chambers, October 9 and October 31, 1900, and Diehl to Chambers, October 11, 1900, Chambers papers, Box 2.

3. Logbook *Texas,* NARG 24; *New York Times,* May 24, 1900, 14; Chambers to W. J. Burns, June 10, 1924, Chambers papers, Box 4.

4. Chambers to Bureau of Navigation, October 17, 1900, and Crowninshield to Chambers, October 22 and October 31, 1900, Chambers papers, Box 2; Train to Bureau of Navigation, October 29, 1900, Chambers Correspondence, NARG 24.

5. Logbook *Annapolis,* NARG 24.

6. Sawyer, *Sons of Gunboats,* v–vi; Brian McAllister Linn, *The Philippine War, 1899–1902* (Lawrence: University Press of Kansas, 2000), 35 and 325–26; R. Blake Dunnavent, *Brown Water Warfare* (Gainesville: University Press of Florida, 2002), 89–103.

7. Sawyer, *Sons of Gunboats,* 16.

8. Logbook *Annapolis,* NARG 24; Chambers, *Annapolis* Journal, Chambers papers, Box 43.

9. John Morgan Gates, *Schoolbooks and Krags: The United States Army in the Philippines, 1898–1902* (Westport, CT: Greenwood Press, 1973), 241.

10. Chambers, *Annapolis* Journal.

11. Quartermaster General M. I. Ludington to the Secretary of War, December 12, 1901, and Secretary of War to Rohrer and Chambers, December 18, 1901, Chambers Correspondence, NARG 24; Chambers, *Annapolis* Journal; Secretary of War, *Annual Report,* 1901, 233; A. P. Niblack, "Operations of the Navy and the Marine Corps in the Philippine Archipelago, 1898–1902," USNIP 30 (December 1904): 751.

12. Brian McAllister Linn, *The U.S. Army and Counterinsurgency in the Philippine War* (Chapel Hill: University of North Carolina Press, 1989), 152–59; Glenn Anthony May, *Battle for Batangas: A Philippine Province at War* (New Haven, CT: Yale University Press, 1991).

13. Chambers Fitness Reports, 1902, NARG 24.

14. Stuart Creighton Miller, *Benevolent Assimilation: The American Conquest of the Philippines, 1899–1903* (New Haven, CT: Yale University Press, 1982), 219–20; Gates, *Schoolbooks and Krags,* 254–63; and Linn, *The Philippine War,* 306–14.

15. Secretary of War, *Annual Report,* 1902, 256–57; Logbook *Frolic,* NARG 24; Chambers, "Petition to Congress"; Linn, *The Philippine War,* 321; and SONAR, 1902, 396 and 441.

## Chapter 11

1. W. J. Coggeshall and J. E. McCarthy, *The Naval Torpedo Station* (Newport, RI: Training Station Press, 1920), 2–15.

2. Mason to Chambers, October 2, 1902, Chambers papers, Box 2.

3. Gray, *Devil's Device,* 159; Bureau of Navigation to Chambers, September 20, 1904, Chambers Correspondence, NARG 24.

4. Chambers, "Torpedo Lecture Notes," Chambers papers, Box 35; Bradley Fiske, "American Naval Policy," USNIP 31 (1905): 1–80; Chambers, "Discussion of American Naval Policy," USNIP 31 (1905): 183–84; SONAR, 1902, 27–29.

5. Norman Friedman, *Submarine Design and Development* (Annapolis, MD: Naval Institute Press, 1984), 27–28.

6. *New York Times,* July 26, 1899, 4; and Frank T. Cable, *The Birth and Development of the American Submarine* (New York: Harper and Brothers, 1924), 160–65.

7. Chambers, "Memorandum on Submarine Boats and the Principal Military Advantages of the Lake Type," Chambers papers, Box 35; Cable, *Birth and Development of the American Submarine,* 260–65; John J. Poluhowich, *Argonaut: The Submarine Legacy of Simon Lake* (College Station: Texas A&M University Press, 1999), 18–21, 80.

8. Cable, *Birth and Development of the American Submarine,* 170–71; SONAR, 1904, 4–7; Chambers, "Memorandum on Submarine Boats and the Principal Military Advantages of the Lake Type."

9. Chambers, "Memorandum on the Evolution of the All Big Gun Ship," January 23, 1911, Chambers papers, Box 35; and Chadwick to Chambers, July 17, 1903, in Doris D. Maguire, *French Ensor Chadwick: Selected Papers and Writings* (Washington, DC: University Press of America, 1981), 301–2.

10. Sperry to Chambers, undated, Chambers papers, Box 34; William McBride,

*Technological Change and the United States Navy, 1865–1945* (Baltimore, MD: Johns Hopkins University Press, 2000), 66–71; Homer Poundstone, "The Size of Battleships for the U.S. Navy," USNIP 29 (1903): 161–74; R. D. Morris, "Homer Clark Poundstone and the All-Big-Gun Ship," USNIP 74 (1948): 707–21; and Bradley Fiske, "Compromiseless Ships," USNIP 31 (1905): 693–98.

11. Chambers, "Memorandum on the Evolution of the All-Big-Gun Battleship in the U.S. Navy"; Vittorio Cuniberti, "An Ideal Warship for the British Navy," in *All the World's Fighting Ships,* ed. Fred T. Jane, 803–7 (London: Sampson, Low, 1903); Daniel Costello, "Planning for War: A History of the General Board of the Navy, 1900–1914" (PhD diss., Tufts University, 1968), 252–53.

12. Sperry to Chambers, February 2, 1904, Chambers papers, Box 2; Ronald Spector, *Admiral of the New Empire: The Life and Career of George Dewey* (Baton Rouge: Louisiana State University Press, 1974), 174; G. B. No. 420–22, January 26, 1904, Chambers papers, Box 35.

13. Costello, "Planning for War," 254; SONAR, 1904, 571–73.

14. Costello, "Planning for War," 24–31, quote on page 24; George Dewey, *Autobiography of George Dewey* (New York: Scribner's, 1913), 291–92.

15. Paul T. Heffron, "Secretary Moody and Naval Administrative Reform: 1902–1904," *American Neptune* 29 (January 1969): 30–48.

16. Spector, *Dewey,* 175; Chambers, "The Study of Ship Designs, Memorandum in re. Lieutenant Commander Sims' Comments on Our Methods of Determining the Designs of Men-of-War," October 18, 1904, Chambers papers, Box 35.

17. SONAR 1905, 391–92.

18. Sims, "The Inherent Tactical Qualities of All-Big-Gun Battleships," *USNIP* 32 (December 1906): 1337–66; Elting E. Morison, *Admiral Sims and the Modern American Navy* (Boston: Houghton Mifflin, 1942), 180–84; McBride, *Technological Change,* 74–78.

19. Fiske, "American Naval Policy," 1–80, and "Compromiseless Ships," 549–53; and William McBride, "The Rise and Fall of a Strategic Technology: The American Battleship from Santiago Bay to Pearl Harbor, 1898–1941" (PhD diss., Johns Hopkins University, 1989), 90–94 and 130–35.

20. Philip Towle, "The Evaluation of the Experience of the Russo-Japanese War," in *Technical Change and British Naval Policy, 1860–1939,* ed. Bryan Ranft (London: Hodder and Stoughton, 1977), 71; McBride, *Technological Change,* 70–71.

21. Chambers, "The Study of Ship Designs, Memorandum in re. Lieutenant Commander Sims' Comments."

22. Chambers, "Memorandum on the Evolution of the All-Big-Gun Battleship."

23. Spector, *Dewey,* 175–76.

24. Thomas A. Bailey, "Dewey and the Germans at Manila Bay," *American Historical Review* 45 (October 1939): 59–81; George W. Baer, *One Hundred Years of Sea Power* (Stanford, CA: Stanford University Press, 1994), 39.

25. Chambers to General Board, October 17, 1903, "Memorandum Referring to General Board no. 420," Chambers papers, Box 3; Baer, *One Hundred Years of Sea Power,* 39.

26. Dewey to Secretary of the Navy, March 31, 1905, Maury to Chambers, May 24,

1905, and Chambers to Swift, "In re—Martin's Mooring Board and Battenberg's Course Indicator," undated, Chambers papers, Box 2; Chambers, "Memorandum on the New Floating Dock for the Philippine Naval Station," March 1905, Chambers papers, Box 30; and Dewey to Chambers, February 4, 1905, NARG 24, Chambers Correspondence.

27. Chambers, "Directions for Making Turning Trials and Obtaining Tactical Maneuvering Data," Chambers papers, Box 35; Chambers, "Notes on Tactical Diameters," Chambers papers, Box 29.

28. Chambers, "Memorandum on Increase of Personnel," October 25, 1904, Chambers papers, Box 36.

## Chapter 12

1. Moody to Commander-in-Chief, North Atlantic Squadron, October 4, 1902, Area File 8, NARG 45.

2. David Healy, *Drive to Hegemony: The United States in the Caribbean, 1898–1917* (Madison: University of Wisconsin Press, 1988), 100–115; and Dana G. Munro, *Intervention and Dollar Diplomacy in the Caribbean, 1900–1921* (Princeton, NJ: Princeton University Press, 1964), 88–100.

3. Crosely to Taylor, May 6, 1903, Area File 8, NARG 45.

4. Damon E. Cummings, *Admiral Richard Wainwright and the United States Navy* (Washington, DC: GPO, 1962), 146; Healy, *Drive to Hegemony,* 115; Lester Langley, *The Banana Wars* (Lexington: University Press of Kentucky, 1985), 26–30; Richard D. Challener, *Admirals, Generals, and American Foreign Policy, 1898–1914* (Princeton, NJ: Princeton University Press, 1973), 120.

5. Powell to Hay, February 24, 1904, NARG 45, Area File 8; Langley, *Banana Wars,* 29–33; Donald Yerxa, *Admirals and Empire: The United States Navy and the Caribbean, 1898–1945* (Columbia: University of South Carolina Press, 1991), 23; and Healy, *Drive to Hegemony,* 117.

6. Munro, *Intervention and Dollar Diplomacy,* 100.

7. J. Fred Rippy, "The Institution of the Customs Receivership in the Dominican Republic," *Hispanic American Historical Review* 17 (November 1937), 419–57; and Munro, *Intervention and Dollar Diplomacy,* 101–2.

8. Logbook *Nashville,* NARG 24.

9. Elting Morrison, ed., *The Letters of Theodore Roosevelt* (Cambridge, MA: Harvard College Library, 1951–54), 5:10; Chambers to Bradford, October 5, 1905, Chambers papers, Box 2; and Bradford to the Secretary of the Navy, October 11, 1905, Area File 8, NARG 45.

10. Logbook *Nashville,* NARG 24; Bonaparte to Roosevelt, September 4, 1905, and Bradford to the Secretary of the Navy, October 11, 1905, Area File 8, NARG 45.

11. Root to Dawson, *Papers Relating to the Foreign Relations,* 1905, 408.

12. Chambers to the Secretary of the Navy, December 26, 1905, Chambers papers, Box 2; Chambers to the Secretary of the Navy, December 27, 1905, Area File 8, NARG

45; Southerland to the Secretary of the Navy, December 24 and 30, 1905, Area File 8, NARG 45.

13. Southerland to Chambers, January 1, 1906, Area File 8, NARG 45.

14. Chambers to Chief of the Bureau of Medicine and Surgery, January 4, 1906, Area File 8, NARG 45; Chambers Fitness Report, June 1906, NARG 24; Southerland to Chambers, June 30, 1906, Chambers papers, Box 13.

15. Chambers, January 9, 1906, Memorandum, Area File 8, NARG 45; Chambers to U.S. Consul I. T. Petit, January 12, 1906, Chambers papers, Box 3.

16. Chambers to Southerland, January 13, 1906, Chambers papers, Box 3.

17. Chambers to Enrique Leroux (U.S. consular agent), January 17, 1906, Chambers papers, Box 3; Chambers to Southerland, January 18, 1906, Area File 8, NARG 45.

18. Logbook *Nashville,* NARG 24; Chambers to Secretary of the Navy, February 13, 1906, Southerland to Chambers, February 26, 1906, and Dewey to Chambers, November 10, 1905, Chambers papers, Box 3; Evans to Chambers, March 18, 1906, Chambers papers, Box 2; Costello, "Planning for War," 143.

19. Harry A. Ellsworth, *One Hundred Eighty Landings of the United States Marines, 1800–1934* (Washington, DC: GPO, 1974), 62–63; Allan R. Millett, *The Politics of Intervention: The Military Occupation of Cuba, 1906–1909* (Columbus: Ohio State University Press, 1968), 91.

20. Schroeder to Chambers, September 30, 1906, and Chambers to Senior Officer Present (Cuba), October 16, 1906, Chambers papers, Boxes 2 and 3; Logbook *Newport,* NARG 24.

21. Metcalf to Chambers, February 27, 1907, Chambers papers, Box 3; Chambers, "Petition to Congress," 8–9.

22. Chambers, "Petition to Congress," 8–9; SONAR, 1908, 417; and Chambers, "Military Characteristics of Battleships," undated circa 1908, Chambers papers, Box 35.

23. SONAR, 1907, 27; SONAR, 1908, 420–21; SONAR, 1909, 395–401.

24. Chambers to the Secretary of the Navy, September 4, 1907, Chambers Correspondence, NARG 24; Chambers, "Consolidation of Bureau Duties," undated circa 1909, Chambers papers, Box 32.

25. Chambers Physical Exam Report, May 1909, NARG 24; George Van Deurs, *Anchors in the Sky: Spuds Ellyson, the First Naval Aviator* (San Rafael, CA: Presidio Press, 1978), 13.

## Chapter 13

1. Logbook *Louisiana,* NARG 24; Meyer to Chambers, October 21, 1909, and Chambers to Bureau of Navigation, October 20, 1909, Chambers papers, Box 3.

2. Chambers Fitness Report, July 1, 1909 to December 6, 1909, NARG 24.

3. Henry P. Beers, "The Development of the Office of the Chief of Naval Operations," *Military Affairs* 10 (Spring 1946): 59–64; and SONAR, 1909, 8–11.

4. Swift to Chambers, November 11, 1909, Chambers papers, Box 3.

5. Ibid.

6. R. D. Layman, *To Ascend from a Floating Base: Shipboard Aeronautics and Aviation, 1783–1914* (Rutherford, NJ: Fairleigh Dickinson University Press, 1979), 92–93; Tom Crouch, *The Bishop's Boys* (New York: Norton, 1989), 256–58.

7. Archibald Turnbull and Clifford Lord, *History of United States Naval Aviation* (New Haven, CT: Yale University Press, 1949), 2–6.

8. Glenn Curtiss and Augustus Post, *The Curtiss Aviation Book* (New York: Frederick A. Strokes, 1912), 105–6.

9. Turnbull and Lord, *History of United States Naval Aviation,* 4–8; and Layman, *To Ascend from a Floating Base,* 110.

10. Dewey to Secretary of the Navy, October 14, 1910, General Board File 449.

11. Costello, "Planning for War," 271–73; George Van Deurs, *Wings for the Fleet* (Annapolis, MD: Naval Institute, 1966), 14; Layman, *To Ascend from a Floating Base,* 110.

12. R. M. Watt to the Secretary of the Navy, October 11, 1910, and Winthrop to Watt, October 12, 1910, both in "Letters Sent Concerning the Navy's Early Use of Aircraft," NARG 24.

13. Van Deurs, *Wings for the Fleet,* 35–37.

14. Chambers, "Aviation and Aeroplanes," USNIP 37 (March 1911): 162–208; Turnbull and Lord, *History of United States Naval Aviation,* 9.

15. Mary C. Welborn, "Naval Contributions to Aeronautical Science," USNIP 74 (August 1948): 965–74.

16. Chambers, "Aviation and Aeroplanes"; Van Deurs, *Wings for the Fleet,* 15–17; Theodore Roscoe, *On the Seas and in the Skies: A History of the U.S. Navy's Air Power* (New York: Hawthorne Books, 1970), 25.

17. Wainwright to Chambers, October 12, 1910, Chambers papers, Box 4; Van Deurs, *Wings for the Fleet,* 17.

18. Curtiss and Post, *Curtiss Aviation Book,* 116–19; Van Deurs, *Wings for the Fleet,* 18; Chambers to the Secretary of the Navy, November 23, 1910, Chambers papers, Box 4.

19. Meyer to Ely, November 17, 1910, Chambers papers, Box 15.

20. Pond to Secretary of the Navy, January 18, 1911, Chambers papers, Box 21; Ely to Chambers, January 30, 1911, Chambers papers, Box 15; Van Deurs, *Wings for the Fleet,* 29.

21. Clark G. Reynolds, *Admiral John H. Towers: The Struggle for Naval Air Supremacy* (Annapolis, MD: Naval Institute Press, 1991), 32–33; Curtiss and Post, *Curtiss Aviation Book,* 119, 148–50; House Committee on Naval Affairs, Hearings on H.R. 10106, 70th Cong., (1930), 2220.

22. Chambers, "Brief Summary of the First Steps in the Development of Naval Aeronautics," Chambers papers, Box 10; Stirling to Secretary of the Navy, January 31, 1911, Chambers papers, Box 4; Harold B. Miller, *Navy Wings* (New York: Dodd, Mead, 1937), 77; Turnbull and Lord, *History of United States Naval Aviation,* 13.

23. Chambers to A. E. Tangren, January 21, 1911, Chambers papers, Box 20; Chambers, "Aviation and Aeroplanes," 162–208; Chambers to the Secretary of the Navy, April 3, 1911, Chambers papers, Box 4; SONAR, 1910, 23.

24. Chambers to Russell, March 11, 1911, NARG 24: Letters sent concerning the

navy's early use of aircraft; Chambers to Ely, February 9, 1911, Chambers papers, Box 15; "Washington News," *Aero and Hydro* 2 (March 11, 1911): 192.

25. Meyer to Chambers, March 13, 1911, Chambers papers, Box 4.

26. Fletcher to Nicholson, April 7, 1911, Chambers papers, Box 4; Chambers, Typescript of Testimony to the House Committee on Naval Affairs, May 10, 1930, Chambers papers, Box 24.

27. Chambers, Typescript of Testimony to the House Committee on Naval Affairs, May 10, 1930; Chambers, "Brief Summary"; Turnbull and Lord, *History of United States Naval Aviation,* 15; Van Deurs, *Wings for the Fleet,* 38.

28. Chambers to C. A. Dorriss, February 7, 1912, Chambers to Findley, undated, Chambers to W. J. Darby, March 2, 1911 and March 25, 1912, and Lee S. Burridge to M. B. Sellers, undated, Chambers papers, Boxes 13–15; Chambers to William R. Rose (U.S. Aerial Navigation Company), June 26, 1912, Chambers papers, Box 21; Chambers to B. C. Riblet, January 10, 1913, Chambers papers, Box 9.

29. Bureau of Navigation to Chambers, April 29, 1911, Chambers papers, Box 4.

30. Herbert A. Johnson, *Wingless Eagle: U.S. Army Aviation through World War I* (Chapel Hill: University of North Carolina Press, 2001), 108–9.

31. Chambers to Curtiss, June 2, 1911, Chambers papers, Box 13; Chambers, "Brief Summary," 6.

32. Chambers, "Brief Summary," 10.

33. Ibid.; Chambers to the Chief of the Bureau of Navigation, May 1, 1911, Secretary of the Navy to the Superintendent of the Naval Academy, June 27, 1911, and Bureau of Navigation to Chambers, July 6, 1911, all in Chambers papers, Box 4.

34. Reynolds, *Towers,* 53; Van Deurs, *Wings for the Fleet,* 51.

35. Chambers to Ellyson, January 11, 1911, Chambers papers, Box 14.

36. Chambers to Ely, February 9, 1911, Chambers papers, Box 15; Chambers, "Memorandum on the Employment of Aeroplanes," June 29, 1912, Chambers papers, Box 18; Chambers, "Brief Summary," 7; Chambers to Curtiss, October 17, 1911, Chambers papers, Box 13; Chambers to Russell, November 27, 1911, Chambers papers, Box 21.

37. Van Deurs, *Anchors in the Sky: Spuds Ellyson,* 118–24; Towers to Chambers, April 5, 1912, Chambers papers, Box 22.

38. Chambers to Russell, undated, Chambers papers, Box 21; Chambers to Wright, May 25, 1912, Chambers papers, Box 17; Chambers, "Safety in Aviation as Viewed by French Officers," *Aero and Hydro* 4 (June 22, 1912): 275; Chambers, "Revival of Aviation in the United States," *Aero Club Bulletin* 6 (May 1912): 1–4; and Chambers, "Aviation at Home and Abroad Reviewed," *Aero and Hydro* 5 (1913): 266–76.

39. Chambers to Curtiss, January 3, 1912, Chambers papers, Box 13; Chambers to F. H. Russell, November 27, 1911, Chambers papers, Box 21; Towers to Chambers, September 16, 1912, Chambers papers, Box 22; Chambers to Means, December 30, 1913, Chambers papers, Box 18.

40. Chambers to Curtiss, December 31, 1911, Chambers papers, Box 13.

41. On the detrimental effects of the Wright-Curtiss patent dispute see Johnson, *Wingless Eagle,* 104–15.

42. Turnbull and Lord, *History of United States Naval Aviation,* 20.

43. Chambers to the Chief of the Bureau of Navigation, October 7, 1911, Chambers papers, Box 10; Turnbull and Lord, *History of United States Naval Aviation,* 20.

44. Chambers, "Brief Summary," 9; Chambers to the Chief of the Bureau of Navigation, "Memorandum on Aeronautic Progress," December 18, 1911, Chambers papers, Box 4.

## Chapter 14

1. Ellyson to Chambers, September 7, 1911, Chambers papers, Box 15.

2. Chambers, "Brief Summary," 12–13; Turnbull and Lord, *History of United States Naval Aviation,* 19; Van Deurs, *Wings for the Fleet,* 69–70; Henry Wisewood to Chambers, December 6, 1912, Chambers papers, Box 23; and Chambers to the Secretary of the Navy, December 16, 1912, Chambers papers, Box 4.

3. *New York Herald,* June 9, 1912, Chambers papers, Box 21.

4. Chambers to R. E. Gillmore, June 29, 1912, Sperry to Chambers, December 31, 1912, Chambers to Sperry, October 20, 1913, and Chambers to Sperry, December 16, 1913, Chambers papers, Box 22; Chambers, "Brief Summary," 7–8; Charles Keller, "Automatic Pilot, 1913 Version," *American Aviation Historical Society Journal* 20 (1975): 130–32.

5. Chambers to the Chief of the Bureau of Navigation, May 22, 1912; Chambers to Senator Benjamin Tillman, April 23, 1913; Chambers to George Perkins (Chair House Naval Affairs Committee), May 24, 1912; House of Representatives, Hearings, Committee on Naval Affairs, January 9, 1913, 543, all in Chambers papers, Box 4.

6. Chambers, "Report on Aviation," in SONAR, 1912, 155–70.

7. Secretary of the Navy to Commandant USMC, March 4, 1912, and Chambers to the Aide for Personnel, February 29, 1912, Chambers papers, Box 18.

8. See Chambers's penciled notes on his copy of Major Dion Williams, *The Naval Advance Base,* GPO, 1912, Chambers papers, Box 47; Chambers, "Brief Summary," 17–18.

9. *New York Herald,* June 9, 1912, Chambers papers, Box 21.

10. General Board 449, August 30, 1913, General Board to Chambers, June 26, 1912, General Board memorandum on aeroplanes, December 20, 1912, Chambers papers, Box 18; Chambers to the Bureau of Navigation, January 29, 1913, Chambers papers, Box 6.

11. Van Deurs, *Wings for the Fleet,* 64–65; Reynolds, *Towers,* 45–47; Chambers, "Brief Summary," 11.

12. The ONI to Chambers, August 15, 1911, Chambers papers, Box 22; Reynolds, *Towers,* 55–56; Chambers "Brief Summary," 11.

13. Chambers, "Report on Aviation," in SONAR, 1912, 155–70.

14. Chambers to Wanneck, March 12, 1913, and Chambers to Woodhouse, October 29, 1912, Chambers papers, Box 17; Chambers, "Airships and Naval Policy," unpublished manuscript, Chambers papers, Box 12.

15. Chambers, "Airships and Naval Policy," Chambers to Ernest L. Jones (editor of *Aeronautics*), December 5, 1911, Chambers papers, Box 17; Chambers to Thomas A. Wal-

ton, July 10, 1911, Chambers papers, Box 23; Chambers to H. Henry Klinker, December 10, 1912, Chambers papers, Box 11.

16. Chambers to Thomas A. Walton, July 10, 1911, and Chambers to Woodhouse, October 29, 1912, Chambers papers, Box 23; ONI translation of German Document, "Protective Measures against Bombs Dropped from Aircraft," October 2, 1912, Chambers papers, Box 12; Chambers to L. P. Cole, May 5, 1913, Chambers papers, Box 10.

17. Layman, *Floating Base,* 187; *New York American,* June 30, 1912, Chambers papers, Box 46; Chambers, "A Hanger Ship," *Aero Club of America Bulletin* 1 (August 1912): 25–26. Chambers's comments on Lieutenant Lapoint, "Aviation in the Navy," USNIP 38 (1912): 744–46; and Chambers to Navy Department, June 29, 1912, Chambers papers, Box 18.

18. Russell to Chambers, May 30, 1912, Chambers papers, Box 21.

19. Albert F. Zahm, "On the Need for an Aeronautical Laboratory in America," *Aero Club of America Bulletin* 1 (February 1912): 35; Zahm to Henry A. Wisewood, December 20, 1912, Chambers papers, Box 7; SONAR, 1912, 155–70; Chambers, "Aviation Today, and the Necessity for a National Aerodynamic Laboratory," USNIP 39 (December 1912): 329–36; Alex Roland, *Model Research: The National Advisory Committee for Aeronautics, 1915–1958* (Washington, DC: GPO, 1985), 5–8.

20. Turnbull and Lord, *History of United States Naval Aviation,* 27; Roland, *Model Research,* 10–11.

21. Roland, *Model Research,* 10–12.

22. Rodney P. Carlisle, *Where the Fleet Begins: A History of the David Taylor Research Center, 1898–1998* (Washington, DC: Naval Historical Center, 1998), 74–75.

23. Turnbull and Lord, *History of United States Naval Aviation,* 16; Roland, *Model Research,* 13–15; Chambers to Sirsch, January 21, 1919, Chambers papers, Box 21; Chambers, "Brief Summary," 13–14.

24. Gray, *Devil's Device,* 205–6; Curtiss to Chambers, August 3, 1912, Chambers papers, Box 13; Chambers, "Report on Aviation," September 21, 1912, Chambers papers, 3, Box 4; Turnbull and Lord, *History of United States Naval Aviation,* 21; Layman, *To Ascend from a Floating Base,* 151.

25. Reynolds, *Towers,* 52–57; Van Deurs, *Anchors in the Sky: Spuds Ellyson,* 143–49; Van Deurs, *Wings for the Fleet,* 71.

26. Chambers Fitness Report, January–March, 1912, NARG 24; Chambers to Chief of the Bureau of Navigation, October 5, 1912, Chambers papers, Box 28; Chambers, "Brief Summary," 15.

27. Andrews to Meyer, October 5, 1912, and Meyer to Andrews, October 7, 1912, Chambers papers, Box 28.

28. Chambers to Towers, February 13, 1913, and Towers to Chambers, February 1 and 8, and March 5, 1913, Chambers papers, Box 22.

29. E. David Cronon, ed., *The Cabinet Diaries of Josephus Daniels* (Lincoln: University of Nebraska Press, 1963), 6.

30. Cummings, *Wainwright,* 238–39; Bradley A. Fiske, *From Midshipman to Rear-Admiral* (New York: Century, 1919), 481; Richard Wainwright, "The General Board," USNIP 48 (January 1922): 188–98.

31. Costello, "Planning for War," 99–101; Chambers to Sirsch, January 21, 1919, Chambers papers, Box 21.

32. Coletta, *Admiral Bradley A. Fiske,* 104–5; Fiske, *Midshipman,* 531–32.

33. Van Deurs, *Wings for the Fleet,* 90–92.

34. Reynolds, *Towers,* 57–60.

35. Chambers to Daniels, April 23, 1913, Chambers papers, Box 4; House Committee on Naval Affairs, Hearings, January 9, 1913; Twombly (President of the Aeronautical Society) to Chambers, April 17, 1913, Chambers papers, Box 23; Chambers to the Bureau of Navigation and the Secretary of the Navy, March 13, 1913, Chambers papers, Box 13.

36. Turnbull and Lord, *History of United States Naval Aviation,* 27–28; Roland, *Model Research,* 17–25.

37. Reynolds, *Towers,* 65–68; Chambers, "Aviation at Home and Abroad Reviewed," 248; Chambers, "Brief Summary," 18.

38. Reynolds, *Towers,* 68; Van Deurs, *Wings for the Fleet,* 85–87.

39. Chambers, handwritten note on Chambers to Chief of the Bureau of Navigation, October 5, 1912, Chambers papers, Box 28; Chambers, "Brief Summary," 15; House of Representatives, 70th Cong. (1930), Hearing 499 on H.R. 10106, 2212.

40. Mason to Secretary of the Navy, May 29, 1912, and Secretary of the Navy to Mason, June 1, 1912, Chambers papers, Box 4; House of Representatives, 70th Cong. (1930), Hearing 499, 2216–17.

41. Chambers to Pond, August 28, 1913, Chambers papers, Box 21; Mayo to Chambers, June 20, 1916, Chambers papers, Box 18.

42. Chambers to Secretary of the Navy, May 18, 1913, Chambers papers, Box 4.

43. Bureau of Navigation to Secretary of the Navy, June 3, 1913, Chambers papers, Box 4; Secretary of the Navy to the Bureau of Navigation, June 7, 1913, Chambers papers, Box 4.

44. House of Representatives, Hearing 499, 70th Cong. (1930), 2216–18. The other captains plucked were J. M. Ellicott, C. M. Knepper, C. C. Marsh, and J. C. Quinby.

45. Secretary of the Navy to Chambers, July 1, 1913, Chambers to Bureau of Navigation, July 2, 1913, Daniels to Chambers, July 11, 1913, Chambers papers, Box 4.

46. Chambers to Sirsch, January 21, 1919, Chambers papers, Box 21; Van Deurs, *Wings for the Fleet,* 9; Fiske, *Midshipman,* 538.

47. Coletta, *Patrick N. L. Bellinger,* 72.

48. William McBride makes a similar point, arguing that Fiske removed Chambers because Chambers was willing to work with the technical bureaus rather than fight for line officer supremacy. McBride, "The Rise and Fall of a Strategic Technology," 208–9.

49. Chambers, "Brief Summary," 18; Johnson, *Wingless Eagle,* 38–41.

50. Chambers Fitness Reports, 1911–13, NARG 24.

## Chapter 15

1. Van Deurs, *Wings for the Fleet,* 94–95; Reynolds, *Towers,* 68–69; Chambers to Towers, July 4, 1913, Box 22.

2. Fiske, *Midshipman,* 538; Coletta, *Admiral Bradley A. Fiske,* 109.

3. Van Deurs, *Wings for the Fleet,* 97; Chambers, "Aviation at Home and Abroad Reviewed," *Aero and Hydro* 45 (1913), 267; Robert G. Albion, *Makers of Naval Policy, 1798–1947* (Annapolis, MD: Naval Institute Press, 1980), 362.

4. Reynolds, *Towers,* 70–71; Minutes of the Aeronautic Board, Chambers papers, Box 7.

5. Minutes of the Aeronautical Board; Van Deurs, *Wings for the Fleet,* 97.

6. House Naval Affairs Committee, 53rd Cong. (1914), Hearings, 1794–1803; Roscoe, *On the Seas and in the Skies,* 42; Turnbull and Lord, *History of United States Naval Aviation,* 33–34; Chambers, "Brief Summary," 16.

7. McBride, "Rise and Fall of a Strategic Technology," 209; Van Deurs, *Wings for the Fleet,* 98–99; Chambers to Burridge, December 26, 1913, Chambers papers, Box 13.

8. Chambers, "Brief Summary," 19; Chambers to Fiske, January 10, 1914, Chambers papers, Box 4.

9. Fiske to Chambers, January 5, 1914, Chambers to the Secretary of the Navy, January 6, 1914, Chambers to Fiske, January 10, 1914, Fiske to Chambers and Bristol, January 14, 1914, all in Chambers papers, Box 4.

10. Van Deurs, *Wings for the Fleet,* 99–100.

11. Sue to Chambers, July 28, 1913, Irving Chambers to W. I. Chambers, July 4, 1913, Gove to Chambers, July 3, 1913, Pond to Chambers, August 15, 1913, Peary to Chambers, July 3, 1913, Lee Burridge to Chambers, July 2, 1913, and Bellinger to Chambers, July 7, 1913, all in Chambers papers, Box 13; Chambers, 1913 form letter, Box 21.

12. Chambers to Dewey, September 24, 1913, Chambers papers, Box 4.

13. Chambers to the Secretary of the Navy, February 14 and 18, 1914, Secretary of the Navy to Chambers, February 16, 1914, Fiske to Chambers, February 18, 1914, Chambers papers, Box 4.

14. Chambers, Petition, Chambers to Burridge, March 29, 1914, Chambers papers, Box 13; Woodhouse to Chambers, February 4, 1914, Chambers to Andrews, January 24, 1914, Andrews to Chambers, January 31, 1914, all in Chambers papers, Box 7.

15. Jack Sweetman, *The Landing at Veracruz: 1914* (Annapolis, MD: U.S. Naval Institute, 1968); Turnbull and Lord, *History of United States Naval Aviation,* 41–43.

16. Chambers, "Brief Summary," 16.

17. Cronon, *Cabinet Diaries of Josephus Daniels,* 272; Mary Klachko, *Admiral William Shepherd Benson, First Chief of Naval Operations* (Annapolis, MD: Naval Institute Press, 1987), 25, 30–33.

18. Van Deurs, *Wings for the Fleet,* 136; Turnbull and Lord, *History of United States Naval Aviation,* 50–51; Albion, *Makers of Naval Policy,* 362–75.

19. Karsten, *Naval Aristocracy,* 360; Chambers, "Universal Peace, Naval Efficiency, and the 'Plucking' System," *The Navy* 9 (March–April, 1915).

20. Fletcher to Chambers, September 20, 1915, Chambers papers, Box 4; Chambers to Reed, May 30, 1917, and May 28, 1918, Chambers papers, Box 21.

21. Chambers, "Aircraft in Warfare," September 30, 1914, Chambers papers, Box 12; Chambers to Representative William E Humphrey, October 15, 1912, Chambers papers, Box 16.

22. Chambers to John O'Leary, February 10, 1913 and February 18, 1913, Chambers

papers, Box 20; Turnbull and Lord, *History of United States Naval Aviation,* 60; Chambers to O'Leary, May 5, 1916 and May 30, 1916, Chambers to Molly O'Leary, March 2, 1917, Molly O'Leary to Chambers, July 28, 1918, Chambers to Molly O'Leary, July 1918, all in Chambers papers, Box 20.

23. Chambers Fitness Report, April 1 to September 30, 1917, NARG 24; Chambers, "Typescript of Testimony to the House Committee on Naval Affairs," May 10, 1930, Chambers papers, Box 24.

24. Reynolds, *Towers,* 122; Chambers to William Ford, April 9, 1918, and Chambers to Gove, January 8, 1919, Chambers papers, Box 15.

25. Paolo E. Coletta and Bernarr B. Coletta, *Admiral William A. Moffett and U.S. Naval Aviation* (Lewiston, NY: Mellon Press, 1997), 23–24; Chambers to Moffett, September 14, 1925, Moffett papers, Naval Academy Library; Bellinger to Chambers, July 28, 1919, Chambers papers, Box 12.

26. Chambers to Gove, January 8, 1919, Chambers to Kenneth Clark, April 25, 1918, Grace Cole to Chambers, December 29, 1918, and Lucile Belknap to Chambers, undated, all in Chambers papers, Box 13; *New York Herald,* April 3, 1918; F. Law Olmstead to Chambers, December 14, 1918; Colonel Leon Osterrieth to Chambers, October 3, 1918, July 15, 1919, and August 30, 1921, all in Chambers papers, Box 20; and Sims to Chambers, May 15, 1912, Chambers papers, Box 21.

27. Fiske, *Midshipman,* 481; Coletta, *Admiral Bradley A. Fiske,* 98–99.

28. Coletta, *Admiral Bradley A. Fiske,* 193–97; Paolo Coletta, "The Perils of Invention," *American Neptune* 37 (1977): 111–27.

29. Chambers to Workman, April 8, 1929, Chambers papers, Box 4.

30. House of Representatives, 70th Cong. (1930), Hearing 499; Frank Slifer to Chambers, June 7, 1930, Clearwater (Chambers attorney) to Pratt, January 14, 1930, both in Chambers papers, Box 4; Charles Melhorn, *Two-Block Fox: The Rise of the Aircraft Carrier, 1911–1929* (Annapolis, MD: Naval Institute Press, 1974), 119.

31. House of Representatives, 71st Cong. (1932), Hearing 638; Moffett to Chambers, March 22, 1932, Bristol to Upham, January 4, 1932, F. B. Upham to Judge Advocate General, February 3, 1932, Pratt to Judge Advocate General, February 9, 1932, all in Chambers papers, Box 4.

## Conclusion

1. Lee S. Burridge to M. B. Sellers, undated, Chambers papers, Box 21.

2. Reynolds, *Towers,* 115–16.

3. Chambers, "The U.S. Navy's Splendid Aeronautic Record Reviewed," *Aero and Hydro* 7 (1914): 228–39.

# Bibliography

## Primary Sources

### *Government Archives and Manuscript Collections*

Library of Congress Manuscript Division
- Mark L. Bristol papers
- Washington Irving Chambers papers
- William E. Chandler papers
- Grover Loening papers
- Stephen B. Luce papers
- Henry T. Mayo papers
- Holden C. Richardson papers
- Wilbur and Orville Wright papers

National Archives
- RG 24: Records of the Bureau of Naval Personnel
- RG 38: Office of Chief of Naval Operations
- RG 45: Office of Naval Records and Library
- RG 71: Records of the Bureau of Yards and Docks
- RG 72: Bureau of Aeronautics
- RG 80: General Records of the Department of the Navy
- RG 181: Records of Naval Districts and Shore Establishments (New York branch)

Naval War College Library
- RG 1: Early Records
- RG 8: Intelligence and Technology

RG 14: Faculty and Staff Presentations
RG 15: Guest Lecturers

United States Naval Academy, Nimitz Library
Academic and Conduct Records of Cadets
William A. Moffett papers
Naval Academy Registers
Physical Exam Reports
William S. Schley papers
Subject Files

## *Published Government Documents*

Annual Register of the U.S. Naval Academy, 1871–76
Annual Report of the National Advisory Committee for Aeronautics, 1915
Annual Reports of the Secretary of the Navy, 1872–1919
Annual Reports of the Secretary of War, 1901–2
Papers Relating to the Foreign Relations of the United States, 1885 and 1904–6
U.S. Congress. Congressional Record, 1872–1917
U.S. Congress. Senate. The Nicaragua Canal. Senate Executive Document 57, 43rd Congress, 1st session (1875).
U.S. Congress. Senate. Reports of Naval Officers on Panama Canal. Senate Executive Document 123, 48th Congress, 1st session (1885).
U.S. Congress. Senate. Report of the U.S. Nicaragua Surveying Party, 1885. Senate Executive Document 99, 49th Congress, 1st session (1886).
U.S. Congress. House. Survey of the Darien Canal Routes. House Miscellaneous Document 113, 42d Congress, 3rd session.
U.S. Congress. House. Report of the Armor Factory Board. House Document 95, 54th Congress, 2nd session (1897).
U.S. Congress. House. Committee on Naval Affairs. Aviation Hearings. 62nd Congress, 2nd session (January 9, 1913).
U.S. Congress. House. Committee on Naval Affairs. Hearing on H.R. 10106. 70th Congress.
U.S. Congress. House. Committee on Naval Affairs. Hearing on H.R. 4327. 71st Congress.

## *Memoirs, Diaries, and Collected Letters*

Ammen, Daniel. *The Old Navy and the New.* Philadelphia: J. B. Lippincott, 1891.
Coontz, Robert E. *From the Mississippi to the Sea.* Philadelphia: Dorrance, 1930.
Cronon, David E., ed. *The Cabinet Diaries of Josephus Daniels, 1913–1921.* Lincoln: University of Nebraska Press, 1963.
Dewey, George. *The Autobiography of George Dewey, Admiral of the Navy.* New York: Scribners, 1913.
Evans, Robley D. *An Admiral's Log.* New York: Appleton, 1910.

———. *A Sailor's Log.* Annapolis, MD: Naval Institute Press, 1993. Reprint, New York: Appleton, 1901.
Fiske, Bradley A. *From Midshipman to Rear-Admiral.* New York: Century, 1919.
Goodrich, Caspar. *Rope Yarns from the Old Navy.* New York: Naval History Society, 1931.
Greely, A. W. *The Lady Franklin Bay Expedition.* Washington, DC: GPO, 1885.
Maguire, Doris D., ed. *French Ensor Chadwick: Selected Letters and Papers.* Washington, DC: University Press of America, 1981.
Mahan, Alfred Thayer. *From Sail to Steam.* New York: Harper and Brothers, 1907.
Morison, Elting E., ed. *The Letters of Theodore Roosevelt.* Cambridge, MA: Harvard University Press, 1951.
Schley, Winfield Scott. *Forty-Five Years under the Flag.* New York: Appleton, 1904.
Schroeder, Seaton. *A Half Century of Naval Service.* New York: Appleton, 1922.
Seager, Robert II, and Doris D. Maguire. *The Letters and Papers of Alfred Thayer Mahan.* 3 vols. Annapolis, MD: Naval Institute Press, 1975.
Selfridge, Thomas O. *What Finer Tradition: The Memoirs of Thomas O. Selfridge, Jr., Rear Admiral, USN.* Columbia: University of South Carolina Press, 1987.
Stirling, Yates. *Sea Duty: The Memoirs of a Fighting Admiral.* New York: Putnam, 1939.

## *Articles*

Ammen, Daniel. "The Proposed Inter-Oceanic Ship Canal." *Bulletin of the American Geographical Society* 3 (1878).
Belknap, Charles. "The Naval Policy of the United States." USNIP 6 (1880): 375–71.
Bellinger, Patrick. "Sailors in the Sky." *National Geographic* 120 (1961): 276–96.
Chambers, Washington I. "Aviation and Airplanes." USNIP 37 (March 1911): 162–208.
———. "Aviation at Home and Abroad Reviewed." *Aero and Hydro* 5 (1913): 266–76.
———. "Aviation Today, and the Necessity for a National Aerodynamic Laboratory." USNIP 39 (December 1912): 329–36.
———. "The Best Method for Reconstruction and Increase of the Navy." USNIP 11 (1885): 3–83.
———. "A Hanger Ship." *Aero Club of America Bulletin* 1 (August 1912): 25–26.
———. "A Modified Monitor, with a New Method for Mounting and Working the Guns." USNIP 7 (1881): 437–46.
———. "Naval Aviation." *Scientific American* 105 (July 8, 1911): 26–27.
———. "Notes on the Nicaraguan Ship Canal as Relocated and Revised by the U.S. Surveying Expedition of 1885." USNIP 11 (1885): 807–14.
———. "Rescue of the *Trinity's* Crew from Heard's Island." USNIP 9 (March 1883): 121–29.
———. "Revival of Aviation in the United States." *Aero Club of America Bulletin* 6 (May 1912): 1–4.
———. "Safety in Aviation as Viewed by French Officers." *Aero and Hydro* 4 (June 22, 1912): 275.

———. "The U.S. Navy's Splendid Aeronautic Record Reviewed." *Aero and Hydro* 7 (1914): 228–29.

———. "Universal Peace, Naval Efficiency, and the 'Plucking' System." *The Navy* 9 (March–April, 1915).

Craven, Thomas T. "Naval Aviation." USNIP 46 (1920): 181–91.

———. "Naval Aviation and a United Air Service." USNIP 47 (1921): 307–22.

Cuniberti, Vittorio. "An Ideal Warship for the British Navy." In *All the World's Fighting Ships,* edited by Fred T. Jane, 803–7. London: Sampson, Low, 1903.

Fiske, Bradley. "American Naval Policy." USNIP 31 (March 1905): 1–80.

———. "Compromiseless Ships." USNIP 31 (1905): 549–53.

———. "Naval Power." USNIP 37 (September 1911): 683–736.

———. "The Naval Profession." USNIP 33 (June 1907): 475–578.

Fullam, William F. "The System of Naval Training and Discipline Required to Promote Efficiency and Attract Americans." USNIP 16 (1890): 480–99.

Kelley, J. D. J. "Our Merchant Marine: The Causes of Its Decline, and the Means to Be Taken for Its Revival." USNIP 8 (1882): 3–47.

Little, William McCarty. "The Strategic Naval War Game or Chart Maneuver." USNIP 38 (December 1912): 1213–33.

Luce, Stephen B. "Naval Administration," USNIP 29 (1903): 1–13.

———. "On the Study of History." USNIP 15 (1887): 175–201.

———. "On the Study of Naval Warfare as a Science." USNIP 14 (1886): 527–46.

———. "War Schools," USNIP 11 (1883): 633–657.

Mason, T. B. M. "The United States Naval Institute." *The United Service* (April 1879): 290–96.

Menocal, Aniceto G. "Discussion upon Inter-Oceanic Canal Projects." *American Society of Civil Engineers Transactions* 9 (November 1880): 429–46.

Murdock, J. B. "Torpedo Tubes in Battleships." USNIP 29 (1903): 547–51.

Niblack, A. P. "Operations of the Navy and the Marine Corps in the Philippine Archipelago, 1898–1902," USNIP 30 (December 1904): 745–53, 31 (June 1905): 463–64, and 31 (September 1905): 698.

———. "The Tactics of the Gun." USNIP 38 (1902): 925–36.

Parker, Foxhall A. "Our Fleet Maneuvers in the Bay of Florida and the Navy of the Future." USNIP 1 (1874): 163–76.

Poundstone, Homer. "The Size of Battleships for the U.S. Navy." USNIP 29 (1903): 161–74.

Reuterdahl, Henry. "Needs of Our Navy." *McClure's* 30 (January 1908): 251–63.

Rogers, Charles C. "Naval Intelligence." USNIP 9 (1883): 659–92.

Saufley, "Naval Aviation: Its Values and Needs" USNIP 40 (1914): 1459–72.

Sims, William S. "The Inherent Tactical Qualities of All-Big-Gun Battleships." USNIP 32 (December 1906): 1337–66.

Stockton, Charles H. "The Inter-Oceanic Canal." USNIP 25 (December 1899): 753–97.

———. "Notes upon the Necessity and Utility of the Naval War College in Connection with the Preparation for Defense and War." USNIP 19 (August 1893): 407–13.
Taylor, Henry C. "The Control of the Pacific." *Forum* 3 (June 1887).
———. "The Fleet," USNIP 29 (December 1903).
———. "The Future of the Navy," *Forum* 27 (March 1899).
———. "Memorandum on a General Staff for the Navy," USNIP 26 (1900).
———. "The Study of War," *North American Review* 162 (1896).
Very, Edward W. "The Type of (I) Armored Vessel, (II) Cruiser, Best Suited to the Present Needs of the United States." USNIP 7 (1881): 43–83.

## Books

Benjamin, Park. *The Naval Academy: Being the Yarn of the American Midshipman.* New York: G. P. Putman's Sons, 1900.
Bennett, Frank M. *The Monitor and the Navy under Steam.* Boston: Houghton Mifflin, 1900.
———. *The Steam Navy of the United States.* Pittsburgh: Warren, 1896.
Cable, Frank T. *The Birth and Development of the American Submarine.* New York: Harper, 1924.
DeLong, George. *The Voyage of the Jeannette: The Ship and Ice Journals of George W. DeLong, Lieutenant-Commander U.S.N. and Commander of Polar Expedition of 1879–1883.* Boston: Houghton Mifflin, 1883.
Gleaves, Albert. *The Life of an American Sailor: Rear Admiral William Hemsley Emory.* New York: George H. Doran, 1923.
———. *The Life and Letters of Rear Admiral Stephen B. Luce.* New York: Putnam, 1925.
Greely, Adolphus W. *Three Years of Arctic Service: An Account of the Lady Franklin Bay Expedition of 1881–84 and the Attainment of the Farthest North.* New York: Scribners, 1886.
King, James W. *The War-Ships and Navies of the World, 1880.* Washington, DC: GPO, 1880. Reprint, Annapolis, MD: Naval Institute Press, 1982.
Long, John D. *The New American Navy.* 2 vols. New York: Outlook, 1903.
Mahan, Alfred Thayer. *The Influence of Sea Power upon the French Revolution and Empire, 1793–1812.* Boston: Little, Brown, 1892.
———. *The Influence of Sea Power upon History.* Boston: Little, Brown, 1890.
———. *The Interest of America in Sea Power, Present and Future.* Boston: Little, Brown, 1897.
———. *Naval Administration and Warfare.* Boston: Little, Brown, 1908.
Niblack, Albert P. *History and Aims of the Office of Naval Intelligence.* Washington, DC: GPO, 1920.
Schley, Winfield Scott. *Report of Winfield S. Schley: Commanding Greely Relief Expedition of 1884.* Washington, DC: GPO, 1887. Originally published as 49th Congress, 2d sess. H. Misc. Doc. 157.

———, and J. R. Soley. *The Rescue of Greely.* New York: Scribners, 1885.

Seager, Robert, and Doris D. Maguire, eds. *Letters and Papers of Alfred Thayer Mahan.* 3 vols. Annapolis, MD: Naval Institute Press, 1975.

Strong, Josiah. *Our Country: Its Possible Future and Its Present Crisis.* New York: American Home Missionary Society, 1885.

## Secondary Sources

### *Articles*

Angevine, Robert G. "The Rise and Fall of the Office of Naval Intelligence." *Journal of Military History* 62 (April 1998): 291–312.

Barnes, James. "Rear Admiral John G. Walker." *American Review of Reviews* 16 (September 1897): 298–302.

Beers, Henry L. "The Development of the Office of the Chief of Naval Operations: Part I." *Military Affairs* 10 (Spring 1946): 40–68.

———. "History of the Bureau of Navigation, 1862–1942." *American Archivist* 6. (1943): 212–52.

Coletta, Paolo E. "French Ensor Chadwick: The First American Naval Attaché, 1882–1889," *American Neptune* 39 (1979): 126–41.

———. "The 'Nerves' of the New Navy." *American Neptune* 38 (1978): 122–30.

———. "The Perils of Invention." *American Neptune* 37 (1977): 111–27.

Colwell, David G. "The Navy and Greely: The Rescue of the 1881–1884 Arctic Expedition." USNIP 84 (January 1958): 71–79.

Crosley, Walter S. "The Naval War College, the General Board, and the Office of Naval Intelligence." USNIP 39 (1913): 965–74.

Crowell, Jackson. "The United States and a Central American Canal, 1869–1877." *Hispanic American Historical Review* 49 (1969): 27–52.

Dennett, Tyler. "Early American Policy in Korea, 1883–1887: The Services of Lieutenant George T. Foulk." *Political Science Quarterly* 37 (1923): 82–103.

Duncan, Donald B., and H. M. Dater. "Administrative History of U.S. Naval Aviation." *Air Affairs: An International Quarterly* 1 (Summer 1947): 526–39.

Ellicott, John M. "Greely, Victim of Amphibious Noncooperation." USNIP 71 (March 1945): 311–13.

———. "The Passing of Cadet Engineers," USNIP 64 (August 1938): 1123–34.

———. "Theodorus Bailey Meyers Mason: Founder of the Office of Naval Intelligence." USNIP 78 (March 1952): 265–67.

———. "Three Navy Cranks and What They Turned." USNIP 51 (October 1924): 1615–28.

Field, R. L. "The Black Midshipman at the U.S. Naval Acad." USNIP 99 (April 1973): 28–30.

Gross, C. J. "George Owen Squire and the Origins of American Military Aviation." *Journal of Military History* 54 (1990): 281–305.

Hattendorf, John. "Technology and Strategy: A Study in the Professional Thought of the U.S. Navy, 1900–1916," *Naval War College Review* 24 (November 1971): 25–48.

Heffron, Paul T. "Secretary Moody and Naval Administrative Reform, 1902–1904." *American Neptune* 29 (January 1969): 30–53.

Hill, Rodcoe R. "The Nicaraguan Canal Idea to 1913." *Hispanic American Historical Review* 28 (May 1948): 197–211.

Karsten, Peter. "Armed Progressives." In *The Military in America from the Colonial Era to the Present,* edited by Karsten, 229–71. New York: Free Press, 1980.

———. "No Room for Young Turks?" USNIP 99 (March 1973): 37–50.

Keller, Charles L. "Automatic Pilot, 1913 Version," *American Aviation History Society Journal* 20 (Summer 1975): 130–32.

Lasby, Clarence G. "Science and the Military." In *Science and Society in the United States,* edited by David D. Van Tassel and Michael G. Hall, 251–82. Homewood, IL: Dorsey Press, 1966.

McBride, William M. "The Greatest Patron of Science?: The Navy-Academia Alliance and U.S. Naval Research, 1896–1923." *Journal of Military History* 56 (1996): 7–33.

McCandless, Bruce. "The Howell Automobile Torpedo." USNIP 92 (October 1966): 174–76.

Merril, James M. "The Greely Relief Expedition, 1884." USNIP 77 (September 1951): 969–75.

Morison, Elting E. "Naval Administration in the United States." USNIP 72 (October 1946): 1303–13.

Morris, D. R. "Homer Clark Poundstone and the All-Big-Gun Ship." USNIP 74 (June 1948): 707–21.

Rippy, Fred J. "The Initiation of the Customs Receivership in the Dominican Republic." *Hispanic American Historical Review* 20 (May 1940): 190–97.

Roland, Alex. "The Impact of War upon Aeronautical Progress: The Experience of the NACA." In *Air Power and Warfare,* edited by Alfred E. Hurley and Robert C. Ehrhart. U.S. Air Force Academy Military History Symposium 1978. Washington, DC: U.S. Air Force Academy, 1979.

Seager, Robert, II. "Ten Years before Mahan." *Mississippi Valley Historical Review* 40 (December 1953): 491–512.

Smart, Larry. "Evolution of the Torpedo Boat." *Military Affairs* 23 (1959): 97–101.

Stillson, Albert C. "Military Policy without Political Guidance: Theodore Roosevelt's Navy." *Military Affairs* 26 (Spring 1962): 18–31.

Welborn, Mary C. "Naval Contributions to Aeronautical Science, 1908–1913." USNIP 74 (August 1948): 965–74.

West, Richard S. "The Superintendents of the Naval Academy." USNIP 72 (April 1946): 59–67.

Wicks, Daniel H. "The First Cruise of the Squadron of Evolution." *Military Affairs* 44 (1980): 64–68.

*Books*

Abrahamson, James L. *America Arms for a New Century.* New York: Free Press, 1981.

Albion, Robert G. *Makers of Naval Policy, 1798–1947.* Annapolis, MD: Naval Institute Press, 1980.

Alden, John D. *The American Steel Navy.* Annapolis, MD: Naval Institute Press, 1972.

Arpee, Edward. *From Frigates to Flat-Tops: Rear Admiral William A. Moffett.* Lake Forest, IL: Privately published, 1953.

Arthur, Reginald Wright. *Contact: Careers of Naval Aviators Assigned Numbers 1 to 2000.* Washington, DC: Naval Aviator Register, 1967.

Baer, George W. *One Hundred Years of Sea Power.* Stanford, CA: Stanford University Press, 1994.

Blisten, Roger. *Flight in America.* Baltimore, MD: Johns Hopkins University Press, 1984.

Bowers, Peter M. *Curtiss Aircraft, 1907–1947.* Annapolis, MD: Naval Institute Press, 1987.

Bradford, James C., ed. *Admirals of the New Steel Navy: Makers of the American Naval Tradition, 1880–1930.* Annapolis, MD: Naval Institute Press, 1990.

———. *Captains of the Old Steam Navy: Makers of the American Naval Tradition, 1840–1880.* Annapolis, MD: Naval Institute Press, 1986.

Brodie, Bernard. *Sea Power in the Machine Age.* Princeton, NJ: Princeton University Press, 1941.

Canney, Donald L. *The Old Steam Navy: Frigates, Sloops, and Gunboats.* Annapolis, MD: Naval Institute Press, 1990.

Carlisle, Rodney P. *Where the Fleet Begins: A History of the David Taylor Research Center, 1898–1998.* Washington, DC: Naval Historical Center, 1998.

Casey, Louis. *Curtiss: The Hammondsport Era, 1907–1915.* New York: Crown, 1981.

Caswell, John. *Arctic Frontiers: United States Explorations in the Far North.* Norman: University of Oklahoma Press, 1956.

Calvert, Monte. *The Mechanical Engineer in America, 1830–1910.* Baltimore, MD: Johns Hopkins Press, 1967.

Challener, Richard D. *Admirals, Generals, and American Foreign Policy, 1898–1914.* Princeton, NJ: Princeton University Press, 1973.

Coggeshall, W. J., and J. E. McCarthy. *The Naval Torpedo Station.* Newport, RI: Training Station Press, 1920.

Coletta, Paolo E. *Admiral Bradley A. Fiske and the American Navy.* Lawrence: Regents Press of Kansas, 1979.

———. *Bowman Hendry McCalla: A Fighting Sailor.* Washington, DC: University Press of America, 1979.

———. *French Ensor Chadwick: Scholarly Warrior.* Lanham, MD: University Press of America, 1980.

———. *Patrick N. L. Bellinger and U.S. Naval Aviation.* Lanham, MD: University Press of America, 1987.

———, ed. *American Secretaries of the Navy.* Annapolis, MD: Naval Institute Press, 1980.

———, and Bernarr B. Coletta. *Admiral William A. Moffett and U.S. Naval Aviation.* Lewiston, NY: Mellen Press, 1997.

Cooling, Benjamin Franklin. *Benjamin Franklin Tracy.* Hampden, CT: Archon Books, 1973.

———. *Gray Steel Blue Water Navy.* Hampden, CT: Archon Books, 1979.

Crane, John, and James F. Kieley. *The United States Naval Academy: The First Hundred Years.* New York: McGraw-Hill, 1945.

Crouch, Tom. *The Bishop's Boys: A Life of Wilbur and Orville Wright.* New York: Norton, 1989.

Cummings, Damon E. *Admiral Richard Wainwright and the United States Navy.* Washington, DC: GPO, 1962.

Curtiss, Glenn H., and Augustus Post. *The Curtiss Aviation Book.* New York: Frederick A. Strokes, 1912.

Dewey, A. M. *The Life and Letters of Admiral Dewey from Montpelier to Manila.* New York: The Woolfall Company, 1909.

Dorwart, Jeffery. *The Office of Naval Intelligence: The Birth of America's First Intelligence Agency, 1865–1918.* Annapolis, MD: Naval Institute Press, 1979.

Drake, Frederick C. *The Empire of the Seas: A Biography of Rear Admiral Robert Wilson Shufeldt, USN.* Honolulu: University of Hawai'i Press, 1984.

Dunnavent, R. Blake. *Brown Water Warfare: The U.S. Navy in Riverine Warfare and the Emergence of a Tactical Doctrine, 1775–1970.* Gainesville: University Press of Florida, 2003.

Dupree, Hunter. *Science in the Federal Government: A History of Policies and Activities to 1940.* Cambridge, MA: Harvard University Press, 1957.

Ellsworth, Harry A. *One Hundred Eighty Landings of the United States Marines, 1800–1934.* Washington, DC: GPO, 1974.

Gates, John Morgan. *Schoolbooks and Krags: The United States Army in the Philippines, 1898–1902.* Westport, CT: Greenwood Press, 1973.

Goetzmann, William H. *New Lands, New Men: America and the Second Great Age of Discovery.* New York: Penguin, 1986.

Gray, Edwin. *The Devil's Device: The Story of Robert Whitehead, Inventor of the Torpedo.* London: Seely, 1975.

Haber, Samuel. *Efficiency and Uplift: Scientific Management in the Progressive Era, 1890–1920.* Chicago: University of Chicago Press, 1974.

Hagan, Kenneth J. *American Gunboat Diplomacy and the Old Navy, 1877–1889.* Westport, CT: Greenwood Press, 1973.

———. *This People's Navy: The Making of American Sea Power.* New York: Free Press, 1991.

———, ed. *Naval Technology and Social Modernization in the Nineteenth Century.* Manhattan, KS: Military Affairs and the American Military Institute, 1976.

Hammond, Paul. *Organizing for Defense: The American Military Establishment in the Twentieth Century.* Princeton, NJ: Princeton University Press, 1961.

Harrod, Frederick S. *Manning the New Navy.* Westport, CT: Greenwood Press, 1978.

Hatch, Alden. *Glenn Curtiss: Pioneer of Naval Aviation.* New York: Julian Messner, 1942.

Hattendorf, John B. *Sailors and Scholars: The Centennial History of the U.S. Naval War College.* Newport, RI: Naval War College Press, 1984.

Hayes, John, and John Hattendorf. *The Writings of Stephen B. Luce.* Newport, RI: Naval War College Press, 1966.

Healy, David. *Drive to Hegemony: The United States in the Caribbean, 1898–1917.* Madison: University of Wisconsin Press, 1988.

Herrick, Walter R. *The American Naval Revolution.* Baton Rouge: Louisiana State University Press, 1966.

Hirsch, Mark D. *William C. Whitney, Modern Warwick.* New York: Dodd, Mead, 1948.

Hobbs, William H. *Peary.* New York: Macmillan, 1936.

Hoeling, Adolph. *The Jeanette Expedition.* New York: Abelard and Schuman, 1967.

Holley, I. B. *Ideas and Weapons.* New Haven, CT: Yale University Press, 1953.

Hovgaard, William. *Modern History of Warships.* New York: Spon and Chamberlain, 1920.

Howe, M. A. D. *George von Lengerke Meyer.* New York: Dodd, Mead, 1920.

Hunt, Thomas. *The Life of William Henry Hunt.* Brattleboro, VT: E. L. Hildreth, 1922.

Johnson, Herbert A. *Wingless Eagle: U.S. Army Aviation through World War I.* Chapel Hill: University of North Carolina Press, 2001.

Karsten, Peter. *The Naval Aristocracy: The Golden Age of Annapolis and the Emergence of Modern American Navalism.* New York: Free Press, 1972.

Keller, Morton. *Affairs of State: Public Life in Late Nineteenth Century America.* Cambridge, MA: Belknap Press of Harvard University Press, 1977.

Klachko, Mary. *Admiral William Shepherd Benson, First Chief of Naval Operations.* Annapolis, MD: Naval Institute Press, 1987.

LaFeber, Walter. *The New Empire.* Ithaca, NY: Cornell University Press, 1963.

Langley, Lester. *The Banana Wars: United States Intervention in the Caribbean, 1898–1934.* Lexington: University Press of Kentucky, 1985.

Layman, R. D. *Before the Aircraft Carrier: The Development of Aviation Vessels, 1849–1922.* Annapolis, MD: Naval Institute Press, 1989.

———. *To Ascend from a Floating Base: Shipboard Aeronautics and Aviation, 1783–1914.* Rutherford, NJ: Fairleigh Dickinson University Press, 1979.

Linn, Brian McAllister. *The Philippine War, 1899–1902.* Lawrence: University Press of Kansas, 2000.

———. *The U.S. Army and Counterinsurgency in the Philippine War.* Chapel Hill: University of North Carolina Press, 1989.

Livingston, Dorothy. *Master of Light: A Biography of Albert A. Michelson.* New York: Scribners, 1973.

Mack, Gerstle. *The Land Divided: A History of the Panama Canal and Other Isthmian Canal Projects.* New York: Alfred A. Knopf, 1944.

May, Ernest R. *Imperial Democracy: The Emergence of America as a Great Power.* New York: Harcourt, Brace, 1961.

May, Glenn Anthony. *Battle for Batangas: A Philippine Province at War.* New Haven, CT: Yale University Press, 1991.

McBride, William M. *Technological Change and the United States Navy, 1865–1945.* Baltimore, MD: Johns Hopkins University Press, 2000.

McCullough, David G. *The Path between the Seas: The Creation of the Panama Canal, 1879–1914.* New York: Simon and Schuster, 1977.

Melhorn, Charles. *Two-Block Fox: The Rise of the Aircraft Carrier, 1911–1929.* Annapolis, MD: Naval Institute Press, 1974.

Mersky, Peter B. *Wings over the Seven Seas: The Story of Naval Aviation's Fight for Survival.* South Brunswick, NJ: A. S. Barnes, 1975.

Miller, Harold Blaine. *Navy Wings.* New York: Dodd, Mead, 1937.

Miller, Stuart. *Benevolent Assimilation: The American Conquest of the Philippines, 1899–1903.* New Haven, CT: Yale University Press, 1982.

Millett, Allan R. *Military Professionalism and Officership in America.* Columbus: The Mershon Center of the Ohio State University, 1977.

———. *The Politics of Intervention: The Military Occupation of Cuba, 1906–1909.* Columbus: Ohio State University Press, 1968.

Mirsky, Jeanette. *To the Arctic!* Chicago: University of Chicago Press, 1970.

Morison, Elting E. *Admiral Sims and the Modern American Navy.* Boston: Houghton Mifflin, 1942.

———. *Men, Machines, and Modern Times.* Cambridge: Cambridge University Press, 1966.

———. *The War of Ideas: The United States Navy, 1870–1890.* Colorado Springs, CO: U.S. Air Force Academy, 1969.

Morris, Richard. *John P. Holland.* Annapolis, MD: Naval Institute Press, 1966.

Munro, Dana G. *Intervention and Dollar Diplomacy in the Caribbean, 1900–1921.* Princeton, NJ: Princeton University Press, 1964.

O'Connell, Robert L. *Sacred Vessels: The Cult of the Battleship and Rise of the U.S. Navy.* Boulder, CO: Westview Press, 1991.

O'Gara, G. C. *Theodore Roosevelt and the Rise of the Modern Navy.* Princeton, NJ: Princeton University Press, 1943.

Packard, Wyman H. *A Century of U.S. Naval Intelligence.* Washington, DC: GPO, 1996.

Paullin, Charles Oscar. *Paullin's History of Naval Administration, 1775–1911.* Annapolis, MD: Naval Institute, 1968.

Perkins, Dexter. *The History of the Monroe Doctrine.* Boston: Little, Brown, 1963.

Plesur, Milton. *America's Outward Thrust: Approaches to Foreign Affairs, 1865–1890.* DeKalb: Northern Illinois University Press, 1971.

Puleston, William. *Annapolis: Gangway to the Quarterdeck.* New York: D. Appleton-Century, 1942.

———. *History of the United States War College.* Newport, RI: Unpublished typescript, Naval War College, 1916.

———. *Mahan, the Life and Work of Captain Alfred Thayer Mahan.* New Haven, CT: Yale University Press, 1939.

Reynolds, Clark G. *Admiral John H. Towers: The Struggle for Naval Air Supremacy.* Annapolis, MD: Naval Institute Press, 1991.

Richardson, Leon Burr. *William E. Chandler, Republican.* New York: Dodd, Mead, 1940.

Roland, Alex. *Model Research: The National Advisory Committee for Aeronautics, 1915–1958.* Washington, DC: GPO, 1985.

Roscoe, Theodore. *On the Seas and in the Skies: A History of the U.S. Navy's Air Power.* New York: Hawthorne Books, 1970.

Roseberry, Cecil. *Glenn Curtiss: Pioneer of Flight.* Garden City, NY: Doubleday, 1972.

Sawyer, Frederick L. *Sons of Gunboats.* Annapolis, MD: U.S. Naval Institute, 1946.

Seager, Robert, II. *Alfred Thayer Mahan: The Man and His Letters.* Annapolis, MD: Naval Institute Press, 1977.

Shulman, Mark Russell. *Navalism and the Emergence of American Sea Power.* Annapolis, MD: Naval Institute Press, 1995.

Soley, James R. *Historical Sketch of the United States Naval Academy.* Washington, DC: GPO, 1876.

Spector, Ronald. *Admiral of the New Empire: The Life and Career of George Dewey.* Baton Rouge: Louisiana State University Press, 1974.

———. *Professors of War: The Naval War College and the Development of the Naval Profession.* Newport, RI: Naval War College Press, 1977.

Sprout, Harold, and Margaret Sprout. *The Rise of American Naval Power, 1776–1918.* Annapolis, MD: Naval Institute Press, 1990. Reprint, Princeton, NJ: Princeton University Press, 1939 and 1966.

Still, William N. *American Sea Power in the Old World.* Westport, CT: Greenwood Press, 1980.

Studer, Clara. *Sky Storming Yankee: The Life of Glenn Curtiss.* New York: Stackpole, 1937.

Swanborough, Frederick Gordon, and Peter M. Bowers. *United States Navy Aircraft since 1911.* London: Putnam, 1968.

Swann, Leonard. *John Roach, Maritime Entrepreneur.* Annapolis, MD: Naval Institute Press, 1965.

Sweetman, Jack. *The Landing at Veracruz: 1914.* Annapolis, MD: Naval Institute Press, 1968.

———. *The U.S. Naval Academy: An Illustrated History.* Annapolis, MD: Naval Institute Press, 1979.

Todd, Alden. *Abandoned: The Story of the Greely Arctic Expedition of 1881–1884.* New York: McGraw-Hill, 1961.

Trimble, William F. *Admiral William A. Moffett: Architect of Naval Aviation.* Annapolis, MD: Naval Institute Press, 1994.

Turnbull, Archibald, and Clifford Lord. *History of United States Naval Aviation.* New Haven, CT: Yale University Press, 1949.

Valle, James. *Rocks and Shoals: Naval Discipline in the Age of Fighting Sail.* Annapolis, MD: Naval Institute Press, 1996.

Van Deurs, George. *Anchors in the Sky: Spuds Ellyson, the First Naval Aviator.* San Rafael, CA: Presidio Press, 1978.

———. *Wings for the Fleet.* Annapolis, MD: Naval Institute Press, 1961.

West, Richard S. *Admirals of American Empire.* Indianapolis: Bobbs-Merrill, 1948.

———. *The Second Admiral: A Life of David Dixon Porter, 1813–1891.* New York: Coward-McCann, 1937.

White, Leonard D. *The Republican Era.* New York: Macmillan, 1958.

Yerxa, Donald. *Admirals and Empire: The United States Navy and the Caribbean, 1898–1945.* Columbia: University of South Carolina Press, 1991.

## *Unpublished Theses and Dissertations*

Costello, Daniel. "Planning for War: A History of the General Board of the Navy, 1900–1914." PhD diss., Tufts University, 1968.

Green, James R. "The First Sixty Years of the Office of Naval Intelligence." Master's thesis, American University, 1963.

McBride, William M. "The Rise and Fall of a Strategic Technology: The American Battleship from Santiago Bay to Pearl Harbor, 1898–1941." PhD diss., Johns Hopkins University, 1989.

Stein, Stephen K. "Washington Irving Chambers: Innovation, Professionalization, and the New Navy, 1872–1919." PhD diss., Ohio State University, 1999.

Wicks, Daniel H. "New Navy and New Empire: The Life and Times of John Grimes Walker." PhD diss., University of California, Berkeley, 1979.

Wilson, Ray Thomas. "The First Year of United States Naval Aviation." Master's thesis, American University, 1959.

# Index